Joel A. Allen

The American bisons, living and extinct

Joel A. Allen

The American bisons, living and extinct

ISBN/EAN: 9783337716790

Printed in Europe, USA, Canada, Australia, Japan

Cover: Foto ©ninafisch / pixelio.de

More available books at **www.hansebooks.com**

Memoirs of the Museum of Comparative Zoölogy,

AT HARVARD COLLEGE, CAMBRIDGE, MASS.

VOL. IV. No. 10.

THE AMERICAN BISONS,

LIVING AND EXTINCT.

BY J. A. ALLEN.

PUBLISHED BY PERMISSION OF N. S. SHALER, DIRECTOR OF THE KENTUCKY GEOLOGICAL SURVEY.

WITH TWELVE PLATES AND A MAP.

UNIVERSITY PRESS, CAMBRIDGE:
WELCH, BIGELOW, & CO.
1876.

PRELIMINARY NOTE.

THIS Memoir of Mr. Allen was prepared for the Kentucky Geological Survey, with special reference to the large collection of fossil Bison remains found at Big Bone Lick, and now in the Museum of Comparative Zoölogy at Harvard University. This collection was made by me in 1868 and 1869. A part of the expense of the costly excavations whence the specimens were taken was kindly borne by Mr. James M. Barnard, of Boston, Mass.

The revival of the Kentucky Geological Survey has made it possible to begin the study of the remains from this renowned locality, with a view to their complete elucidation. Mr. Allen, having been for some time engaged in the study of the American Bisons, generously offered to undertake the study of the remains of these animals from Big Bone Lick.

As this work was soon found to be intimately connected with the whole history of the Buffalo, it has seemed to me best, for the interests of the Survey and of science generally, to have this Memoir include the whole of Mr. Allen's admirable studies on the subject.

The Act of 1874, providing for the continuance of the geological survey, allows "that the scientific results of the Survey may be published in any scientific journal, by permission of the Director." Although this monograph will form the second part of the first volume of the Memoirs of the Kentucky Geological Survey, it seems to me highly desirable that it should secure the wider circulation that will be given it by simultaneous publication in the Memoirs of the Museum of Comparative Zoölogy, at the same time the Survey is fortunate in being able, by this arrangement, to repay in part the large debt it owes to the Museum of Comparative Zoölogy for aid in every step of its scientific work.

N. S. SHALER,
Director of the Kentucky Geological Survey.

INTRODUCTION.

The following monograph consists essentially of two quite distinct parts. The first embraces descriptions of the species, while the second is devoted to the consideration of the geographical distribution of *Bison americanus*. The first part of Part I, or that portion relating to the extinct species, is the least satisfactory, owing to the scantiness of the materials for their description. It has been my good fortune, however, to have the opportunity of examining nearly all the material thus far described from the United States relating to these interesting forms, including the original specimens of *Bison latifrons* and *Bison antiquus*, as well as the later-described bison remains from California. The specimens from Eschscholtz Bay, described by Richardson, I have not had an opportunity of seeing, but I have had access to a few remains of the extinct bison from other Alaskan localities.

In the following pages two extinct species are recognized, which differ quite widely from each other, the one (*Bison latifrons* Leidy) being much larger than the other (*Bison antiquus* Leidy = *Bison crassicornis* Richardson), with disproportionately larger horn-cores. Neither of the species is as yet known from satisfactory material, although enough of their remains have been found to indicate the existence of two widely differing forms. Without knowing positively more of *Bison latifrons* than the three cranial fragments thus far discovered represent, it is difficult to assign some other specimens to the one species rather than to the other, owing to our lack of knowledge of the sexual difference in size this large species may present. The female of the larger extinct species, judging from the sexual differences seen in the living species, would apparently about equal in size the male of the smaller one, and hence it is difficult to positively specifically assign such specimens as detached teeth or single bones of the extremities. Again, the female of the smaller extinct species being of about the size of the male of *Bison americanus* (perhaps a little smaller) still further complicates the problem.

The material for the description of *Bison americanus*, and for its comparison with the aurochs (*Bison bonasus*), has, on the other hand, been nearly all that could be desired, far exceeding that ever before brought together. To complete, in a measure, the history of this species, several pages are devoted to an account of its habits, based mainly on personal observation; while Part II — embracing by far the greater part of the paper — has been devoted entirely to the subject of its geographical distribution, including a history of its extirpation from the greater part of its former vast habitat. As bearing upon this general subject, a chapter has been devoted to an account of its products, another to the means and methods used for its destruction, not only by the different Indian tribes, but also by white men, and a third to the few attempts that have been made for its domestication. The preparation of this part of the paper has been very time-taking, the necessary research having absorbed the leisure time of many months. Although extended to so great a length, it cannot be considered as an exhaustive essay on the subject, but it is believed that the conclusions reached will not be much affected by future investigations, though many important details respecting particular districts may yet be added.

The problem of the best manner of presenting the historical part of the subject has offered many difficulties. I have, however, deemed it best to give the data in full, at the risk of prolixity, rather than to briefly summarize the facts, without giving the basis for the conclusions reached. I have hence often made copious quotations, *verbatim*, instead of giving simple references to authorities, thereby presenting in full whatever bears upon the special points at issue. As a geographical arrangement of the matter seemed clearest and most logical I have adopted that method of presentation, dividing the area under discussion into several minor geographical regions. After stating in a somewhat general way the boundaries of the habitat of the American bison at the time when the different regions of the continent were first explored by Europeans (as indicated by the facts presented in the pages which follow), every portion of this boundary is afterwards discussed in detail, since the original limits of its range in different directions has been more or less the subject of discrepant opinions. Its original limit to the eastward has especially been a matter of dispute, or at least of conflicting statements, and to a less degree also its original limitation to the southward and westward. Taking, for instance, that portion of the United States east of the Mississippi River, — the first region treated in

Part II, — it was found necessary to examine in detail the alleged evidences of its former existence along the whole Atlantic seaboard from New England to Florida, over which many writers have assumed that it formerly ranged, — as well as southward to the Gulf coast, — but which a critical examination of the evidence fails to substantiate. Its actual eastern limit at the time of the first exploration of the Atlantic slope by Europeans being settled with as much certainty as available evidence will allow, the region of the Ohio Valley is next considered, where its former limits and relative abundance are traced with considerable fulness, together with its gradual total extirpation therefrom. Subsequently its former range and final extirpation over the trans-Rocky Mountain region is similarly treated. An effort is then made to define its former range south of the Rio Grande. A brief sketch is then given of its extirpation over the greater part of the vast region included between the Rio Grande on the south, the Platte River on the north, the Mississippi River on the east, and the Rocky Mountains on the west, with a definition of its present limited range within this area. The region lying between the Platte River on the south, the United States and British boundary on the north, the Mississippi River on the east, and the Rocky Mountains on the west, is next similarly treated. Finally its former vast range to the northward of the United States is defined, with a history of its extirpation over much of this area, and the limits of its present circumscribed range in the region north of the Platte River.

The accompanying map is designed to show not only the extreme limits of the known range of the buffalo (which was presumably about its range at the middle of the eighteenth century), but also its range at several different subsequent periods, as well as its habitat at the present time. The outer border of the blue area shows the extreme known range of the buffalo, while the space colored blue represents the area over which this animal had disappeared prior to the year 1800. The outer border of the pink area shows approximately its extreme limits of distribution at this date, and the area colored pink the portion of country over which it disappeared during the succeeding twenty-five years. The portion colored green represents in like manner its restriction during the next succeeding twenty-five years, or between the years 1825 and 1850. The yellow area similarly shows its restriction between the years 1850 and 1875, and the orange spaces the limited areas over which it still exists. Other tints indicate the localities at which the remains of the extinct species have been found. The boundaries given cannot, of course, be more than approximate, but are believed to be as nearly correct as the data extant will permit.

No indigenous animal has perhaps figured so prominently in the history of Kentucky as the buffalo. It not only formed for a time the chief subsistence of some of the early pioneers of this State, but its fossil remains form large deposits at several localities about its numerous Salt Licks; while it is only in this State that any efforts for its domestication worthy of the name have as yet been made. Both of the extinct species were also first described from remains found in Kentucky; and it is to the great valley of the Ohio that we must mainly still look for further materials to furnish us with a clew to their fuller histories and distinctive characters.

In Part II will be found not only references to narratives of exploration and the records of the early settlement of the country, but also much matter hitherto unpublished. While due credit is given in each case for the information received from my many correspondents,—the name of the contributor being always given as the authority for the facts communicated,—it gives me pleasure to mention here a few of those to whom I am especially indebted for valuable contributions. Among these are Dr. F. V. Hayden, Geologist-in-charge of the United States Geographical and Geological Survey of the Territories; Dr. Elliott Coues, U. S. A., Naturalist of the United States and British Boundary Commission; Prof. S. F. Baird, Assistant Secretary of the Smithsonian Institution; Professor George M. Dawson of McGill College, Montreal; J. S. Taylor, Esq., late U. S. Consul at Winnipeg, B. N. A.; Hon. Wm. N. Byers, Editor of the Rocky Mountain News; Mr. W. H. Dall, Assistant United States Coast Survey; Dr. W. S. Tremaine, U. S. A., of Fort Dodge, Kansas; Mr. J. Boll of Dallas, Texas; Dr. W. J. Hoffman, late Assistant Surgeon U. S. A.; Prof. B. F. Mudge of Kansas; Professor O. C. Marsh of New Haven, Conn.; Dr. J. G. Cooper of California; Mr. C. E. Aiken of Colorado Springs, Col.; Prof. J. R. Loomis of Lewisburg, Pa.; Mr. C. W. Pritchett of Glasgow, Mo.; Mr. George Graham of Cincinnati, Ohio; E. T. Bowen, Esq., late General Superintendent of the Kansas Pacific Railway; C. F. Morse, Esq., Superintendent of the Atchison, Topeka, and Santa Fé Railroad; E. P. Vining, Esq., General Freight Agent of the Union Pacific Railroad; and to various officers of the United States Army.

I am also especially indebted for the use of material to the Museum of Comparative Zoölogy, Cambridge, without access to whose collections the preparation of this monograph would have been impossible. Also to the

Smithsonian Institution, Washington; to the Academy of Natural Sciences of Philadelphia; to the California Academy of Sciences; to the Boston Society of Natural History; and to Mrs. Romeo Elton of Boston, for the use of valuable specimens. Finally I wish to express my gratitude to Mr. N. S. Shaler, Director of the Geological Survey of Kentucky, and to Mr. Alexander Agassiz, Curator of the Museum of Comparative Zoölogy, for their liberality in providing for the accompanying plates and map, and to the former for valuable suggestions and information. I also wish to return thanks to Mr. Louis Trouvelot and to Mr. Paul Roetter for the careful manner in which they have executed the map and plates.

An unexpected delay in the completion of the plates having occurred, several months have elapsed since the main part of the paper was put in type, which has afforded an opportunity to include in the Appendix several valuable communications which were received too late to be inserted in their proper connection. These relate chiefly to the occurrence of the buffalo in Union County, Pennsylvania, and to the date of its extirpation in the Ohio Valley. Matter is also added in respect to the southern limit of the buffalo east of the Mississippi River, especially south of the Tennessee River, which somewhat modify statements made respecting this point in the main body of the paper. Hence the attention of the reader is especially called to these supplemental notes. In the Appendix will also be found an important communication by Mr. Shaler, "On the Age of the Bison in the Ohio Valley."

J. A. ALLEN.

Museum of Comparative Zoölogy, Cambridge, Mass., May 24, 1876.

THE AMERICAN BISONS.

PART I.

1. — Distinctive Characteristics and Affinities of the Bisons.

Genus **BISON** *Smith.*

Bos (in part) of many authors.
Bison H. Smith, Griffith's Cuvier's An. King., V, 373, 1827.
Urus Bojanus, Nov. Act. Acad. Nat. Cur., XIII, 2, 427, 1827. — Owen, Rep. British Assoc., 1843, 232.
Harlanus Owen, Proc. Acad. Nat. Sci. Phila., 1846, 94.
Bisontina Rütimeyer, Verhandl. d. naturforsch. Gesells. in Basel, IV, iii, 335, 1865.

The bisons are easily distinguished osteologically from the other members of the bovine family by the peculiar conformation of the skull. These distinctive features, as Cuvier * long since pointed out, consist in the forehead of the ox being flat or slightly concave, while that of the bison is convex, though somewhat less so than in the buffalo; in the ox the forehead is also quadrate, its length being equal to its breadth, while in the bisons the breadth, measured at the same point, exceeds the height in the proportion of three to two; in the ox the horns are attached to the extremity of the highest salient line of the head, or that which separates the forehead from the occiput, while in the bisons the horns are placed considerably in front of this line; finally in the ox the plane of the occiput is quadrangular, and forms an acute angle with the forehead, while in the bison it is semicircular and forms an obtuse angle with the forehead. The genus *Bison*, as Dr. J. E. Gray † was the first to point out, differs also from *Bos* in the peculiar form of the intermaxillaries, which, as in the genera *Poëphagus* and *Bibos*, are short, triangular, and acute behind, not reaching to the nasals, as they do in *Bos*, *Bubalus*, and *Anoa*. They gradually decrease in length from *Poëphagus* to *Bison*, in which latter genus they are much shorter than in the others.

* See Ossem. Foss., troisième édition, Tome IV, p. 109, 1825.

† Ann. and Mag. Nat. Hist., Vol. VIII, p. 229, 1846; Cat. Mam. Brit. Mus., Part III, p. 16, 1852.

Prof. Owen * later made this the chief distinction between the bison and the ox. In the bisons the short premaxillaries do not rise to join the nasals, and therefore six bones enter into the formation of the external nasal opening instead of four, as is the case in *Bos* and *Bubalus*. Owen also calls attention to the projecting orbital processes, which with the lachrymal and malar processes form a projecting orbital cylinder. The ribs, Owen also says, "never exceed in number thirteen pairs in any species of *Bos* proper; [while] the European bison or aurochs has fourteen, and the American bison fifteen pairs of ribs." The last statement, however, is erroneous, the American bison having the same number of pairs of ribs and the same number of lumbar vertebræ as the European, notwithstanding numerous statements to the contrary.†

* Descrip. Cat. Ost. Series in Mus. Roy. Coll. Surgeons of England, p. 622, 1853.

† This oft-repeated misstatement affords a striking instance of the persistency of error. In this case the error had a singular origin, and its repetition is to some degree justifiable. The first skeleton of the American bison known in Europe was that obtained from a living specimen received at the Paris Menagerie in 1819, and which was described by Cuvier in his Ossemens Fossiles (tome IV, p. 118, of third edition). This specimen — one instance probably in thousands — chanced to have *fifteen pairs of ribs*, and consequently but four lumbar vertebræ. Cuvier of course called attention to this fact as affording an important distinction between the American and European bisons. Says Cuvier: "Quant au reste du squelette, la femelle envoyée d'Amerique par M. Milbert a quinze paires de côtes, tandis que l'aurochs de Pologne n'en a que quatorze, et les autres bœufs treize seulement. Cette femelle n'a en revanche que quatre vertèbres lombaires, tandis que l'aurochs en a cinq, et les autres bœufs six." It is hence not strange that mere compilers, and even authorities of some eminence, should for a time perpetuate the error, especially since it was many years before a second skeleton of the American bison fell under the eye of a comparative anatomist. Yet it seems a little strange to find it repeated by leading English anatomists and zoologists for many years after several of the leading museums of Great Britain contained skeletons of the American bison. Owen, as late as 1866, in his great work on the Comparative Anatomy of the Vertebrates (Vol. II, p. 462), says: "The European bison has fourteen dorsal and five lumbar vertebræ; the American bison has fifteen dorsal and four lumbar, and this is the extreme reached, in the Ruminant order, of movable ribs, equalling in number those of the Hippopotamus."

Hamilton Smith in Griffith's Cuvier (Vol. IV, p. 404 and Vol. V, p. 374), published in 1825, of course gave the same number as Cuvier, as did also Fischer, in 1828, in his Synopsis Mammalium (p. 496); and Wagner (Suppl. to Schreber's Sauget., V, 472), in 1855. Dr. J. E. Gray, in 1852, in his Catalogue of the Mammalia of the British Museum (Part III, Ungulata Furcipeda, p. 35), says under *Bison*, "Ribs fourteen or fifteen pairs," although there were then two skeletons in the British Museum. Edward Blythe, in Orr's translation of Cuvier's Animal Kingdom (p. 143), in 1846 and in 1851, reiterated the same error, as did Owen in 1846, in his British Fossil Mammals and Birds, as above cited, and in the Proceedings of the Zoological Society of London for 1848 (p. 130), as it was also by authors of lesser fame. Gerrard, in 1862, in his Catalogue of the Bones of Mammals in the British Museum (p. 230), gave for the first time the correct number. Lilljeborg, in 1874 (Fauna öfver Sveriges och Norges Ryggradsdjur), refers to Owen's statement on this point, and cites the number given by Gerrard. Rutimeyer in 1867 also refers to a skeleton in Amsterdam which presented only fourteen pairs of ribs and five lumbar vertebræ (Versuch einer Natürlichen Geschichte des Rindes, II, p. 68).

As compared with the species of *Bos* proper, the bisons also differ in their more slender limbs, smaller ribs, and less massive bones, as well as in their much longer dorsal spines, and relatively longer canon-bones of the hind limbs as compared with those of the fore limbs. Externally they differ in having the head heavily clothed with long bushy hair; they also possess a heavy barb, and the fore legs are heavily fringed with coarse long hair. The clothing hair of the body also differs from that of the representatives of the restricted genus *Bos* and most of its allies in consisting mainly of short, curled, crisp wool in place of straight hairs. On the whole the bisons proper, or the restricted genus *Bison*, form a strongly marked natural group, the different members of which exhibit a close interrelation. Their nearest ally is probably the yac (*Poëphagus grunniens*), which was considered by Turner as congeneric with the bisons, though by others as more allied to the musk ox. The other nearest allies of the bisons are the gaurs (*Bibos gaurus* and *Bibos frontalis*), but none of these forms very closely approach the bisons.

The name *Bison* was first applied to this group in a generic sense by Hamilton Smith in 1827. In the same year Bojanus used the name *Urus* for the designation of the aurochs and the larger extinct bisons. Prof. Owen in 1843 also used the name *Urus* in a generic sense for the designation of this group. The name *Harlanus*, given to a supposed new tapiroid pachyderm, was based on what proved on later investigation to be an imperfect ramus of an extinct bison, the teeth of which had become so much worn as to obscure their true character. Rütimeyer has recently used the name *Bisontina* in a super-generic sense for the same group.

2. — General historical Account of the Remains of Extinct Bisons hitherto found in North America.

As introductory to the following pages, a brief historical notice of the hitherto known remains of extinct North American bisons may not be wholly out of place.

The first remains of an extinct bison discovered in North America * were

* The first-discovered remains of a fossil bison seem to have been the skull obtained near Dantzic, and described by Klein in 1732 (in Philosoph. Transact., XXXVII, No. 426, figs. 1 – 3). In 1803 Faujas, and later Brocchi and Cuvier described others from Northern Italy and the valley of the Rhine, and numerous

found in the bed of a small creek about a dozen miles north of Big-bone Lick, Kentucky, and consisted of a part of a cranium with a considerable portion of one horn-core attached. This specimen was presented by Samuel Brown of Kentucky to the American Philosophical Society, and was first described and figured by Rembrandt Peale, in a paper entitled "Account of Some Remains of a Species of gigantic Oxen found in America and other parts of the World." * This specimen Peale believed indicated a species of the ox tribe of gigantic proportions whose horns must have had a spread of nearly twelve feet, — a conjecture that subsequent discoveries have proved well founded.

This fragment, now deposited in the Museum of the Academy of Natural Sciences of Philadelphia, was repeatedly figured and described by different authors during the next thirty years, and has hence acquired great historic interest, being also the only remains of the larger extinct bison recognized from this continent for nearly half a century. Mr. Peale presented a plaster cast of this specimen to the Museum of Natural History of Paris at about the time of the publication of his essay on the subject of fossil oxen, and it was hence noticed almost simultaneously by M. Faujas-Saint-Fond,† who believed it specifically identical with a younger specimen discovered on the banks of the Rhine near Bonn, which he describes and figures in the same paper, without, however, giving the species a distinctive name.‡ Peale's specimen was next noticed by Cuvier § in 1808, who redescribed and figured it from the cast sent by Mr. Peale to the Paris Museum. Cuvier regarded it as not only identical with the fossil bison of Europe, but referred both to the living aurochs (*Bison bonasus*), from which the fossil animal seemed to

others were subsequently made known by other writers from many other localities. In 1832 Hermann von Meyer was able to give measurements of numerous skulls and a figure and description of the pelvis. J. F. Brandt, in his Zoographische und Palaeontologische Beiträge, published in 1867, gave a list of the localities at which its remains have been found, from which it appears to have been already met with in nearly every country of Europe and in Siberia. The most southerly point at which its remains have been found is in Upper Italy, skulls having been obtained near Pavia, on the Po. They have also been found in France, Switzerland, the British Islands, in Holland, Belgium, and Germany, especially about Mannheim on the Rhine, as well as in Sweden, Poland, Hungary, European Russia, and Greece. They have also been found at several localities in Asiatic Russia.

* Philosophical Magazine, Vol. XV, pp. 325 - 327, pl. vi, 1803.

† Ann. du Museum, Vol. II, p. 190, 1803.

‡ It forms the "Première Espèce" of his essay, and is placed under the descriptive heading, "*Bœuf fossil à cornes disposées presque horizontalement,*" etc.

§ Ann. du Museum, Vol. XII, p. 382, pl. xxxiv, fig. 2.

him to differ only in its somewhat larger size and longer, less curved horns. Cuvier repeated his figure and description of the American specimen in the first and subsequent editions of his "Ossemens Fossiles," and retained the same opinion respecting the affinities of the living and extinct bisons until the edition of 1825, when he admitted, in view of the slight differences which distinguish the aurochs from the American bison (*Bison americanus*), the fossil bison as a third species.*

In 1825 the same specimen was also described by Dr. Richard Harlan,† who, believing it to be a species distinct from the aurochs, gave it the name of *Bos latifrons*, which, as will be shown later, forms the first systematic name any of the extinct species received. In 1827 Bojanus,‡ in his memoir on fossil oxen, in the description of his *Urus priscus* (seu *Urus nostras*), cites the specimen "ex America septentrionalis" described by Cuvier; it is also referred to by H. v. Meyer in 1832, as well as by other authors, being always regarded as specifically identical with the European fossil bison (*Bos priscus*, seu *Bison priscus* auct.).

In 1831 Buckland, in his list of the vertebrate fossils brought by Captain Beechey from the ice-cliffs of Eschscholtz Bay, enumerates the remains of "fossil oxen," some of which he refers to a "*Bos urus*" (probably meaning the *Bison priscus* of other authors), and which constitute the first remains of an extinct bison found in America after the original specimen described by Peale. They received no further notice, however, for many years.

In 1846 the greater portion of the skull of a large extinct bison was discovered on the Brazos River, near San Felipe, Texas, together with a molar tooth. These were described by Dr. W. M. Carpenter,§ and formed the second specimens discovered in the United States. The skull seems to have lacked only a part of the facial bones, and the horn-cores were nearly entire. The specimen was of the same gigantic proportions as the one made known by Mr. Peale.

In 1852 Dr. Leidy ‖ described five molar teeth of a fossil bison, discovered near Natchez, Mississippi, "in association with remains of *Mastodon*, *Equus*,

* Oss. Foss., 3d Ed., Vol. IV, p. 148.

† Fauna Amer., p. 273.

‡ Nov. Acta, Acad. Nat. Cur., XIII, 2.

§ Amer. Journ. Sci., 2d Ser., I, 245.

‖ Proc. Acad. Nat. Sci. Phila., 1852, p. 117.—Memoir on the Extinct Species of American Ox, p. 8, pl. ii, figs. 2–7.

Ursus, Cervus, Megalonyx, and *Mylodon*"; and also a humerus, tibia, atlas, and metatarsus, found in excavating the Brunswick Canal, in Georgia. A fragment of a jaw, with the teeth very much worn, belonging to the same collection, was subsequently identified as belonging to an extinct bison, though in the mean time wrongly referred by Harlan and Owen to other genera. In 1852 Dr. Leidy * also described the greater part of a right horn-core, having a small fragment of the frontal bone attached, found at Big-bone Lick, Kentucky, which he "with some hesitation" described as belonging to a new species (*Bison antiquus* Leidy), but which he later regarded as the female of the larger form (*Bison latifrons*).

In 1854 the fossil bison remains from the ice-cliffs of Eschscholtz Bay collected by Captain Beechey, together with others collected later by Captain Kellet, were described by Sir John Richardson,† who believed them to represent two species. One of these he regarded as new (*Bison crassicornis* Richardson), while he regarded the other as doubtfully identical with the fossil bison of Europe (*Bison priscus* auct.). Altogether the fossil bison remains from this locality included portions of several skulls, several additional horn-cores, most of the bones of the limbs, and the greater part of the vertebræ. None of the skulls, however, embraced the facial portions of the cranium.

In 1860 Dr. Leidy ‡ described and figured a second premolar tooth from the post-pliocene formation of the Ashley River, South Carolina, which he believed to be referable to *B. latifrons*. In 1867 the same writer § described a skull from Pilarcitos Valley, California, and also several teeth from the same State, which he redescribed and figured in 1873.‖ He also described and figured at the same time a molar tooth found at Pittston, on the Susquehanna River, in Luzerne County, Pennsylvania, and another molar from a crevice in the lead-bearing rocks of Jo Daviess County, Illinois, both of which he also referred, though somewhat doubtfully, to the same species.

It thus appears that the hitherto described remains of extinct bisons known from the United States consist of three or four very imperfect skulls, (none of them embracing the very characteristic facial portions,) an atlas, a tibia and humerus and a few detached molar teeth. The remains

* Proc. Acad. Nat. Sci. Phila., 1852, 117.

† Zoölogy of the Voyage of the Herald.

‡ Holmes's Post-Pliocene Fossils of South Carolina, p. 109, pl. xxii. figs. 15, 16, 1860.

§ Proc. Acad. Nat. Sci. Phila., 1867, p. 85.

‖ Contrib. to Extinct Vert. Faun. Western Territories, pp. 253, 318, pl. xxviii, figs. 4–6.

from other parts of North America consist of the specimens already mentioned as obtained from the ice-cliffs of Eschscholtz Bay. These, however, as well as those from California, belong mainly, as will be shown later, to a smaller animal than the remains from which *Bison latifrons* was first described.

In addition to the above there are described in the following paper several fragments of lower jaws and a skull from California, a horn-core from the Tatlo River, Alaska, an imperfect skull, and a metacarpus from the valley of the Yukon, and two entire horn-cores from Adams County, Ohio. The latter belong to the large species first described by Peale, the others to the smaller extinct bison of Western and Northwestern North America.

3. — Description of the Extinct Species.

BISON LATIFRONS (Harlan) Leidy.

Great Extinct American Bison.

Bos latifrons Harlan, Fauna Americana, 273, 1825; Edinb. New Philos. Journ. XVII, 359, 1834; Med. and Phys. Res., 276, 1835; Trans. Geol. Soc. Penna., 1835, 71. — Cooper, Month. Am. Journ. Geol., 1831, 174. — DeKay, Ann. Lyc. Nat. Hist. New York, 1828, 286; New York Faun. Zool., Pt. I. 10, 1842. (Not the *Bos latifrons* of Fischer, Bull. Soc. Imp. des Nat. de Moscow, 1830, p. 81, based wholly on Siberian specimens.)

Bison latifrons Leidy, Proc. Acad. Nat. Sci. Phila., 1852, 117; 1854, 89, 210; 1867, 85; Mem. Ext. Sp. Amer. Ox, in Smith Contrib., 1852, 8 (pls. i, ii, in part only); Wailes's Rep. Agric. and Geol. Mississippi, 286, 1854; Holmes's Post-pliocene Fos. of South Carolina, 109, pl. xvii, figs. 15, 16, 1860 (doubtfully referable to *B. latifrons*); Ext. Mam. N. Amer. (Journ. Acad. Nat. Sci. Phila. Soc., 2d Ser., VII), 371, 1869 (in part only); Contr. Ext. Vert. Faun. Western Territories, 253, 318, pl. xxviii, figs 4 – 8, 1873, (in part only).

Urus priscus Bojanus, Nov. Act. Acad. Nat. Cur., XIII, ii, 427, 1827; Owen, Rep. British Assoc., 1843, 232. — Cat. Fos. Mam. etc., Mus. Roy. Col. Surg., 271, 1845 (the American reference only).

Bos (Bison) priscus Meyer, Palæologica, 96, 1832.

Bos priscus Meyer, Nov. Act. Acad. Nat Cur., 141, 1835 (in part only). — Giebel, Fauna der Vorwelt, 153, 1847 (in part only). — Rütimeyer, Verhand. Naturf. Gesells. in Berlin, IV, iii, 339, 1865 (in part only).

Bos bonasus Lilljeborg, Fauna öfver Sveriges och Norges Ryggradsdjur, I, 877, 1874 (in part only).

? *Bos*, Couper, Proc. Acad. Nat. Sci. Phil., 1842, 190, 216. — Owen, Journ. Acad. Nat. Sci. Phila., 2d Ser., I, 18, 1847.

Taurus gigas Rafinesque, Enumeration of Remark. Natural Objects, etc., 1831.

Taurus latifrons Rafinesque, Enumeration of Remark. Nat. Obj., etc., 1831; Atlantic Journ., 1832 – 33, 29.

? *Sus americana* Harlan, Amer. Journ. Sci. & Arts, XLIII, 143, pl. iii, fig. 1, 1842. — Couper, Proc. Acad. Nat. Sci. Phila., 1842, 190, 216.

? *Lophiodon bathygnathus* OWEN, Cat. Fos. Mam. etc. Mus. Roy. Col. Surg., 197, 1845.

? *Harlanus americanus* OWEN, Proc. Acad. Nat. Sci. Phila., 1846, 96; Journ. Acad. Nat. Sci. Phila., I, 18, pl. vi, 1847; Amer Journ. Sci. & Arts, 2d Ser., III, 125, 1847.

Great Indian Buffalo, PEALE, Philos. Mag., 1803, 325; Hist. Disq. on the Mammoth, 84, 1803.

Aurochs, CUVIER, Ann. du Mus. d'Hist. Nat., XII, 382, pl. xxxiv, fig. 2, 1808; Ossem. Fos., IV, 50, pl. iii, fig. 2, 1812; 2d Ed., 1824; 3d Ed., 143, pl. xii, fig 2, 1825; 4th Ed., VI, 287, pl. xxii, fig. 2, 1835 (the American specimen only).

Great Fossil Ox, sp. *latifrons*, GODMAN, Am. Nat. Hist., III, 243, pl., 1828.

Fossil Ox, CARPENTER, Amer. Journ. Sci. & Arts, 2d Ser., I, 245, figs. 1, 2, 1846; 3d Ser., X, p. 336, 1875.

? *Ox*, COOPER, Proc. Acad. Nat. Sci. Phila., 1842, 217.

Bœuf fossile à cornes disposées presque horizontalement, etc., FAUJAS, Ann. du Mus., II, 190, 1803; Essais de Géologie, I. 329, pl. xvii (only the reference to the American specimen).

The present species of *Bison* seems to be well distinguished from all others of the genus, either living or extinct, by its gigantic size, far exceeding even the *Bison priscus* of the Old World. Our knowledge of it rests at present on portions of three skulls. Other remains have been attributed to it, but most of them apparently improperly. For a long time the species was known only from the original specimen first made known by Peale, and subsequently redescribed by Harlan and Leidy, under the names respectively of *Bos latifrons* and *Bison latifrons*. The second specimen was found in Texas and described by Dr. Carpenter in 1846, simply as the skull of an extinct ox. Dr. Leidy subsequently referred it to the *Bison latifrons*. The third specimen, consisting of a pair of horn-cores, found together but disconnected, was recently dug up in Adams County, Ohio, and was first noticed in the American Journal of Science (November, 1875), as the remains of a gigantic extinct ox. Dr. Leidy has described and figured at different times several molar teeth that seem to have belonged to the same species, but other remains latterly doubtfully attributed to the same form belong to a smaller species.

Dr. Leidy's very excellent description of the first specimen is as follows: "The *Bison latifrons* is established upon the fragment of cranium before referred to, presented by Dr. Samuel Brown to the American Philosophical Society. The specimen consists of the hinder portion of the cranium with a fragment fourteen inches in length of the left horn-core, and indicates a species as large as the existing arnee, or buffalo (*Bubalus buffelus* Gray), of India and Java. The sutures of the remaining bones of the specimen are anchylosed; but the positions of the frontal and fronto-parietal sutures are yet distinguishable as slightly elevated zigzag lines. The form of the cranial fragment with its attached portion of horn-core is almost a repetition of the corresponding part of the skull of the buffalo. The base of the horn-core is situated five inches in a curved line outwards and forwards, or two inches and a half in a straight line, in advance of the position of the occipito-parietal crest. The forehead is slightly more flat antero-posteriorly than in the buffalo, arising from the occipito-parietal crest being a little less below its level. The lateral margins of the inion are broken away in the specimen, but the remaining portion exhibits the same appearances in detail as the buffalo, though in an exaggerated degree corresponding to its much greater size. The base of the specimen is very much broken, but that which is preserved indicates the form to have been the same as in the last-mentioned animal. The occipital condyles are alike in both, and, at their anterior part, advance in a concave manner to the posterior muscular protuberances of the basilar process. Between the condyles and paramastoid, a large deep fossa exists, having at its inner side the foramen condyloideum. The foramen magnum occipitis is slightly wider than high, being two inches one line by one inch eleven lines. The basilar process in the fossil, at its posterior muscular protuberances, is four inches wide and two inches and a quarter at those joining the body of the sphenoid. The os tympanica has been large and inflated, as in the buffalo, and a portion of one glenoid articulation remaining in the specimen presents the same form as in the latter."

The additional measurements given by Dr. Leidy are as follows: —

Breadth of forehead between the bases of the horn-cores, 15 inches, or 380 mm.
Height of the inion from the upper edge of the occipital foramen, 5½ inches, or 140 mm.
Circumference of the horn-core at its base, 20½ inches, or 520 mm.
" " " ten inches from its base, 17½ inches, or 445 mm.

This specimen is still in the museum of the Academy of Natural Sciences of Philadelphia. Through the kindness of the curators of the Museum I was enabled recently to examine the specimen at my leisure. I found the circumference of the horn-core fourteen inches from the base (the point at which it is broken off) to be sixteen inches, or only four inches and a half less than at the base, and three and a half inches less than at ten inches from the base. Mr. Peale, in his description of the same specimen nearly three fourths of a century ago, expressed his belief that "the horn itself could not have been less than six feet in length," and thought it "a reasonable conjecture that the buffalo to which it belonged was about ten or eleven feet high." *

The least breadth of the forehead (at the narrowest point between the orbits and horn-cores) is fifteen inches, or about two inches greater than the corresponding measurement of old males of *Bison americanus*. The occipital condyles show that the skull would require an atlas having an articular cup with a transverse axis of not less than seven and a half to eight inches, or more than two inches (more than one third) greater than that of the fossil atlas from Darien, Georgia, doubtfully referred by Dr. Leidy to *Bison latifrons*. If referable to that species it must be considered as having belonged to a female, the skull above described being undoubtedly that of a male.

The second skull referable to *Bison latifrons* is that described by Dr. Carpenter from the banks of the Brazos River, near San Felipe, Texas. Dr. Carpenter's description is as follows: —

"*Fossil Ox.*—This specimen consists of the frontal bone, with portions of the bony nuclei of the horns. The frontal portion of the orbit of one eye is nearly entire; the margins of the other are broken. None of the bones of the lower portions of the head are left, being replaced by a conglomerate mass of sand and pebbles. . . . . The frontal bone is nearly plane anteriorly, and the horns arise laterally from a level with this plane; but the bone bulges about two and one half inches in the occipital portion above the horns, as shown in the figure." The figure is a rude wood-cut, representing the specimen "one sixteenth its linear dimensions."

According to Dr. Carpenter's measurements this specimen nearly equalled in size the one described by Dr. Leidy. The circumference of the horn-cores at the base was seventeen inches, or about three and a half inches less, if measured actually around the base of the horn-core and not around the neck of the horn-core. This measurement in Dr. Leidy's specimen is only eighteen inches, or one inch greater than the measurement given by Dr. Carpenter. The circumference of the horn-core of Carpenter's specimen, at the distance of eighteen inches from the base, is given as fourteen and a half inches, which indicates a size at this point fully as great as Dr. Leidy's specimen could have had. In Dr. Carpenter's specimen considerable portions of the horn-cores were still attached to the skull, namely, eighteen inches of the left horn-core and two feet of the right horn-core. "The bones of the horns," says Dr. Carpenter, "are nearly round, and they have a slight curvature

* Historical Disquisition on the Mammoth, etc., pp. 84, 85.

upwards and forwards (*sic*) [backward, as shown in the figure]; and when entire the bony parts must have measured, at a reasonable estimate, about four feet; and allowing the increase in length by the addition of the horny parts to have been only a foot, it would give a probable distance between the tips of the horns to be at least eleven feet."

Dr. Carpenter also figures "the second true molar of the left upper jaw," found with the skull but not attached to it, which measured along the crown one inch and six tenths by one inch and two tenths. The specimen, however, is too much worn to show any distinctive features. In size it corresponds with the teeth from Natchez, Mississippi, described by Dr. Leidy.

The third specimen of cranial remains thus far known to me as unquestionably referable to the *Bison latifrons* consists of two nearly perfect horn-cores, with small fragments of the frontal bones attached. These remains were exhumed about three years since, in Adams County, Ohio, in digging in the gravel on Brush Creek, preparatory to laying the abutments of a bridge, and were first brought to the notice of the scientific world by Dr. O. D. Norton, to whom I am indebted for a small photograph of them, and for the subjoined measurements. They were found about eighteen feet below the surface with remains of the mastodon, and are now in the museum of the Natural History Society of Cincinnati. These horn-cores are nearly entire (see Plate I), lacking only a little of the apical portions, and give the following measurements: —

Total length measured along the upper or concave side, 32 inches, or 813 mm.
" " " lower or convex side, 34 inches, or 853 mm.
Circumference at base, 20 inches, or 510 mm.
" ten inches from the base, 16 inches, or 407 mm.
" fourteen inches from the base, 14½ inches, or 368 mm.
" twenty-four inches from the base, 9½ inches, or 240 mm.
Width of skull between bases of horn-cores (estimated), 16 inches, or 407 mm.

They thus about equal in size the specimens above described, and undoubtedly represent the same species. They indicate also a species so immensely superior in size to the *Bison priscus* of the Old World as to leave little reason for questioning their distinctness. The largest specimens of the latter rarely exceed a breadth of three to three and a half feet between the tips of the horn-cores, while the same breadth in *Bison latifrons* must have exceeded twice those dimensions, with proportionally greater thickness. If the proximal two feet of the horn-core were to be removed, the remaining portion would just about equal in length and thickness the average size of the horn-cores of the adult male of either the aurochs or the American bison.

Several teeth that apparently belong to this species have been described by Dr. Leidy, together with some that represent a smaller species. The five molar teeth from Natchez, Mississippi, found in association with the remains of *Mastodon*, *Equus*, *Ursus*, *Cervus*, *Megalonyx*, and *Mylodon*, are the largest teeth belonging to any known species of *Bison*, being considerably larger than those of *Bison priscus* described by H. von Meyer, from Mannheim, Germany, as well as much larger than those from California, which are referable to the species next described in the present paper. The specimens from Natchez Dr. Leidy thus describes: "In the upper molars the external side exhibits six folds, relatively not more prominent than in the common ox. Internally, between the principal lobes, the accessory column is very well developed and robust. The crescentic enamel pits or islands of the grinding surface are more simple than in the ox, and appear relatively more capacious as a result of their greater simplicity or less degree of inversion of the sides of the pits [a difference common to all the members of the bison group, as compared with the representatives of the restricted genus *Bos*]. The last lower molar also presents a well-developed accessory column between the anterior pair of the principal lobes externally, and in the worn-down specimen, upon the triturating surface forms a correspondingly larger fold. In the unworn specimen the summit of the posterior lobe bifurcates anteriorly, one portion joining the postero-internal fold of the middle lobe, the other the postero-external angle of the same lobe."

These are the only teeth thus far described that seem to me to be referable to the *Bison latifrons*. Those described by Dr. Leidy, from California,* evidently belong to the smaller western form (*Bison antiquus*), of which Dr. Leidy has also figured and described the skull. The tooth from Pittston, Luzerne County, Pennsylvania,† found with remains of *Mastodon americanus* and *Equus major*, seems to wholly lack the accessory column, judging from the figure, "the oval islet" being apparently *not* formed by the wearing down of the accessory column. In other respects the tooth also resembles the corresponding tooth of *Ovibos*, and it seems to me is undoubtedly referable to the extinct musk-ox and not to any form of *Bison*. It is in any case too small for a tooth of *Bison latifrons*.

* Ext. Vert. Fauna, etc., p. 254, pl. xxviii, figs. 6, 7.

† Ibid., p. 255, pl. xxviii, fig. 8.

The tooth from the lead-bearing crevices of Elizabeth, Jo Daviess County, Illinois,* is undoubtedly, it appears to me, a tooth of *Bison americanus*, as Dr. Leidy himself deemed "not improbable."

A second upper premolar tooth from the post-pliocene beds of the Ashley River, South Carolina,† is described by Dr. Leidy as presenting "nothing characteristically different from the corresponding tooth of the recent bison," but is provisionally referred by him to *Bison latifrons*. It is, however, not larger than the corresponding tooth of *Bison americanus*, and it seems to me may have belonged to this species, or — and perhaps with greater probability — to the domestic ox, other remains identified as such by Dr. Leidy having been found in the same beds.‡

The bison remains from Darien, Georgia, consisting of an atlas, part of a humerus, a tibia and a metatarsal bone, referred by Dr. Leidy to *Bison latifrons*, nearly correspond in size with the remains of the smaller extinct bison from the ice-cliffs of Eschscholtz Bay and California, and are hence too small to belong to the male of the large *Bison latifrons*, but they may perhaps be regarded as representing the female of that species. The atlas is one third too small to fit the condyles of the original specimen of *B. latifrons*. Since, however, the Georgia remains indicate an animal about one tenth larger than the species represented by the remains from Eschscholtz Bay, described by Dr. Richardson they are here provisionally referred to *Bison latifrons*, although it seems almost equally probable that they may belong to *B. antiquus*. The following detailed description and the accompanying measurements and figures (see Plate II) will perhaps aid in determining the matter whenever additional material is discovered.

The atlas from Georgia is a little larger than the largest atlas described by Richardson, and referred by him to his *Bison crassicornis*; it, however, closely resembles it in form, apparently not differing more from it than atlases of different individuals of the same species often differ. There is only one important discrepancy, namely, the length of the centrum measured on the dorsal aspect, which is disproportionately short, being scarcely longer than that of a female *B. americanus*. Neither the Georgia specimen nor that referred by Richardson to *B. crassicornis* differs much in form or proportions from the atlas of *Bison americanus*, though materially in some respects from that of *Bison bonasus*. All the atlases of the bisons of which measurements

* Ext. Vert. Fauna, etc., p. 355, pl. xxxvii, fig. 4.

† Holmes's Post-pliocene Fossils, p. 109, pl. xvii, figs. 15, 16.

‡ Ibid., p. 110.

are given in the subjoined table differ from the atlases of domestic cattle in the very much greater size of the articular cup, and in the form of the pleurapophyses or "wings" of the atlas.

TABLE I.*

MEASUREMENTS OF ATLASES.

	1	2	3	4	5	6	7	8
Transverse axis of brim of articular cup	133	137	133	128	115	117	118	118
Sterno-dorsal " " "	70	65	62	60	51	57	61	53
Transverse axis of post-articular surface	136	126	130	119	112	102	128	114
Greatest transverse breadth of atlas	240	215	227	200	....	170	237	204
Greatest breadth sterno-dorsally of distal end of atlas	100	90	116	96	....	85	105	97
Greatest length near the lateral edge of wing	127	120	130	115	....	110	135	116
Length of centrum, mesial line of sternal aspect	59	51	50	55	54	50	53	47
" " " " dorsal "	84	58	75	68	....	56	74	....

* The measurements in this and all the following tables are given in millimetres.

Explanation of Table I.

1. *Bison latifrons.* Darien, Georgia.
2. *Bison "crassicornis."* Eschscholtz Bay. (Measurements from Richardson.)
3. *Bison bonasus.* Large adult male. (M. C. Z. No. 165.)
4. *Bison americanus.* Large old male. (M. C. Z. No. 10.)
5. *Bison "priscus?"* Eschscholtz Bay. (No. 21,576 of Richardson.)
6. *Bison americanus.* Adult female. (M. C. Z. No. 105.)
7. Old domestic bull.
8. Domestic ox. (Measurements from Richardson.)

From the above table it will be seen that the Georgia specimen is the largest of the series; that the atlas of *B. "crassicornis"* is next in size, while that of *B. bonasus* is third, though exceeding in some of its proportions either of the above-named specimens; the latter differs more from them in its proportions than does the atlas of the male *B. americanus.* This, though fourth in size, corresponds quite nearly in form with the fossil specimens. The atlas of *B. bonasus* has a considerably greater sterno-dorsal thickness than either of the others. The atlas of Richardson's "*Bison priscus?*" it will be noticed, corresponds very nearly in size with that of the *female* of *B. americanus,* being apparently *a little smaller,* while from Richardson's measurements and description it seems to differ but slightly from it in form. All the parts referred by Richardson to his "*B. priscus?*" except the skull (No. 24,589 of Richardson) and a horn-core (No. 105 of Richardson) correspond in size with similar parts of *Bison americanus,* and seem not to differ essentially in any point from them.

The imperfect humerus from Georgia is rather larger (about one tenth) than the humerus from Eschscholtz Bay referred by Dr. Richardson to his *Bison crassicornis*, as shown by Dr. Leidy's measurements. The tibia has also about the same proportional size as the humerus.

The metatarsal bone from Georgia is also a little stouter than the metatarsal attributed by Dr. Richardson to *Bison crassicornis*, though of about the same length, but, as shown by the subjoined table of measurements, neither differs much in size from the corresponding part of a large old male aurochs, all of which much exceed in size the metatarsal of an old very large male *Bison americanus*.

TABLE II.

MEASUREMENTS OF METATARSAL BONES.

	1	2	3	4	5	6	7	8	9
Greatest length	268	264	266	256	261	218	250	283	270
Greatest transverse diameter of proximal end	63	65	66	57	57	44	68	....	....
Greatest antero-posterior diameter of proximal end	61	62	60	55	50	40	63	....	....
Transverse diameter of shaft 3½ in. from proximal end	39	44	46	35	37	25	43	....	45
Antero-posterior diam. of shaft 3½ in. from proximal end	39	44	35	40	39	28	42	....	....
Circumference of shaft 3½ in. from proximal end	142	145	150	124	133	92	147	150	....

Explanation of Table II.

1. *Bison "crassicornis."* "No. 70" of Richardson.
2. *Bison latifrons.* Dr. Leidy's specimen, Darien, Georgia.
3. *Bison bonasus.* Large old male. (M. C. Z. No. 165.)
4. *Bison americanus.* Large old male. (M. C. Z. No. 10)
5. *Bison americanus.* Specimen (fossil?) from Dubuque, Iowa. (See Wyman, in Whitney's Rep. on the Upper Mississippi Lead Region, p. 421.)
6. *Bison americanus.* Adult female. (M. C. Z. No. 1735.)
7. Domestic Bull, "Baron of Oxford."
8. *Bison priscus.* Specimen from Clacton, England. Professor Owen's measurements.
9. *Bison "bonasus."* "Sub-fossil" specimen from Lilljeborg's measurements.

The fragment of a ramus from Georgia is the only portion of the lower jaw' supposed to belong to any of the extinct American bisons thus far described. The teeth in this fragment being very much worn and their original characters thereby disguised, the specimen was at first referred to the genus *Sus*, and was subsequently made the basis of a new genus for a supposed new "tapiroid pachyderm." Still later it was determined by Dr. Leidy to belong to an extinct bison, being referred by him to *Bison* *latifrons.* Its size, however, as given by Dr. Harlan,* shows it to have been of about the size of or at least not larger than corresponding parts of *Bison antiquus* from California.

As already remarked, the horn-cores of *Bison latifrons* have fully twice the dimensions of the largest horn-cores of *Bison priscus* of Europe, this discrepancy at once indicating the two species to be animals possessing very diverse characters. In the subjoined table is given in a single comparative view the measurements of the skulls and cranial fragments of all the forms of fossil bisons thus far described, which in the present paper are referred to three species, namely, *Bison antiquus, Bison priscus,* and *Bison latifrons.* The first-named is the smallest, with relatively small, short, much curved, and abruptly conoidal horns; the second is but little larger, apparently, in general size, but has somewhat longer, less curved, slenderer, and more gradually tapering horns; the third is apparently considerably larger even than the second, with immensely greater horn-cores, which when covered by the horns must have had a spread at the tip of between ten and twelve feet.

TABLE III.

MEASUREMENTS OF SKULLS OF EXTINCT BISONS.

	Bison antiquus.			Bison priscus.													Bison latifrons.		
	1	2	3	4	5	6	7	8	9	10	11	12	13	14	15	16	17	18	19
Anterior border of premaxillæ to occipital crest	...	...	...	646	649	...	...	...	...	...	...	...	...	...	...	630	...	...	...
Fronto-nasal suture to occipital crest	...	343	...	...	323	...	...	...	...	...	...	...	...	...	304	[illegible]	...	...	...
Width of forehead at narrowest part (between orbits and horn cores)	...	287	...	...	...	...	...	...	...	...	...	...	...	...	348	351	380	...	...
Distance between edges of the orbits	...	430	...	356	350	359	...	374	379	341	340	...	351	358	[illegible]	...	...	...	...
Distance between bases of horn cores	...	31[illegible]	290	283	355	[illegible]	360	457	404	307	310	345	366	379	350	...	418	...	467
Width of occiput	...	330	...	...	297	291	280	291	310	...	270	...	301	...	...	...	...	...	...
Length of horn-cores, upper side	...	338	...	...	614	684	730	548	487	609	496	728	632	456	436	...	...	...	813
Circumference of horn-cores at base	370	330	338	391	369	413	417	354	393	377	374	418	375	309	350	...	520	497	530
Distance between extreme tips of horn-cores	...	900	936	...	1650	986	1303	1326	1623	1624	891	1066	1086	900	1036	...	...	...	...
Length of nasals	...	...	...	234	223	...	...	...	...	...	...	...	...	...	...	...	...	...	...
Length of molar series of maxilla	...	...	...	...	166	...	...	...	...	...	...	...	...	...	...	...	...	...	...

Explanation of Table III.

1. *Bison antiquus* Leidy. Big-bone Lick specimen.
2. *Bison antiquus.* Specimen from California described by Dr. Leidy.
3. *Bison antiquus.* California. Measurements communicated by Dr. J. G. Cooper.
4. *Bison priscus* Meyer. Specimen from Bjersjöholm, Scania. Measurements from Nilsson, as quoted by Dr. Richardson.

* Amer. Journ. Sci. Vol. XLIII, p. 143, 1842.

5. *Bison priscus.* Specimen from Sandhofen, Province of Mannheim. Measurements from Meyer's *Ueber fossile Reste von Ochsen* (Nov. Act. Acad. Nat. Cur., Vol. XIII), No. 7 of Meyer's Memoir.
6. *Bison priscus.* Specimen from Pavia, on the Po. No. 8 of Meyer's Memoir (l. c.).
7. *Bison priscus.* Believed to be from Hungary. No. 9 of Meyer's Memoir (l. c.).
8. *Bison priscus.* Banks of the Rhine near Erfelden. No. 10 of Meyer's Memoir (l. c.).
9 – 15. *Bison priscus.* Banks of the Rhine. Nos. 11 – 16 of Meyer's Memoir (l. c.).
16. *Bison priscus.* Cast of specimen from Austrian Italy, in the Museum of Parma. (No. 1199 of Ward's Series of Casts.)
17. *Bison latifrons* Leidy. Peale's original specimen.
18. *Bison latifrons.* San Felipe, Texas. Specimen described by Dr. Carpenter.
19. *Bison latifrons.* Adams County, Ohio. Measurements communicated by Dr. O. D. Norton.

Synonymy and Nomenclature. — By European writers the remains of the extinct bisons found in North America have been always referred to the *Bison priscus* of the Old World. Dr. Leidy, who is almost the only American author who has written about them, has always viewed them as not only distinct from the European, but has at different times regarded them as belonging to several different species.

The first specific systematic name, however, bestowed upon any species of extinct bison was that of *latifrons*, given by Dr. Harlan (see the preceding table of synonymy) in 1825. The specimen described by Harlan was the now historic one described first by Peale, and subsequently by Cuvier and Leidy; but Harlan adds, "Similar fossil skulls have been found in Europe, on the borders of the Rhine, near to Cracovie, in Bohemia," etc. Previously the remains of the fossil bisons had all been universally referred to the aurochs (*Bison bonasus* Gray), although in this same year Cuvier, in the third edition of his "Ossemens Fossiles," admitted the fossil bison as a third species, without, however, giving it a distinctive name.* Two years later Bojanus applied to the extinct bisons, including the American, the specific name of *priscus* (*Urus priscus*).†

* Dans ma première édition, j'avois considéré les crânes fossiles d'Europe comme appartenant à l'aurochs ordinaire, et ceux de Sibérie comme provenant d'une espèce perdue; maintenant que j'ai reconnu les uns et les autres pour être de la même espèce, il s'agiroit de savoir s'ils seroient tous de l'aurochs; mais comme je viens de constater aussi qu'ils ne ressemblent pas plus à l'aurochs que celui-ci ne ressemble au bison d'Amérique, et comme ces deux animaux sont distincts par l'espèce, on ne voit pas pourquoi celui qui a produit les grands crânes fossiles ne seroit pas d'une troisième espèce, aussi distincte que les deux premières, et dont les caractères auroient tenu à d'autres parties qu'à la tête. La grandeur de ses cornes pourroit déjà le faire soupçonner, car les plus vieux bisons et les plus vieux aurochs n'ont que des cornes médiocres. M. Hacquet m'écrit que les plus grands individus n'ont pas de noyaux de cornes de plus d'un pied de long." — *Ossemens Fossiles*, 3d Ed., Tome IV, p. 148.

† Bojanus's words are as follows: "Quam prisci aevi terrarum etiam, a quibus hoc tempore prorsus

In 1830 Fischer also gave the name *latifrons* to a species of fossil bison described from remains found in Siberia, which he appears to have regarded as new, without, however, apparently being aware that the same name had been already given to fossil bison remains from America, or that the name *priscus* had been proposed for the extinct bison of Europe, he referring to only Cuvier's works in his discussion of the subject.

In 1832 H. v. Meyer, recognizing the fossil bison as a species distinct from the aurochs, gave references to the literature of the subject, and a list of the countries in which its remains had been found. He alludes to it under the name "*Bos* (*Bison*) *priscus* Bojanus," referring it for the first time to Hamilton-Smith's "subgenus" *Bison*. Meyer appears also to have been the first author who associated the name *priscus* with either *Bos* or *Bison*. Neither of these generic terms were used by Bojanus in connection with the specific name *priscus*, although Bojanus is almost invariably cited as the author of this association.*

Owen, in 1843, used the name *Urus*, in a generic sense, for the bison, without reference, however, to Bojanus, Owen employing it in this sense entirely independently of any previous author.

In 1842 Dr. Harlan referred a fragment of jaw, having very much worn teeth, found in digging the Brunswick Canal, Georgia, to the genus *Sus*, believing it to represent a new species of that genus, which he called *Sus americanus*. The same specimen was afterwards referred to *Lophiodon* by Professor Owen, who still later regarded it as forming a new genus, which he

abest, indigenam, Rhinocerotis staturae belluam. *Uri prisci* nomine, aliis auctoribus iam recepto, designamus."—*Nov. Act. Acad. Nat. Curios.*, Vol. XIII, Part II, p. 427. The date usually quoted for Bojanus's name of *priscus* is 1825, which is the date of writing; the volume is dated 1827.

* The phraseology used by Bojanus, as already shown, was "*Urus priscus*," but only once have I been able to find the name *Urus priscus* Bojanus given among the synonymes of any species of *Bison*. Meyer, in 1832, wrote "*Bos* (*Bison*) *priscus* Bojanus," and in 1835, simply "*Bos priscus* Bojanus," evidently citing Bojanus as the authority for only the specific name. In 1846 Owen, in his synonymy (Brit. Fossil Mam. and Birds, p. 491) of *Bison priscus*, wrote "*Bos* (*Bison*) *priscus* Bojanus, Nov. Act. Acad. Nat. Cur., t. XIII."! In 1854 Richardson said, "Bojanus, in 1825, bestowed the name of *Bos* (*Bison*) *priscus* on the fossil species" (Zool. Voy. Herald, p. 31), while Dr. J. E. Gray, in 1852, in his synonymy of the genus *Bison*, cites "*Bison* Bojanus, N. Act. Acad. Nat. Cur., XIII"; but Bojanus, as above stated, did not use the word *Bison* at all in a generic sense in the article in question. Lilljeborg is the only author who has, so far as I have seen, given the references to Bojanus properly. In his Fauna öfver Sveriges och Norges Ryggradsdjur (Upsala, 1874), p. 877, under *Bos bonasus* Linné, he cites Bojanus as follows: "*Urus nostras* L. H. BOJANUS. De uro nostrate ejusque sceleto, Commentatio; Nova Acta Physico-Medica Acad. Caesar. Leop. Carol. Nat. Curios., T. XIII, pars IIda, pag. 413,—1827." He also gives "*Urus priscus*, IDEM: ibm, pag. 427."

named *Harlanus*, and considered it as a form allied to the tapiroid pachyderms. In 1854 Dr. Leidy accidentally came across the same specimen, and found it to be not only *not* suiline but to belong to "a true ruminant, and this the *Bison latifrons*." *

In 1846 Professor Owen † wrote respecting the affinities of the fossil bison with the aurochs as follows: "The remains of the ancient European bisons attest their larger size, and larger and somewhat less bent horns than are manifested by the individuals of the present race, but no satisfactory specific distinction has been detected in the fossils compared with the bones of the Lithuanian aurochs." Later, after comparing the bones of the existing wild aurochs with "those of the fossil aurochs," and pointing out the observable differences, he says: "Admitting with Cuvier, that such characters are neither constant nor proper for the distinction of species, we may recognize in the confined sphere of existence to which the aurochs has been progressively reduced, precisely the conditions calculated to produce a general loss of size and strength, and a special diminution of the weapons of offence and defence. I cannot perceive, therefore, any adequate ground for abandoning the conclusion to which I had arrived from a study of the less perfect materials available to that end, before the arrival of the entire skeleton of the Lithuanian aurochs, namely, that this species was contemporary with the mammoth, the tichorhine rhinoceros, and other extinct mammals of the pliocene period." ‡

Professor Nilsson, in 1847, also considered the fossil and living aurochs as one and the same species; the living aurochs differing from the extinct form mainly (as he believed) in its smaller size, he regarded as the degenerate descendant of the fossil aurochs. M. Gervais, § a year or two later, also took substantially the same view, referring the *B. priscus* of authors to the *B. bonasus* Linn.

Dr. Leidy in 1852 considered the remains of the large extinct bison found in America as specifically distinct from the European, to which view he seems to have ever since adhered. He also at this time referred another specimen, which from its size seemed to represent a smaller animal, to a second species, which he called *Bison antiquus*. This he has since

* Proc. Acad. Nat. Sciences, Phila., 1854.

† Hist. British Fossil Mammals and Birds, p. 493.

‡ Ibid., p. 515.

§ Zool. et Paléont. Françaises, I, 73, 1848 - 1852.

regarded as only the female of *B. latifrons*, although as late as 1873 he deemed the question as to the number of species of American fossil oxen as not satisfactorily settled.*

Sir John Richardson, in 1854, in his report on the bison remains from Eschscholtz Bay, expressed himself as inclined to believe in a greater number of fossil species of bison than previous writers had been willing to admit. He had convinced himself, he says, that in the collections from Eschscholtz Bay were "remains of one, and perhaps two, species of the bison type, related as closely to the American bison as to the aurochs." Again he says that some of the remains *more closely* resemble corresponding parts of the American bison than the aurochs, though differing decidedly from both, and inclines to the opinion that what he calls "*Bison priscus?*" together with the remains from Big-bone Lick, Dr. Leidy had described and referred doubtfully to *Bison americanus*, should be regarded as a distinct species and receive a new name. The remains from Big-bone Lick referred to by Richardson prove, however, to belong unquestionably to *Bison americanus*. The larger specimens from Eschscholtz Bay Richardson regarded as belonging to a species distinct from any that had been previously described, to which he gave the name *Bison crassicornis*. Most authors have since regarded these larger specimens as representing only the female of *B. latifrons*, — a view wholly untenable, as sufficiently shown in the preceding pages.

In 1854 Dr. Leidy recognized five species of bisons from America as more or less well established, namely: 1. *Bison americanus* (recent and fossil). 2. *Bison latifrons*. 3. *Bison priscus?* Richardson. 4. *Bison crassicornis* Richardson. 5. *Bison antiquus* Leidy. Later, however, as already noticed, he referred his own *B. antiquus*, and also *B. crassicornis*, to *B. latifrons*. In 1860 he recognized *Bison priscus* as distinct from *B. latifrons*, referring to the former the remains from Eschscholtz Bay, doubtfully referred by Richardson to *B. priscus*. In 1873, however, as already stated, he considered the question as to the number of species of American fossil bisons as still unsettled.

All European writers of note have always regarded the American and Old World fossil bison remains as pertaining to one and the same species. Recent authorities, particularly Professor L. Rütimeyer and Dr. J. F. Brandt, as previously noticed, have regarded this fossil species as the immediate progenitor of the European aurochs and the American bison, Brandt † at the

* Contr. to Ext. Vertebrates, Fauna, etc., p. 253.

† Zoogeog. und Palaont. Beiträge, pp. 101 – 152 (Verhandl. mineral. Gesells. St. Petersburg, II, 1865).

same time regarding all the bisons, recent and fossil, as belonging to the same species!

Lilljeborg, in 1874, also very strangely referred all the bisons, both living and extinct, to the *Bos bonasus* of Linnæus, ignoring alike the prominent osteological as well as external features that distinguish the aurochs from the American bison, and the enormous differences that distinguish the *Bison latifrons* Leidy, not only from both the *B. americanus* and *B. bonasus*, but also from the other extinct species, *B. priscus* and *B. antiquus*, — a thing he could not have done had he worked from specimens or duly weighed the published evidence.

BISON ANTIQUUS Leidy.

The Smaller Extinct American Bison.

Bos urus Buckland, Beechey's Voy. to the Pacific, II, 539, pl. iii, fig. 1 – 7, 1831.

Bison antiquus Leidy, Proc. Acad. Nat. Sci. Phila., 1852, 117; 1854, 210; 1867, 85; Mem. Ext. Spec. Amer. Ox, 11, pl. ii, fig. 1, 1852 (Smithsonian Contributions, Vol. III).

Bison priscus? Richardson, Zoöl. Voy. of Herald, 33, 139, pls. vi, figs. 5, 6, vii, x, figs. 1 – 6, xiii, fig. 3, 1852 – 54 (female).

Bison priscus Leidy, Proc. Acad. Nat. Sci. Phila., 1854, 210; Ext. Mam. of North America, 371, 1869 (Journ. Acad. Nat. Sci. Phila., new Ser., VII).

Bison crassicornis Richardson, Zoöl. Voy. of Herald, 40, 139, pls. ix, xi, fig. 6, xii, figs. 1 – 4, xiii, figs. 1, 2, xv, figs. 1 – 4, 1852 – 54 (male). — Leidy. Proc. Acad. Nat. Sci. Phila., 1854, 210.

Bison latifrons Leidy, Mem. Ext. Spec. Amer. Ox (in part); Extinct Mam. N. Amer., 371, 1869 (in part); Extinct Vertebrate Fauna, 253 (in part), pl. xxviii, figs. 4 – 7, 1873.

?*Fossil Ox*, Perkins, Amer. Journ. Sci., XLII, 137, 1842.

Bison, Buffalo, Whitney, Geol. Surv. California, Geol., I, 252, 1865.

The *Bison antiquus* of Dr. Leidy was first described from a fragment of horn-core, having a small portion of the frontal bone attached, found at Big-bone Lick, Kentucky. It was at first hesitatingly regarded as a distinct species, Dr. Leidy having suspicions that it might prove to be the female of *Bison latifrons*, and in his later notices of the group he has referred it to that species. The fragment indicates, however, an animal of about the size of the male of the smaller extinct bison, whose remains have thus far been found mainly in California and Alaska, and is probably identical with the species described by Dr. Richardson under the name *Bison crassicornis*, based on remains from the ice-cliffs of Eschscholtz Bay. Of late years all these names have been regarded by Dr. Leidy — the only author who has really given the subject much attention — as synonymes of *Bison latifrons*, on the supposition that these remains, notwithstanding other important differences than that of size existing between them and those of the large *Bison latifrons*, merely represented the female of *B. latifrons*. With the light afforded by additional remains of both forms, a different view now seems tenable, namely, that to the smaller species are referable not only the original fragment on which *B. antiquus* was based, but also other remains from California and Alaska.

Dr. Leidy's original description of the Big-bone Lick fragment is as follows: —

"The specimen is rather too small [a fragment] to determine positively whether it is a distinct species or not from *Bison latifrons*. It did not belong to an aged individual, as the suture is still open between the frontal bone and that portion of the parietal which forms the upper boundary of the temporal fossa. It belonged to a species of *Bison*, as indicated by the advanced position of the horn-core, and resembles more the corresponding part in the *Bison priscus* of Europe, as represented by Cuvier and others, than it does that of *Bison latifrons*. The horn-core is more abruptly conoidal, and relatively more curved than in the latter. It is not improbable, however, that the fragment may have belonged to the female of *Bison latifrons*. The only characteristic measurements to be obtained from it are as follows: —

"Length of the fragment of horn-core, 10 inches [or 255 mm.].
Circumference on a line with the basal margin inferiorly, 14½ inches [or 368 mm.].
" five inches from the basal margin superiorly 10 inches [or 255 mm.]."

In respect to the curvature of the horn-core this fragment bears a strong resemblance to the corresponding part of *Bison crassicornis* of Richardson, and also to specimens from California. So great is this resemblance that Dr. Leidy at first referred the California form to his *Bison antiquus*, and the specimen he described (now in the collection of the Academy of Natural Sciences of Philadelphia) is still thus labelled.

Dr. Leidy described the California specimen as approaching "sufficiently near in size and form to the corresponding fragment of a skull from Big-bone Lick, Kentucky, referred to *Bison antiquus*, that it might be regarded as of the same species. Both probably belong," Dr. Leidy, however, adds, "to the female of *Bison latifrons*, as originally suggested in relation to the Big-bone Lick fragment."* Dr. Leidy later adds that "it [the California specimen]

* Proc. Acad. Nat. Sci. Phila., 1867, p. 85.

also sufficiently resembles the fossil from Eschscholtz Bay, described by Buckland and Richardson, and referred by the latter to an extinct species, with the name *Bison crassicornis*, to render it probable that this may have belonged to the same species";* and in his table of synonymy published at this time he refers both *B. antiquus* and *B. crassicornis* to *B. latifrons*.

Respecting the California specimen, in a fuller account of it published later, with figures,† Dr. Leidy also says: "The specimen resembles the corresponding part of the skull of the living buffalo (*Bison americanus*) so closely that it will be unnecessary to describe it in detail. Besides being larger, the horn-cores are especially disproportionately larger, and are more transverse in their direction, or are less inclined backward. The occiput appears proportionately wider and lower from the less degree of prominence of its summit. The latter is, however, wider, and is more distinctly defined from the posterior occipital surface by the rougher and more prominent protuberance of attachment for the nuchal ligament. The occipital foramen is no larger than in the buffalo, and the notch below, between the condyles, is more contracted. The forehead, near its middle, is rather more protuberant than in the buffalo." At this time he very properly deemed the material insufficient to determine whether the remains from this continent of "large oxen which were contemporaneous with the American mastodon," and which had been referred to several distinct species, really pertain to more than one. He, however, still inclined to the opinion of the specific unity of all the forms; "the more robust specimens," he says again, "probably belonged to males, and the smaller ones to females."‡

This view, however, as already stated, seems to me untenable, the fossil bison remains thus far known apparently indicating two quite distinct extinct species of bison in North America, the larger very much exceeding in size, and doubtless otherwise differing from *Bison priscus* of Europe and Asia, and the other of about the size of *Bison priscus*, but differing from it in important features, and closely resembling in many points the bisons still existing.

The *Bison crassicornis* of Richardson was based on "the fragment of a skull brought home by Captain Beechey, and figured by Dr. Buckland in pl. iii, fig. 1,"§ and "referred by him [Beechey] to *Bos urus*, by which is meant,"

* Ext. Mam. of North America, p. 373, 1869.

† Ext. Vert. Faun., p. 253, pl. xxviii, figs. 4, 5, 1873.

‡ Ibid., p. 253.

§ Beechey's Voyage to the Pacific, Vol. II.

says Richardson, "the aurochs, or *Bison priscus* of more recent palæontologists." * To this form Dr. Richardson referred also a large horn-core, an atlas, several other cervical, dorsal, and lumbar vertebræ, a sacrum, parts of several innominate bones, two humeri, several radii, several imperfect femora, and several metatarsals, chiefly on account of their large size. These remains, together with other bison remains of smaller size, were all from the ice-cliffs of Eschscholtz Bay, the smaller remains of this collection being provisionally referred by Dr. Richardson to "*Bison priscus?*" The remains referred to *Bison crassicornis* are described in great detail by Dr. Richardson (the more important of which are also figured), and seem to differ in no important particular (except in being somewhat larger) from the corresponding parts of *Bison americanus*. Many of the slight differences he points out as existing between his *Bison crassicornis* and *B. priscus?* relate only to what would normally be included within the range of individual and sexual variation of representatives of the same species. All of the remains of his "*Bison priscus?*" are smaller, with perhaps the exception of the fragment of a skull (No. 24,580 of Richardson's work, figured in his plate vii), than the corresponding parts of the male of *Bison americanus*, some, perhaps of not fully grown individuals, being not larger even than the corresponding parts of the female of that species. The differences existing between the remains referred by Richardson to "*B. priscus?*" and "*B. crassicornis*" are not greater than those that obtain between the two sexes of *Bison americanus;* hence it seems possible that all of the bison remains described from Eschscholtz Bay may belong to one and the same species, the larger representing the male and the smaller the female, of the form Richardson named *Bison crassicornis*, which is very probably the same as the *B. antiquus* of Leidy, and to which the California bison remains may be at least provisionally referred.

To the same form I at first referred with much hesitation the bison remains recently discovered by Mr. Dall and others in Alaska. As these pages are passing through the press an imperfect skull † from the vicinity of St. Michael's, Alaska, has also come to hand which seems to confirm the

* Zoöl. of Voy. of Herald, as cited above.

† Received for examination from the California Academy of Sciences and labelled "*Bison americanus*, St. Michael's, Alaska, presented by the Alaska Commercial Company." It is wholly unmineralized, and presents merely a weathered appearance, looking as a specimen might after only a few years' exposure to the elements.

correctness of this reference. This specimen (see Plate IV) embraces the upper surface of the skull except the nasal bones, but lacks the occipital and lower surfaces, including the teeth and the greater portion of the maxillæ. It belonged to a rather young or middle-aged animal, in which the sutures had not closed. This specimen is remarkable for the flatness of the frontal region, which is not elevated above the plane of the base of the horn-cores. As this degree of flatness is nearly equalled in recent specimens of *B. americanus*, among which the range of variation in respect to the convexity of the frontal region is very great, it forms a difference of no great importance. The only prominent difference between it and corresponding specimens of *B. americanus*, is in the disproportionately large size of the horn-cores. The general dimensions of the skull (see Table IV) are not larger than those of large old male specimens of *B. americanus*, but the horn-cores are one third to nearly one half longer and proportionately thicker. The horn-core of a bison from the Tatlo River, Alaska, obtained by Mr. Dall, almost exactly corresponds in size with the one from St. Michael's (compare columns 3 and 7 of Table IV). They agree also very nearly in size with the specimens doubtfully referred by Dr. Richardson to *Bison priscus* (see columns 1 and 2 of Table IV). They differ from Richardson's *B. crassicornis* very much as the female of that species might be expected to differ from the other sex. There are in Alaska certainly the two forms, which may be only male and female of one and the same species, or quite distinct species, the smaller of which would present an almost exactly half-way link between the larger *B.* "*crassicornis*" of Richardson and the existing *B. americanus*. If there are two species we as yet know only the males of each, and it therefore seems more reasonable to regard the two forms as different sexes of the same species.

Considering the above-mentioned remains as conspecific they seem to indicate a species of much larger size than the existing American bison, but one not essentially differing from it in form. The older and larger is most evidently the direct and not very remote progenitor of the existing American bison.

Its affinities are perhaps also as close with the existing aurochs as with the latter. The chief differences, so far as its few known remains will permit one to judge, between the species here recognized as *Bison antiquus* and the existing species of bison, consist in its larger general size, and in the disproportionately larger size of its horn-cores. As shown by the following table of comparative measurements of the horn-cores and skulls of all the hitherto described species of *Bison*, it apparently differs but little in size from the true *Bison priscus* of the Old World.

TABLE IV.

MEASUREMENTS OF HORN-CORES AND SKULLS OF EXISTING AND EXTINCT FORMS OF BISON.

	1	2	3	4	5	6	7	8	9	10	11	12	13	14	15	16
Distance from mesial plane of occiput to tip of either horn-core	420	...	360	325	300	327	320	...	...	390	...	470	...	...	...	...
Distance between tips of horn-cores	760	...	680	650	565	615	647	...	...	...	...	920	1058	...	...	1332
Dist. between bases of horn-cores	305	295	295	300	290	296	278	...	...	320	...	392	355	430	...	407
Least width of forehead (between orbits and horn-cores)	...	...	290	285	260	277	270	278	...	...	...	336	...	380	...	...
Greatest width of occiput	276	280	...	245	245	273	258	...	...	...	...	332	297	...	...	...
L'gth of horn-core along upper side	...	270	260	210	170	198	190	...	...	245	...	336	514	...	...	813
Circumference of horn-core at base	...	215	300	275	245	244	240	318	383	263	370	...	380	320	?445	*510
Circ. of horn-cores 14 in. from base	0	0	0	0	0	0	0	0	?	0	?	0	?	307	307	368

* Estimated.

Explanation of Table IV.

1. "*Bison priscus?*" Rich. Specimen No. 24,589, Zoöl. Voy. of Herald, p. 35. (Measurements from Richardson.)
2. "*Bison priscus?*" Rich. Specimen No. 105, Ibid., p. 35. (Measurements from Richardson.)
3. *Bison antiquus.* Specimen from St. Michael's, Alaska.
4. *Bison americanus.* Big-bone Lick, Kentucky. (M. C. Z., No. 2050.) This specimen has the largest horn-cores I have met with in any specimen of *Bison americanus.*
5. *Bison americanus.* Big-bone Lick, Kentucky. (M. C. Z., No. 2047.)
6. *Bison americanus*, adult male. Specimen No. 91, Mus. Comp. Zoölogy.
7. *Bison bonasus*, adult male. Specimen No. 195, Mus. Comp. Zoology.
8. "*Bison crassicornis*," Rich. Capt. Beechey's specimen, Zool. Voy. of Herald, p. 41. (Measurements from Richardson.)
9. "*Bison crassicornis*," Rich. Specimen No. 91, — the large horn-core figured and described by Richardson, l. c. p. 42. Said to have been somewhat reduced in size by abrasion. (Measurements from Richardson.)
10. *Bison antiquus.* Specimen collected by Mr. W. H. Dall on the Tatlo River, Alaska (No. 7529 of the National Museum).
11. *Bison antiquus* Leidy. Original specimen from Big-bone Lick.
12. *Bison antiquus.* Specimen from California, described by Dr. Leidy.
13. *Bison priscus* Meyer. Specimen No. 7 of Meyer's Memoir, l. c.
14. *Bison latifrons* Leidy. Peale's original specimen.
15. *Bison latifrons.* Carpenter's specimen from Texas.
16. *Bison latifrons.* Adams Co., Ohio.

From the above measurements it appears that the horn-cores of *Bison* "*priscus?*" (= *B. antiquus*, female) are very much larger than those of even the males of either *Bison americanus* or *Bison bonasus*, but the specimens do not appear to be in other respects larger; the horn-cores of "*B. crassicornis*" are one fourth to one third larger than either those of *B. americanus* or *B. bonasus*, about equalling in circumference at base those of *B. priscus*, but are only about two thirds as long as those of *B. priscus*. In none of the above-enumerated forms, except *B. priscus*, do the horns exceed a length of ten to fourteen inches, while in *B. latifrons* they attain a length of nearly *three feet, or nearly twice the length of those* of *B. priscus* with a correspondingly greater thickness.

In the foregoing pages, in discussing the affinities of the bison remains from Georgia, tables of comparative measurements have already been given which include the measurements of some of the remains described by Richardson from the ice-cliffs of Eschscholtz Bay. These tables show, as already noticed, the considerably larger size and heavier character of these remains as compared with those of *Bison americanus* and *Bison bonasus*, and their much smaller size (especially of the horn-cores and skull) as compared with *Bison latifrons*. A few further details are here given, relating more especially to the dentition, the lower jaw, and the metacarpal bones.

The teeth, as shown by the following table, also indicate that *Bison antiquus* is intermediate in size between *Bison latifrons* and *Bison americanus*, or about the size of *Bison priscus*.

TABLE V.

MEASUREMENTS OF THE MOLAR TEETH.

	1	2	3	4	5	6	7
First upper molar, greatest antero-posterior diameter of crown	38	...	...	...	...	31	32
" " " " transverse " "	...	...	...	...	...	...	16
" " " " " " at base	27	...	...	...	...	29	24
" " " " length from base of fangs to crown	63	...	...	...	...	...	69
Second upper molar, greatest antero-posterior diameter of crown	36	34	...	...	...	35	34
" " " " transverse " "	...	25	...	...	...	...	18
" " " " " " at base	...	28	...	...	...	30	26
" " " " length from base of fangs to crown	70	...	...	...	...	...	74
Third upper molar, greatest antero-posterior diameter of crown	44	38	...	...	...	38	33
" " " " transverse " "	...	21	...	...	...	...	16
" " " " " " at base	...	27	...	...	...	30	...
" " " " length from base of fangs to crown	76	...	...	...	...	...	72
First lower molar, greatest antero-posterior diameter of crown	...	...	30	30	...	...	29
" " " " transverse " "	...	...	19	...	...	...	13
" " " " " " at base	...	...	...	...	...	...	18
" " " " length from base of fangs to crown	...	...	...	...	...	...	68
Second lower molar, greatest antero-posterior diameter of crown	...	...	39	36	...	...	32
" " " " transverse " "	...	...	23	23	...	...	14
" " " " " " at base	...	...	...	...	...	...	19
" " " " length from base of fangs to crown	...	...	...	...	...	...	68
Third lower molar, greatest antero-posterior diameter of crown	52	...	53	51	48	...	42
" " " " transverse " "	20	...	21	20	22	...	14
" " " " " " at base	...	...	...	...	...	...	17
" " " " length from base of fangs to crown	69	...	...	...	...	...	69

Explanation of Table V.

1. *Bison latifrons.* Specimen from Natchez, Mississippi. (Measurements from Leidy.)
2. *Bison antiquus.* Specimen from Pilarcitas Valley, California. (Measurements from Leidy.)
3. *Bison antiquus.* Alameda County, California. (Nat. Mus., No. 8,270.)
4. *Bison antiquus.* California. (Prof. Whitney's Collection.)
5. *Bison antiquus.* Darien, Georgia. (Dr. Harlan's measurements.)
6. *Bison priscus.* Specimens from Mannheim, Germany. (Measurements from Meyer.)
7. *Bison americanus.* Specimens from Big-bone Lick, Kentucky.

In the Museum of Comparative Zoölogy are two jaw fragments from California belonging to Prof. J. D. Whitney. One of these is 14 mm. in length, and contains portions of two of the premolars and of the true molars. Its height at the last molar is but little greater than the corresponding measurement in a very large old male *B. americanus* (see Plate III), but its thickness at the same point is nearly one third greater. The other fragment is 18 mm. in length and embraces the portion of the jaw between the inner angle and the first true molar. This belonged to a much smaller animal, perhaps a female, but is still very much larger than the corresponding part in the largest old males of *B. americanus* (see Table VI).

TABLE VI.

MEASUREMENTS OF THE LOWER JAW.

	1	2	3	4	5
Extreme length from tip to angle	400	....	....	....	....
Height at the angle	205	....	....	....	....
" " last molar	76	780	800	....	90
" " first premolar	50	....	....	56	60
Thickness at last molar	29	40	36	....	....
" " " second molar	....	....	....	41	....
" " first premolar	24	27	200	27	....
Circumference at last molar	185	....	....	....	....
" " first premolar	135	....	....	....	....
Length of the alveolar space of molars	152	....	....	195	*165
" " " " the true molars	....	....	....	127	....

* First premolar added by estimate.

Explanation of Table VI.

1. Old male *Bison americanus.*
2. Fragment from California (Whitney's Coll.), 14 mm. long, containing portions of two premolars and portions of the three true molars.

3. Fragment from California (Whitney's Coll.), 18 mm. long, — portion extending from the inner angle to the front edge of first molar.
4. Fragment from California. (National Museum Coll.)
5. Georgia specimen. (Measurements in part from Harlan, and in part from Owen's figure.)

In the National Museum at Washington there is still another fragment of a lower jaw (No. 8270 of the National Museum Register), consisting of a large part of one ramus, from Alameda County, California, presented by Dr. L. G. Yates.* This specimen is of about the size of the larger of the two California specimens already described.

Dr. Harlan's measurements of the Georgia specimen, determined by aid of Prof. Owen's figure,† are also added to the table. As already stated, it indicates a species as large as *Bison antiquus*, the jaw being heavier and thicker even than in the largest known specimen of that species. The length of the molar series seems, however, a little less, but this measurement can be only approximately determined.

Of the metacarpal bones of *Bison antiquus* but a single specimen is known. This was collected by Mr. J. Lockhart, and is contained in the National Museum at Washington. It is about one tenth longer than the largest metacarpal of *Bison americanus* I have been able to find, and is relatively much stouter. It is also rather longer and stouter than the corresponding part in a very large old male *Bison bonasus*. It hence about equals the size of this part in *Bison priscus*. In Table VII will be found measurements of this bone as compared with those of the corresponding part in *Bison americanus* (male and female), *Bison bonasus* (male), and of a large domestic bull.

Having at hand a large series of metacarpal bones of *Bison americanus*, I add here a table of measurements showing the range of variation in this part, resulting from age, sex, and individual differentiation, found in a series of nearly a hundred specimens. This series shows that some of the specimens belonging to females are as long as the average of the males, and

* Since the foregoing was put in type I have received a letter from Dr. Yates, dated "Centreville, Alameda Co., Cal., Jan. 29, 1876," announcing the recent discovery by him of another skull of the fossil bison in California. He says: "I found a splendid specimen last week which I shall preserve. It consists of the skull, with three molar teeth on one side, and the greater portion of the horn-cores. It was so soft that I had to bed it in plaster before I could take it out." He adds that "the skull was found in post-pliocene gravel, about ten feet from the spot where I found the skull of a fossil elephant some ten years ago, and in the same deposit where I have found *Mastodon*, *Equus*, *Auchenia*, etc."

† Journ. Acad. Nat. Sci. Phila., 2d Ser., Vol. I, pl. vi.

TABLE VII.

MEASUREMENTS OF METACARPAL BONES.

	1	2	3	4	5	6
Extreme length	223	207	213	218	194	230
Transverse diameter of proximal end	82	83	75	88	56	87
" " " distal end	84	84	82	76	59	77
Least diameter of shaft	56	52	47	52	30	48
" circumference of shaft	153	145	130	134	87	135

Explanation of Table VII.

1. *Bison antiquus.* Yukon River, Alaska. (No. 6573 of the National Museum Register, J. Lockhart, collector.)
2. *Bison americanus.* Very large old male, — the largest specimen I have ever met with. (No. 12,233 National Museum Register.)
3. *Bison americanus.* Very large old male. (Mus. Comp. Zool., No. 10.)
4. *Bison bonasus.* Large old male. (Mus. Comp. Zool., No. 165.)
5. *Bison americanus.* Adult female. (Mus. Comp. Zoöl., No. 12.)
6. Large Domestic Bull, "Baron of Oxford."

TABLE VIII.

MEASUREMENTS OF METACARPALS OF BISON AMERICANUS FROM BIG-BONE LICK, KENTUCKY.

	1	2	3	4	5	6	7	8	9
Extreme length	174	188	193	184	198	183	192	203	213
Transverse diameter of proximal end	60	50	62	61	61	67	75	69	74
" " " distal end	58	52	63	61	62	69	73	70	73
Least diameter of shaft	35	30	33	37	39	45	48	45	45
" circumference of shaft	93	85	98	104	110	120	128	116	123

Explanation of Table VIII.

1. No. 2463. Full-grown female.
2. " 2475. Young female.
3. " 2470. Adult female.
4. " 2476. Adult female.
5. " 2466. Adult female.
6. No. 2489. Adult male.
7. " 2459. Adult male.
8. " 2488. Adult male.
9. " 2467. Adult male.

exceed some very stout ones that belong to the latter sex. In Table VIII are given measurements of nine specimens, — five male and four female, — selected to show the extremes of individual variation, and also the sexual difference in size and form. These specimens are also figured in Plate X.

From this table it appears that the longest metacarpal of a female *B. americanus* exceeds by ten millimetres the length of the shortest corresponding bone of a male, and is only twenty millimetres — or less than one eighth — shorter than that of the largest male, while the transverse diameter of the stoutest male metacarpal is *one third* greater than that of the smallest female metacarpal. This gives a hint as to the wide differences that may be looked for in the proportions and size of corresponding parts of the two sexes in the extinct species.

Synonymy and Nomenclature. — The remains of *Bison antiquus* were first referred to under the name of *Bos urus* by Dr. Buckland, in 1831, the specimens being those collected by Captain Beechey, at Eschscholtz Bay. Other remains were next mentioned under the name *Bison antiquus* by Dr. Leidy, in 1852, this specimen being the one from Big-bone Lick, Kentucky. During the same year Dr. Richardson gave the name *crassicornis* to remains from Eschscholtz Bay, at the same time doubtfully referring other specimens to the *Bison priscus* of Europe. The name *antiquus* antedates that of *crassicornis* by only a few months, but unquestionably has priority. Dr. Leidy's paper, in which *antiquus* was described, was read July 6, 1852, and published prior to the following October; Dr. Richardson's brochure, containing his description of *B. crassicornis*, is dated October 1, 1852, but was published subsequently to this date. In case future discoveries show that the name *antiquus* refers to a different species, or proves to be the female of *B. latifrons*, the name *crassicornis*, of course, then becomes tenable for the smaller Northern and Western extinct bison.

As already noticed, both the names *antiquus* and *crassicornis* have been regarded, even by Dr. Leidy, as synonymes of *Bison latifrons*, while by all foreign writers, except Richardson, all the remains of extinct bisons found in North America have been regarded as identical with the *B. priscus* of Europe and Asia, and in some cases as specifically undistinguishable from the existing aurochs.

4.—Geographical Distribution and Geological Position of the Remains of the Extinct Bisons of North America.

A. Bison latifrons.

1. *Peale's Specimen.*—As previously stated, the original specimen, first made known by Peale, was discovered in the bed of a small creek, about a dozen miles north of Big-bone Lick, Kentucky, but whether in association with other fossils has not been recorded.

2. *Adams County, Ohio.*—Two entire horn-cores were found a few years since by some workmen on Brush Creek, in Adams County, Ohio, while engaged in digging, preparatory to laying the foundations of the abutments of a bridge. They are said to have been found in gravel eighteen feet below the surface, whether associated or not with other fossil remains I have been unable to learn. Although found several years since, they were but recently brought to the notice of the scientific world, by Dr. O. D. Norton, through whose efforts they have fortunately been secured for the Natural History Society of Cincinnati.

3. *San Felipe, Texas.*—The greater portion of a skull and a molar tooth, described by Dr. W. M. Carpenter in 1846, were from the banks of the Brazos River, Texas, and were supposed to have been found near San Felipe. They appear to have been associated with the remains of an extinct species of tapir, in a formation of "mixed clay, sand and gravel, with much iron."

4. *Natchez, Mississippi.*—Five molar teeth from the vicinity of Natchez, Mississippi, were found, according to Dr. Leidy, in association with the remains of *Mastodon, Equus, Ursus, Cervus, Megalonyx, Mylodon*, and *Felis atrox*.

? 5.—*Darien, Georgia.*—Remains belonging either to the female of *Bison latifrons* or the male of *Bison antiquus* were found some years since, at Darien, Georgia, in excavating the Brunswick Canal. These, according to Mr. J. H. Couper, "were found at the bottom of the alluvial deposit, imbedded in it, and lying on the stratum of sand." They were associated with the remains of "the megatherium, the *Mastodon giganteum, Elephas primogenius*, hippopotamus [= *Mastodon americanus* Leidy], horse, and the *Sus americana* [= *Bison*]."

It thus appears that the remains of the larger Extinct American Bison as yet known are not only few in number, but come from not very widely separated localities. They have generally been found in the beds or banks of streams, and when found with other remains have been associated with extinct species belonging to the Fauna preceding the present. It is worthy of remark that the great deposits of bones found at the Kentucky Salt Licks, especially that of Big-bone Lick, have yielded thus far no remains that have been identified as belonging to this gigantic representative of the ox tribe, although containing the remains of *Mastodon*, *Elephas*, *Megalonyx*, and *Mylodon*, together with those of the fossil horse, the great extinct musk ox, the lesser extinct bison, the extinct peccary, the caribou, and the moose.

B. Bison antiquus.

1. *Big-bone Lick, Kentucky.* — The original specimen on which the *Bison antiquus* was founded came, as is well known, from Big-bone Lick, Kentucky. This, however, remains the sole specimen thus far known from that locality, although thousands of specimens of bison remains have been examined in the search for other relics of this species. In 1869 Professor N. S. Shaler made an extended exploration of this locality, at which time he collected and sent to the Museum of Comparative Zoölogy a very large collection of bison remains, numbering over a thousand specimens. These I have examined with much care, without finding any bison remains differing from the remains of *Bison americanus* sufficiently to warrant their reference to any other form of bison. I have found no trouble in matching the largest specimens with the corresponding parts of large specimens of the living bison from the plains of Kansas.

As previously noticed, the tooth described by Dr. Leidy from the post-pliocene beds of the Ashley River, South Carolina, and the bison remains from Darien, Georgia, may belong either to this species or to the female of *Bison latifrons*.

These remains are all that have thus far been found east of the Rocky Mountains that can be ascribed to *Bison antiquus*, and only the single original specimen can be identified as such with entire certainty.

2. *Eschscholtz Bay, Alaska.* — The ice-cliffs of Eschscholtz Bay have furnished an abundance of the remains of this species, two considerable collections having been made by English explorers, and described by Sir John Richardson in the Zoölogy of the Voyage of the Herald. They were found in association with the remains of *Elephas primigenius* and *Ovibos*, in varying

states of preservation, from those that had wholly lost their animal matter to those that were fresh and unchanged. In some cases the horny coverings still adhered to the horn-cores, and in other cases were found detached but still in a good state of preservation.

3. *Valley of the Yukon and its Tributaries.* — Mr. W. H. Dall reports (verb. com.) the occurrence of the remains of the extinct bison throughout a large part of the valley of the Yukon River, Alaska, and along several of its tributaries. These remains, consisting of horn-cores, crania, lower jaws, and other parts, he informs me are found on or near the surface of the ground, with, and in the same condition as, the remains of *Elephas* and an extinct species of *Equus*. The collection of the National Museum at Washington contains a horn-core with part of the frontal bone attached, brought home by Mr. Dall, and a metacarpal collected by Mr. Lockhart. A skull of this species, belonging to the California Academy of Sciences, and kindly loaned me for examination, is labelled "St. Michael's, Alaska," but may have been brought from some point on the Yukon. It thus appears that the remains of the extinct bison are found throughout a considerable portion of the Territory of Alaska.

4. *California.* — In California the remains of the smaller extinct bison appear to be of rather frequent occurrence, having been already found at several different localities, generally associated with the remains of *Mastodon Elephas*, *Tapirus*, and *Equus*. Dr. Leidy has described a skull from Santa Clara County; Professor Whitney mentions the occurrence of its remains in Tuolumne County, and Dr. J. G. Cooper has sent a description of a skull found by him in Alameda County, where Dr. L. G. Yates has recently discovered another skull, from which locality I have also seen other fragments.

?5. *Oregon.* — A phalangeal bone described by Dr. Perkins is said to have been found twenty feet below the surface, on the "Wolhammet or Multonomah River," a tributary of the Columbia, associated with the remains of *Elephas*. The specimen most likely is referable to the present species.

From the foregoing it appears that the remains of this species have been found rather frequently in California and Alaska, and they probably exist at intermediate points. The single specimen from Big-bone Lick, if really identical with the western type, as there seems to be good reason for believing, extends its range to the valley of the Ohio, and there is hence reason to suppose, aside from the occurrence in Georgia of specimens possibly referable to it, that it may have ranged eastward to the Atlantic coast. Everywhere its remains occur in association with those of the larger extinct mammalia, but it may have survived to a comparatively recent date. There is nothing to indicate whether it was or was not contemporaneous with the larger extinct bison, except that the remains of both species occur with those of the same species of other extinct mammals. Judging by the same evidence, both may also have been contemporaneous with the *Bison priscus* of the Old World.

5. — Relation of the Existing Species of Bisons to the Extinct Species.

European writers seem to have fallen into rather confused and erroneous notions respecting the affinities of the different forms of living and extinct bisons. By the earlier writers all the remains of extinct bisons were referred to the aurochs, which was considered as the modern degenerate race of the older form. Later the extinct bisons were viewed as a species distinct from the living, but all of the extinct ones were referred to the same species. Quite recently Rütimeyer, while maintaining this view respecting the fossil forms,* has considered the *Bison americanus* as the older form, through which *Bison bonasus* has passed in reaching its present estate. This conclusion, based on developmental features of the teeth and skull, has been accepted by Brandt and other writers on the subject, contrary, it appears to me, to the teaching of general facts. Lilljeborg has even carried his generalization to the absurd extreme of referring all the forms of *Bison* to the *Bos bonasus* of Linné!

The evidence bearing upon the question of the actual geological sequence of the different extinct forms is by no means decisive or satisfactory. If we regard, however, the gigantic *B. latifrons*, with its immense horns spreading ten to twelve feet, as the older type, passing into, on the one hand, the *Bison priscus* of the Old World, and on the other, into the *Bison antiquus* of the New World, the former giving origin to the existing *Bison bonasus* and the latter to the existing *Bison americanus*, we have what seems to be a natural transition throughout the series. Both in the Old World and the New, the older form is larger than the more recent, with disproportionately

* Strangely and against all analogy, Rütimeyer regards the small *Bison antiquus* of Leidy as the *male* and the gigantic *Bison latifrons* as the *female*, of one and the same species, and both as identical with the Old World extinct bison.

longer and thicker horn-cores. In respect to the American forms, three stages are represented, each later form being not only smaller than the preceding, but the reduction in the size of the horn-core is relatively greater than that of general size.

The types here recognized as distinct forms under the names *B. priscus* and *B. antiquus*, it should be remarked, differ but slightly from each other,—not more so, probably, than do *B. bonasus* and *B. americanus*, if indeed so much,—and constitute as it were a common circumpolar form from which *B. bonasus* and *B. americanus* have probably been differentiated. It seems to me that the *B. americanus* is really the most differentiated form, *B. bonasus*, in its more massive frame and rather larger horns, more strongly recalling the preceding links (*Bison antiquus* and *B. priscus*) in the chain. It was also until recently the form apparently farthest from extinction. For centuries the *B. bonasus* has had but a few hundred survivors, while its total extermination has been prevented only through royal protection; the *B. americanus*, on the other hand, still has millions of representatives, and a few decades ago swarmed in immense herds over nearly a third of the North American continent.

6.—Description of the Existing Species.

BISON AMERICANUS (Gmelin) Smith.

American Bison or Buffalo.

Bos americanus Gmelin, Syst. Nat., I, 204, 1788.—Desmarest, Nouv. Dict. Hist. Nat., III, 531, 1816; Mammalogie, 496, pl. xliv, 1820.—Harlan, Fauna Amer., 268, 1825.—Godman, Amer. Nat. Hist., III, 4, 1826.—Desmoulin, Dict. Class. Hist. Nat., II, 365, 1822.—Richardson, Fauna Bor. Amer., I, 279, 1829.—Fischer, Synop. Mam., 495, 653, 1829.—Cooper, Month. Am. Journ. Geol. & Nat. Hist., 1831, 44, 174, 207 (remains at Big-bone Lick, Ky.); Amer. Journ. Sci., XX, 371, 1831; Edinb. New Phil. Journ., XI, 353, 1831.—Doughty, Cab. Nat. Hist., II, 169, pl. xiv, 1832.—Sabine, Franklin's Journey, 668, 1833.—Wagner, Schreber's Saugt., V, 472, 1855.—Giebel, Säugt., 271, 1855.—Baird, Mam. N. Amer., 682, 1857; U. S. & Mex. Bound. Survey, Pt. II, 52, 1859.—Newberry, Pacif. R. R. Expl. & Surveys, VI, iv, 72, 1857.—Suckley & Gibbs, Ibid., XII, ii, 138, 1860.—Xantus, Zool. Garten, I, 109.—Allen, Proc. Bost. Soc. Nat. Hist., XIII, 186, 1869; XVII, 39, 1874.

Bison americanus Catesby, Nat. Hist. Carolina, II, App., 20, xxviii, 1754.—Brisson, Reg. Anim., Quad., 1756.—Smith, Griffith's Cuv., V, 374, 1827.—De Kay, Nat. Hist. New York Zool., Pt. I, 110, 1842.—Sundevall, Kong. Sv. Vet. Akad. Handl. for 1844, 203, 1846.—Gray, Knowsley's Menag., 49, 1850; Cat. Mam Brit. Mus., Pt. III, 39, 1852; Hand-List of Edentate, Thick-Skinned, & Ruminant Mam., 85, 1873.—Gerrard, Cat. Bones of Mam. Brit. Mus., 230, 1862.—Turner,

Proc. Zoöl. Soc. London, XVIII, 177, 1850. — AUDUBON & BACHMAN, Quad. N. Amer., II, 32, pls. lvi, lvii, 1851. — BAIRD, Rep. U. S. Pat. Off., Agricult., 1851, 124 (plate), 1852. — LEIDY, Proc. Acad. Nat. Sci. Phila., 1854, 200, 210; Extinct Mam. Faun. N. Amer., 371, 1869. — ALLEN, Bull. Essex Institute, VI, 46, 54, 59, 63, 1874. — RUTIMEYER, Verhandl. Naturf. Gesells. in Berlin, IV, iii, 1865; Versuch einer natürlichen Geschichte des Rindes, II, 58.

Bos bison var. β LINNÉ, Syst. Nat., I, 99, 1766. — KALM, Travels in N. Amer. (Forster's Transl.), I, 297.

Bos bison SCHINTZ, Synop. Mam., 482, 1845 (in part only).

"*Bos urus* var. BODD., Elen. Anim., 1784."

Bos bonasus BRANDT, Zoogeographische und Palæontologische Beiträge, 105, 1867 (in part only). — LILLJEBORG, Fauna öfvers Sveriges och Norges Ryggrad., I, 877, 1874 (in part only).

Taurus mexicanus HERNANDEZ, Mexico, 587.

Taurus quivirensis NIEREMB., Hist. Nat., 181, 182.

Le Bison [*d'Amérique*], BUFFON, Hist. Nat., XI, 284, Suppl. III, pl. v. — F. CUVIER & GEOFFROY, Hist. Nat. des Mam., I, livr. xii, 1819; II, livr. xxxii; III, livr. xliv. — G. CUVIER, Reg. Anim., I, 170, 1817; Oss. Foss., 3d Ed., IV, 117, 1825.

American Bison, AGASSIZ, Proc. Bost. Soc. Nat. Hist., XI, 316, 1867.

Buffalo, COOPER, Month. Am. Journ. Geol., 1831, 174, 207 (remains at Big-bone Lick). — KNIGHT, Amer. Journ. Sci., XXVII, 166, 1835 (remains at Big-bone Lick). — LYELL, Proc. Geol. Soc. London, IV, 36, 1843 (remains at Big-bone Lick).

Description. — An adult male measures about nine feet (two and three fourths metres) from the muzzle to the insertion of the tail, and thirteen and a half feet (about four and one sixth metres) to the end of the tail, including the hairs, which extend about fifteen inches beyond the vertebræ. The female measures about six and a half feet (about two metres) from the muzzle to the insertion of the tail, and about seven feet (two and one sixth metres) to the end of the tail, including the hairs, which extend about ten inches beyond the vertebræ. The height of the male at the highest part of the hump is about five and a half to six feet (about two metres); of the female at the same point about five feet (about one and a half metres). The height of the male at the hips is about four and two thirds feet (nearly one and a half metres); of the female at the same point about four and a half feet (about one and a third metres). Audubon states the weight of old males to be nearly two thousand pounds, that of the full-grown fat females to be about twelve hundred pounds.

The horns of the males are short, very thick at the base, and rapidly taper to a sharp point, which in old individuals becomes worn off on the lower side, and the end is often shortened by the same process and occasionally much splintered. Their direction is outward and upward, finally curving inward. The horns of the females are much smaller at the base but nearly as long as in the males, but they taper very gradually, and are hence much slenderer, and are rather more incurved at the tips, where they are rarely abraded as in the males. The hoofs are short and broad, those of the fore feet abruptly rounded at the end; those of the hind feet are much narrower and more pointed. The muffle is broad and naked, having much the same form as in the domestic ox. The short tail has the long hairs restricted to a tuft at the end.

In winter the head, neck, legs, tail, and whole under parts, are blackish-brown; the upper surface of the body lighter. The color above becomes gradually lighter towards spring; the new short hair in autumn is soft dark umber or liver-brown. In very old individuals the long woolly hair over the shoulders bleaches to a light yellowish-brown. Young animals are generally wholly dark brown, darkest about the head, on the lower surface of the body, and on the limbs. The young calf is at first nearly uniform light chestnut-brown, or yellowish-brown, with scattered darker hairs on the belly, where are also occasionally small patches of white. Toward autumn the light yellowish color is replaced by the darker brown that characterizes the older animals. After the first few months the younger animals are darker than they are later in life, at middle-age the coat, especially over the shoulders, becoming lighter and presenting a bleached or faded appearance, which increases with age. The horns, hoofs, and muffle are black, the hoofs being sometimes edged or striped with whitish. There are no important sexual differences in color.

The woolly hair over the shoulders is much longer and more shaggy than elsewhere on the body; it increases in length on the neck above, gradually losing its woolly character, and between the horns attains a length of ten to fourteen inches, nearly concealing the ears and the bases of the horns, and often partly covers the eyes. The long hair advances also on the face, where it decreases in length and becomes more woolly again, extending far forward in a pointed area nearly to the nose. The chin and throat are also covered with long hair, which under the chin forms an immense beard, eight or ten inches to a foot or more in length. Thick masses of long hair also arise from the inner and posterior surfaces of the upper part of the fore legs, where the hair often attains a length of six or eight inches. A strip of long hair also extends along the crest of the back nearly to the tail. The tail is covered with only short soft hair till near the tip, from which arises a tuft of coarse long hair twelve to eighteen inches in length. The hinder and lower portions of the body and legs are covered with short soft woolly hair. This is moulted early in spring, after which for a few weeks the hinder portions of the animal are quite or nearly naked. The shoulders retain permanently their long shaggy covering, which with the long hair of the neck and head gives them, especially during the moulting season, a singularly formidable aspect.

The female, as already stated, is much smaller than the male, with a less elevated hump, much smaller, slenderer, and more curved horns, less heavily developed beard, less shaggy head, etc., but presents no essential differences in color.

Albinism and Melanism. — Pied individuals are occasionally met with, but they are of rare occurrence.* I have seen but a single specimen, the head of which, finely mounted, is now in the Museum of Comparative Zoölogy. I obtained it of hunters at Fort Hays, Kansas, near which place it was taken in 1870, where it was regarded as a great curiosity. In this specimen, a female, the whole face, from between the horns to the muzzle, is pure white, but in other respects does not differ from ordinary examples. White individuals are still more rare, but are not unknown. A former agent of the American Fur Company, who had had unusually favorable opportunities of judging, informed me that they probably occur in the proportion of not more than one in millions, he having seen but five in an experience of twenty years, although he had met with hundreds of pied ones. Black ones are rather more frequent, but can only be regarded as very rare. The fur of these is usually much softer and finer than that of ordinary individuals, and black robes, from this fact and their great rarity, bring a very large price. They seem to be more frequent at the northward than elsewhere.

Varieties. — There are two commonly recognized varieties of the buffalo, known respectively as the *wood buffalo* and the *mountain buffalo*. The wood buffalo is described by Hind † as larger than the common bison of the plains, with very short soft pelage and soft short uncurled mane, thus more resembling in these points the Lithuanian bison or aurochs. It is said to be very scarce, and to be found only north of the Saskatchewan and along the flanks of the Rocky Mountains, and to never venture into the plains. A supposed variety of the bison, referred to by some of the northern voyagers as occurring north of Great Slave Lake, and known only from vague rumors current among the natives, is in all probability the musk-ox (*Ovibos moschatus*).

The mountain bison, so often referred to by hunters and mountaineers as a

* See Long's Expedition to the Rocky Mts, Vol. I, p. 471.

† Hind (H. Y.), Nar. of Canadian Red River Explor. Exped., etc., Vol. II, pp. 106, 107, 1860.

variety or perhaps a distinct species, seems to agree in all essential particulars with the so-called wood bison of the region farther north. The same characters of larger size, darker, shorter and softer pelage, are usually attributed to it, but one meets with such different, exaggerated, and contradictory accounts of its distinctive features from different observers that it is almost impossible to believe in its existence, except in the imaginations of the hunter and adventurer. I have found that those actually conversant with it, and whose opinions in general matters are most entitled to respect, regard it as but slightly or not at all different from the bison of the plains. Others who know it only from hearsay, and whose notions of it are consequently vague, generally magnify its supposed differences, till some do not hesitate to declare their belief in it as a specifically distinct animal from the common bison of the plains.* Dr. Cooper, speaking of the bisons found formerly in the mountain valleys about the sources of the Snake River, says he "saw no difference in the skulls, indicating a different species, or 'mountain buffalo' of hunters."† The bisons formerly living in the parks and valleys of the central portion of the Rocky Mountain chain doubtless did often grow to a larger size than those of the plains, with rather larger horns, and, being less subjected to the bleaching effects of the elements in their partially wooded retreats, would naturally have a darker and perhaps softer pelage. The weathered bison skulls I met with in 1871 in the upper part of South Park and in the vicinity of the tree-limit in the Snowy Range of Colorado were certainly larger, in the average, by actual measurement, than those of the Kansas plains. The small bands now lingering here and there in the mountains, and now currently known as the mountain buffalo, may be in part the remnants of a former larger mountain form, but certainly a part of them are actually recent migrants from the plains. In 1871 I was able to trace the migration of a small band up the valley of the South Platte and across South Park to the vicinity of the so-called Buffalo Spring, situated considerably to the southward of Fairplay. Specimens of the "mountain bison" sent in a fresh state from Colorado to the Smithsonian Institution during the present winter (December, 1875) certainly presented no appreciable differences from winter specimens from the plains. The mountain race of the bison was apparently a little larger than the buffalo of the plains, and doubtless was nearly identical with the race known farther northward as the "wood buffalo."

* See Bulletin Essex Institute, Vol. VI, p. 55, 1874.

† Amer. Nat., Vol. II, p. 538, 1868.

Their more sheltered and in some other respects somewhat different habitat would tend to develop just the differences claimed to distinguish the mountain and northern woodland race.

Castrated buffaloes are said to be occasionally met with where the buffaloes are abundant, being castrated when quite young by hunters. They are reported to attain an immense size, being so much larger than the others as to be conspicuous from their large size.

Relationship to the Aurochs. — The American bison is a little smaller than the aurochs (*Bison bonasus*), with a much larger chest, a smaller and weaker pelvis, a shorter and smaller tail, more shaggy head, and heavier beard. The more important differences, as shown by a comparison of the skeletons, consist in the chest (see subjoined measurements, Table IX) in *Bison americanus* being absolutely larger than in *Bison bonasus*, while the pelvis is very small and weak. The *B. americanus* is hence greatly developed anteriorly, or in the thoracic portion of the body, with the pelvic portion disproportionately reduced, while in *B. bonasus* just the reverse of this obtains, — a small compressed thorax and a strong heavy pelvis. This gives the aurochs the appearance of standing higher on its legs. The dorsal outline is about equally declined posteriorly in each species, *not* relatively much more declined in *B. americanus*, as generally stated. Neither does the aurochs possess relatively longer hind limbs, as compared with the fore limbs, than *B. americanus*, the proportion being essentially the same in the two, whether the total height of the animal be assumed as the basis of comparison, or whether the comparison be based on the bones of the limbs alone.

Comparing, for example, a fine perfect skeleton of a very large old male of each species, beautifully and correctly mounted,* the height of the American bison at the highest dorsal spine is found to be sixty-six inches; at the anterior end of the sacrum, fifty-two inches; which makes the proportion between the two measurements as 80 to 100. The height of the aurochs at the highest dorsal spine is seventy-three inches; at the anterior end of the sacrum, sixty inches; making the proportion between the two measurements as 82 to 100. This difference is not greater than often occurs

* These skeletons are Nos. 91 (*Bison americanus*) and 165 (*Bison bonasus*) of the osteological collection of the Museum of Comparative Zoölogy, both of which were prepared and mounted in the same manner by the same persons, under the supervision of Professor H. A. Ward of Rochester, and represent two pieces of his best osteological work, which is justly celebrated for its neatness and accuracy.

between two individuals of the same species. A comparison of the anterior and posterior limbs gives a similar result. Thus the proportionate length of the fore limb (excluding the scapula) to the hind limb, in the American bison, is the same as that in the aurochs, namely, as 91 to 100.

While the skeleton of the aurochs is, generally speaking, heavier and more massive than that of the American bison, and considerably larger in all its measurements, the ribs are actually much shorter and straighter, giving a *much smaller thoracic cavity*. The length of the first rib in *B. americanus*, for example, is 452 mm.; in *B. bonasus*, 375 mm.; of the third rib in *B. americanus*, 548; in *B. bonasus*, 492; of the sixth rib in *B. americanus*, 711; in *B. bonasus*, 697; of the ninth rib in *B. americanus*, 910; in *B. bonasus*, 869; of the twelfth rib in *B. americanus*, 783; in *B. bonasus*, 750; of the fourteenth rib (osseous portion only), in *B. americanus*, 437; in *B. bonasus*, 418. The pelvis, on the other hand, is fully one fourth larger in all its dimensions, and the bones that enter into its composition are far more massive in the aurochs than in the American bison. The smaller size of the posterior part of the vertebral column in the American bison is also further seen in its diminutive tail as compared with that of the aurochs. Among other noticeable skeletal differences are the relatively greater length of the dorsal series of the vertebræ, and shorter sternum of the American bison.

While the above-given comparisons are based on a single skeleton of each species, the subjoined measurements (see Table IX) shows that these conclusions are borne out by further material.

As already noticed (p. 2), the American bison is *not* distinguished from the aurochs by the possession of fifteen pairs of ribs and only four lumbar vertebræ, as was formerly supposed, and as has been so often stated, the two species having normally the same number of lumbar vertebræ and the same number of pairs of ribs. Professor Rütimeyer* refers to the greater length of the anterior dorsal spines in *Bison americanus*, but this difference is evidently not constant, as is shown by the measurements given in Table IX. He also regards the differences in the relative length of the different segments of the extremities to each other and to the whole height of the animal as affording differences worthy of note. He gives a table illustrative of these differences, which I subjoin. He says: "Nahm ich die Länge von Metacarpus und Carpus zusammen als Einheit, so verhielten sich dazu die andern Segmente der Extremitäten folgendermassen: —

* Versuch einer natürlichen Geschichte des Rindes, etc., Part II, p. 68.

	Bison americanus.		B. europæus.	
"Carpus — Metacarpus	1.		1.	
Radius (Aussenseite)	1.102	3.387 (1.)	1.254	3.697 (1.)
Humerus mit Trochanter	1.285		1.443	
Scapula vorderer Rand	1.795		1.843	
Metacarpus mit Naviculare	1.151		1.098	
Tibia aussen	1.379	3.999 (1.180)	1.588	4.489 (1.214)."
Femur mit Trochanter	1.469		1.803	

Taking the same method of comparison with five specimens of *B. americanus* and two specimens of *B. bonasus* (= *europæus*) as a basis, gives proportions not differing essentially from Rütimeyer's, though the figures range ten to fifteen per cent larger, being probably based on larger specimens.

Carpus and Metacarpus	1.		1.	
Radius	1.260	3.680 (1.)	1.327	3.901 (1.)
Humerus (with Trochanter)	1.420		1.574	
Scapula	1.940		1.836	
Metacarpus	1.400		1.364	
Tibia	1.680	4.800 (1.130)	1.727	4.834 (1.155)
Femur (with Trochanter)	1.720		1.743	

The differences between the two species in these proportions are very slight, scarcely greater in fact than occur between different individuals of *Bison americanus*.

Dr. J. E. Gray placed the aurochs and American bison in different sections of the genus *Bison*, the first of which, containing the aurochs, is characterized as having the "tarsi elongate, fore and hind quarters subequal," and the other, containing the American bison, as having the "tarsi short, hinder quarters very low." In the description of the aurochs he says again, "fore and hind legs subequal; tarsi elongate," contrasting it with "tarsus short, hinder quarters very low," in his diagnosis of *Bison americanus*. The difference in height between the fore and hind quarters of the aurochs and American bison is, as already shown, more apparent than real, owing to the greater size of the pelvic region in the aurochs. The difference in the relative length of the tarsus is also much less than one might infer from Dr. Gray's diagnosis.

In *Bison americanus* the proportional length of the metatarsal bone to the length of the femur and tibia taken together is (in five specimens) as 29 – 31 to 100; in *Bison bonasus* (two specimens), as 28 to 100, showing an actual slightly greater length of the metatarsal segment in *Bison americanus*. The length of the carpus and metacarpus in *B. americanus* (same specimens) to the length of tarsus and metatarsus is as 74 to 100; in *Bison bonasus* as 73 to 100. The length of the upper portion of the fore limb (humerus and radius) to the upper portions of the hind limb (femur and tibia) in *B. americanus* (same specimens as before) is as 75–83 to 100; in *B. bonasus*, as 80–84 to 100. These proportions coincide with those obtained from comparing the entire fore and hind limbs with each other, as well as the relative height of

TABLE IX.

MEASUREMENTS OF SKELETONS OF BISON AMERICANUS AND BISON BONASUS.

	Bison americanus						Bison bonasus		
	1	2	3	4	5	6	7	8	9
	♂	♂	♂	♂	♀	♀	♂	♂	♂
Whole length of skeleton (including skull)	3338	2080	2916	2920	3120	2789	3375	3416	....
Length of skull	527	550	565	510	500	422	580	565	569
" " cervical vertebræ	527	470	430	480	520	457	590	538	?433
" " dorsal "	1150	950	900	880	1000	868	940	985	....
" " lumbar "	407	340	330	380	370	357	390	400	....
" " sacral	254	190	210	250	245	228	315	293	....
" " caudal	476	500	480	420	485	457	560	635	....
" " first rib	452	350	380	....	....	287	345	375	....
" " " " osseous portion, along external curvature	414	300	330	300	320	274	305	335	....
" " " " cartilaginous portion	38	50	50	....	....	31	40	39	....
" " third rib	548	....	510	....	....	450	470	492	....
" " " " osseous portion	430	385	420	390	430	361	386	418	....
" " " " cartilaginous portion	115	....	80	....	....	88	93	100	....
" " sixth rib	711	....	700	....	....	632	640	609	....
" " " " osseous portion	557	550	560	550	580	503	525	559	....
" " " " cartilaginous portion	154	....	140	....	....	122	115	140	....
" " ninth rib	910	....	920	....	....	780	785	869	....
" " " " osseous portion	670	630	680	635	680	584	600	660	....
" " " " cartilaginous portion	240	....	240	....	....	198	185	210	....
" " twelfth rib	783	....	820	....	....	745	730	750	....
" " " " osseous portion	540	580	500	575	610	532	540	530	....
" " " " cartilaginous portion	243	....	230	....	....	215	190	220	....
" " fourteenth rib	693	....	710	....	....	592	585	....	....
" " " " osseous portion	437	420	520	450	410	396	420	415	....
" " " " cartilaginous portion	254	....	190	....	....	197	165	....	....
" " sternum	460	490	480	490	475	462	510	533	....
" " spine of 6th cervical	114	110	150	90	105	76	180	120	90
" " " 7th "	305	260	370	330	347	244	305	287	266
" " " 1st dorsal	468	470	475	415	453	336	393	470	423
" " " 2d "	477	485	465	430	440	342	420	490	440
" " " 3d "	445	435	430	400	406	317	393	470	435
" " " 4th "	400	420	390	360	370	303	370	437	410
" " " 5th "	348	390	350	320	335	287	350	397	371
" " " 6th "	330	355	315	290	300	248	300	363	343
" " " 7th "	315	310	290	260	265	244	273	325	300
" " " 8th "	284	285	260	235	250	223	240	293	290
" " " 9th "	242	245	225	210	213	197	210	267	247
" " " 10th "	210	210	200	180	185	170	170	217	228
" " " 11th "	173	185	165	155	160	152	158	185	190
" " " 12th "	146	155	140	130	135	128	143	148	154
" " " 13th "	120	120	120	110	118	116	123	134	....
" " " 14th "	108	100	110	100	108	101	90	127	127
Distance between ends of pleurapophyses of 1st lumbar	227	310	280	230	230	268	256	278	297

	Bison americanus.						Bison bonasus.		
	1	2	3	4	5	6	7	8	9
	♂	♂	♂	♂	♀	♀	♂	♂	♂
Distance between ends of pleurapophyses of 2d lumbar	310	335	305	300	314	276	296	325	348
" " " " " " 3d "	356	355	330	333	345	293	345	363	375
" " " " " " 4th "	360	365	340	350	373	313	367	387	381
" " " " " " 5th "	309	295	300	326	350	313	335	343	297
Transverse diameter of proximal end of 1st sacral	240	....	....	240	245	230	250	245	216
Length of innominate bone	515	560	500	510	550	448	590	647	571
Greatest (external) width of pelvis anteriorly	470	490	450	475	497	438	484	560	....
Dist. betw. most lateral parts of post. end of pubic bones	283	284	....	260	273	250	305	315	....
Length of ilium	285	290	290	265	290	258	320	338	320
" " ischio-pubic bones	270	270	250	250	275	234	250	311	288
" " thyroid foramen	115	....	....	115	116	110	115	118	114
Breadth of " "	63	....	....	70	73	70	74	76	65
" " scapula	483	470	460	480	500	427	500	508	478
" " " at proximal end	287	270	235	270	284	217	285	310	....
Length of humerus	380	365	365	350	383	328	395	433	....
Antero-posterior diameter of the proximal end	158	....	....	142	145	128	150	158	....
Transverse " " " "	128	....	....	117	130	113	120	134	....
Greatest breadth of its distal end	110	....	....	88	96	82	90	108	105
Least circumference of its shaft	185	177	183	170	196	141	162	174	190
Length of radius	313	315	320	310	320	293	365	364	340
Transverse diameter of proximal end	100	....	....	95	93	84	95	105	....
" " " distal "	94	....	....	88	88	71	96	90	....
Length of ulna	437	415	420	410	418	381	435	520	457
" " its olecranon	148	130	120	133	140	114	165	270	....
Least breadth antero-posteriorly	74	....	....	65	65	65	68	73	....
Length of carpus	58	50	55	50	62	56	60	51	....
Length of canon bone	197	205	200	200	204	190	220	218	195
Width of proximal end	78	....	....	72	75	65	81	88	76
Width of distal end	80	....	....	76	83	62	71	76	74
Length of inner metatarsal	44	....	....	40	48	36	43	70	62
Length of 1st phalanx (fore limb)	68	60	55	57	64	61	74	74	....
Width " " proximal end	43	....	....	39	45	26	57	43	....
" " " distal "	40	....	....	36	41	27	37	42	....
Length of 2d "	40	40	40	35	38	40	43	44	....
Width " " proximal end	44	....	....	35	40	32	38	42	....
" " " distal "	41	....	....	31	37	31	34	35	....
Length of unguinal phalanx, inner side	63	60	60	53	62	55	52	74	....
Length of femur	431	425	430	420	400	367	490	470	478
Greatest diameter of proximal end	160	....	....	145	140	134	145	150	....
" " " distal "	120	....	....	110	112	110	116	125	....
Least circumference of shaft	158	150	160	142	145	132	165	177	....
" diameter "	46	....	....	43	44	40	44	49	48
Length of tibia	427	395	380	380	390	364	465	476	478
Transverse diameter of proximal end	127	....	....	118	110	106	122	130	125
" " " distal "	78	....	....	74	73	70	74	83	....
Its least circumference	148	....	....	140	144	128	160	150	....
Length of tarsals in situ (inside)	101	90	....	90	105	68	107	108	....
" " calcaneum (outside)	155	....	....	145	160	142	178	181	163
Least circumference of its shaft	120	....	....	110	118	97	118	127	128
Length of metatarsal	250	243	....	248	245	152	264	267	248
Transverse (lateral) diameter of proximal end	65	....	....	55	58	51	68	68	....
" antero-posterior diameter of proximal end	55	....	....	50	57	47	59	58	....
" (lateral) diameter of distal end	70	....	....	63	70	62	70	68	65
" antero-posterior diameter of distal end	36	....	....	30	39	31	33	38	....
Least (lateral) diameter of its shaft	35	....	....	34	35	30	43	44	40
Length of 1st phalanx (hind limb)	75	73	65	60	66	40	73	82	76
Width transversely of proximal end	38	....	....	34	35	28	34	38	38
" of distal end	37	....	....	33	35	27	33	37	37
Length of 2d phalanx	44	40	45	37	41	39	46	50	51
Width of proximal end	38	....	....	33	35	32	35	38	37
" " distal end	32	....	....	27	32	30	30	28	34
Length of unguinal phalanx, inner side	63	60	65	55	66	57	62	70	55

Explanation of Table IX.

1. *Bison americanus.* Male, mounted skeleton (No. 91, Mus. Comp. Zoology), from near Fort Hays, Kansas.
2. *Bison americanus.* Very old male, unmounted skeleton, the bones mostly ligamentously attached (Mus. Comp. Zoölogy), from near Fort Hays, Kansas.
3. *Bison americanus.* Very old male, unmounted skeleton, the bones mostly ligamentously attached (Mus. Comp. Zoölogy), from near Fort Hays, Kansas.
4. *Bison americanus.* Male, disarticulated skeleton (No. 10, Mus. Comp. Zoölogy), from near Fort Hays, Kansas.
5. *Bison americanus.* Female, disarticulated skeleton (No. 11, Mus. Comp. Zoology), from near Fort Hays, Kansas.
6. *Bison americanus.* Female, mounted skeleton (No. 92, Mus. Comp. Zoölogy), from near Fort Hays, Kansas.
7. *Bison bonasus.* Old male, mounted skeleton (No. 165, Mus. Comp. Zoölogy), from the Menagerie of Schœnbrunn, received from the Vienna Museum.
8. *Bison bonasus.* Young male, mounted skeleton (No. 11,514, National Museum, Washington), from the Vienna Museum.
9. *Bison bonasus.* Male (measurements from Richardson's Zoöl. of the Voyage of the Herald).

the animal at the shoulder and hip (as previously given); and show a slightly greater average relative length of the hind limb in *B. bonasus* as compared with *B. americanus.* The differences, however, are really much less than different individuals of either species present when compared with each other.

The skull of *Bison bonasus* is rather longer perhaps than that of *Bison americanus*, but the average difference in length is very slight. It would be often, in fact, almost impossible to decide absolutely as to whether a skull from an unknown locality belonged to one rather than to the other of the two species, especially those of young individuals or females. Neither the teeth nor the relative size and form of any portion of the skull afford any absolutely distinctive characters. The chief difference consists in the rather more massive character of the skull in *Bison bonasus.* The close resemblance in all essential features between the skulls of the two species is sufficiently indicated in the subjoined table of measurements of a considerable number of skulls of each species.

The greater prominence and thickness of the orbital cylinder in the aurochs has been cited by Rütimeyer as a distinctive feature of the aurochs, but in a comparison of skulls of corresponding ages the difference is not apparent, the slightly greater size and thickness corresponding merely with the generally more massive character of the osseous system of the aurochs. The difference in the nasal bones referred to also by the same author is intangible, being equalled in different individuals of *Bison americanus.*

TABLE X.

MEASUREMENTS OF TWENTY-TWO SKULLS OF BISON AMERICANUS AND OF FIVE SKULLS OF BISON BONASUS.

	Bison americanus.																						Bison bonasus.				
	1	2	3	4	5	6	7	8	9	10	11	12	13	14	15	16	17	18	19	20	21	22	23	24	25	26	27
	♂	♂	♂	♂	♂	♂	♂	♂	♂	♂	♂	♂	♂	♂	♂	♂	♀	♀	♀	♀	♀	♀	♀	♂	♂	♂	♂
Anterior border of premaxillæ to occipital crest	540	514	530	500	550	525	505	558	534	510	500	555	550	500	500	600	442	420	450	490	480	422	458	565	570	525	580
" " " anterior edge of orbits	280	290	290	276	273	273	260	270	270	267	285	275	270	250	250	323	240	220	240	253	255	260	230	290	305	...	306
" end of nasal bones to occipital crest	458	463	440	460	452	430	420	460	440	425	415	440	437	420	...	445	368	350	370	390	378	410	393	484	427	...	440
Fronto-nasal suture to occipital crest	247	267	...	263	240	252	230	270	230	227	214	240	245	230	230	255	200	190	198	210	208	216	208	285	257	250	265
Anterior end of nasal bones to base of horn-cores	362	355	...	370	375	350	360	360	365	340	350	356	360	343	...	365	310	300	315	345	340	348	332	394	...	...	375
Breadth of forehead at narrowest point *	270	273	...	270	285	254	270	277	267	252	240	280	272	265	252	290	200	206	208	210	213	220	206	270	245	231	267
Distance between extreme outer edge of orbits	310	305	310	323	345	298	295	333	320	286	290	330	332	335	323	338	250	230	236	267	260	240	230	310	328	310	312
" " bases of horn-cores	266	267	280	280	300	268	284	296	272	260	255	280	286	263	271	283	205	210	214	214	213	220	205	278	282	230	270
Width of skull at the auricular openings	240	267	250	272	270	238	220	273	253	227	238	277	267	260	260	280	174	186	190	220	214	203	193	254	258	240	245
Length of horn-cores measured along upper side	204	197	200	200	215	203	220	196	185	157	146	180	210	176	175	...	146	135	156	132	133	133	153	190	230	...	270
" " a line connecting base and tip	190	163	...	195	200	178	175	176	173	136	132	162	178	161	170	...	126	120	134	125	130	127	127	177	...	...	240
Circumference of base of horn-core	254	254	...	253	260	200	214	240	235	193	200	217	233	255	240	300	138	135	158	163	165	166	178	240	262	...	200
Dist. from mesial plane of skull to tip of horn-core	330	298	...	328	350	314	317	327	298	253	267	300	330	300	290	..	220	205	230	235	233	248	216	320	...	...	310
" between extreme tips of horn-cores	420	684	...	640	680	575	575	615	590	484	515	565	620	585	560	...	418	362	425	468	450	490	395	647	622	...	560
Length of nasals	204	194	195	194	210	206	192	187	197	187	200	195	193	185	...	200	170	163	168	185	172	195	186	220	174	200	183
Greatest breadth of one nasal	60	56	...	57	65	56	53	58	55	57	52	62	55	57	...	65	44	46	46	52	46	40	38	52	52	...	45
Breadth of palatines opposite 2d true molar	108	110	...	100	103	104	97	112	104	89	93	102	98	106	98	113	89	88	90	88	93	102	88	105	102	...	96
Greatest height of skull	158	150	...	154	162	160	152	162	170	147	144	165	168	156	148	117	140	130	137	166	142	146	133	168	...	...	167
Length of molar series of maxilla	140	154	...	140	147	150	157	140	134	144	140	150	136	138	145	143	150	130	152	138	136	146	140	148	142	...	152
" " lower jaw from tip to angle	420	406	400	...	410	400	390	400	400	390	397	410	413	...	...	416	365	362	360	382	380	385	369	433	385	...	406
Height of " " " " "	217	215	200	...	210	215	195	200	208	198	200	215	200	...	...	225	180	170	190	195	195	207	165	230	...	...	203
Length of molar series of lower jaw	155	165	...	...	156	158	160	153	147	160	153	153	148	..	...	146	158	...	...	147	145	156	153	158	157	..	157

* Between orbits and base of horn-cores.

Explanation of Table X.

1. *Bison americanus.* A very old male from Kansas (M. C. Z., No. 95).
2. *Bison americanus.* Male, ten to twelve years old, from Kansas (M. C. Z., No. 91).
3. *Bison americanus.* Very old male, from Kansas.
4. *Bison americanus.* Very old male, from Kansas (M. C. Z., No. 93).
5. *Bison americanus.* Male, about fifteen years old, from Kansas (M. C. Z., No. 10).
6. *Bison americanus.* Male, about six years old, from Kansas (M. C. Z., No. 11).
7. *Bison americanus.* Male, about four years old, from Kansas (M. C. Z., No. 94).
8. *Bison americanus.* Male, about ten years old, from Kansas (M. C. Z., No. 97).
9. *Bison americanus.* Male, about twelve years old, from Kansas (M. C. Z., No. 99).
10. *Bison americanus.* Male, four or five years old, from Kansas (M. C. Z., No. 100).
11. *Bison americanus.* Male, about six years old, from Kansas (M. C. Z., No. 102).
12. *Bison americanus.* Male, about twelve years old, from Kansas (M. C. Z., No. 1770).
13. *Bison americanus.* Male, about twelve years old, from Kansas (M. C. Z., No. 1771).
14. *Bison americanus.* Male, about twelve years old, from Kansas (M. C. Z., No. 1215).
15. *Bison americanus.* Male, about fifteen years old, from Kansas (M. C. Z., No. 1216).
16. *Bison americanus.* Male, ten or twelve years old, from Kansas (National Mus., No. 12,233).
17. *Bison americanus.* Female, four or five years old, from Kansas (M. C. Z., No. 1937).
18. *Bison americanus.* Female, about three years old, from Kansas (M. C. Z., No. 1768).
19. *Bison americanus.* Female, about three years old, from Kansas (M. C. Z., No. 96).
20. *Bison americanus.* Female, about nine years old, from Kansas (M. C. Z., No. 101).
21. *Bison americanus.* Female, about six years old, from Kansas (M. C. Z., No. 105).
22. *Bison americanus.* Female, about six years old, from Kansas (M. C. Z., No. 92).
23. *Bison bonasus.* Female, about five or six years old (M. C. Z., No. 1790).
24. *Bison bonasus.* Old male, from Menagerie of Schœnbrunn (M. C. Z., No. 165).
25. *Bison bonasus.* Male. Measurements as given by Richardson, in Zool. Voy. of the Herald, p. 122.
26. *Bison bonasus.* Old male, from Schœnbrunn. Measurements as given by Cuvier (Ossem. Foss., 3d ed., Tome IV, p. 121)
27. *Bison bonasus.* Male, about six years old, from the Vienna Museum (National Mus., No. 11,514).

Individual Variation. — The American bison presents a considerable range of what may be termed individual variation. This has already been noticed in respect to the metacarpal bones (see Table VIII and Plate X), where it was shown that not always the thickest and stoutest examples are the longest. Thus a metacarpal of a male 192 mm. in length exceeds in all other dimensions another specimen having a length of 213 mm. A similar difference is traceable throughout the skeleton (see Table IX), so that we have individuals that present in all parts of their structure a slender or attenuated form, and others that are relatively thick and stout, the tallest and longest specimens being sometimes exceeded in stoutness, comparing bone with bone, by those of considerably less stature. There are again individuals that differ from the average in general bulk, without presenting any other unusual differences. Variations in the relative length of the different bones of the limbs, of the ribs, the dorsal spines, etc., are of frequent occurrence. As such variations are now so well known to characterize vertebrates in general, — each species having a considerable normal range of osteological variation, — they may be passed over without further remark.

Among more unusual variations are the occasional development of an extra rib, or an extra pair of ribs, which may articulate either with the last cervical or the first lumbar vertebra. A famous instance of the latter was presented by a specimen described by Cuvier (the first skeleton of the American bison that came under the eye of an osteologist), which had fifteen pairs of ribs, and only four, instead of five, lumbar vertebræ (see above, p. 2). The mistake to which this abnormal specimen gave rise in respect to the number of dorsal and lumbar vertebræ and the number of pairs of ribs possessed by the American bison as compared with the aurochs, has already been noticed, — a mistake that still survives in some of our leading text-books of comparative anatomy. In the Museum of Comparative Zoölogy is a male from Kansas possessing a supplemental pair of ribs which articulate with the last cervical vertebra, instead of with the first lumbar, as in the case of Cuvier's specimen.

Variations in the form of the skull are often strikingly apparent, affecting not so much, however, the relative size of the different parts, or the proportion of width to length, as the frontal outline or profile, and the curvature and relative direction of the horns. In respect to the profile, the frontal region varies in different specimens of the same sex and of corresponding ages in the forehead being either flat, or even slightly concave, or very convex (see Plates V, VI, and VII). The horns are usually so much depressed that when the skull is placed on a flat surface with the dorsal aspect downward the points will not touch the surface on which the skull rests, — in other words, do not rise to the plane of the forehead; in other specimens they sometimes rise so high as to prevent the skull from touching the flat surface by a space of one or two inches. The horn-cores are also sometimes directed backward far beyond the plane of the occiput, though usually not reaching it (see Plates V, VI, and VII). Such differences as these are so considerable that they are sometimes, in allied groups, regarded as indicative of specific differences.

The variation in length in a series of a dozen aged male skulls ranges from 500 to 600 mm., but the usual range of variation is between 500 and 550 mm. The extremes in breadth are 240 and 280 mm., ranging usually between 240 and 275 mm. The lower jaw varies in length in the same series from 400 to 420 mm.; the nasals from 194 to 204 mm.; the horn-cores from 180 to 215 mm. The length of the alveolar space of the upper molars varies from 138 to 154 mm.; of the lower, from 148 to 165 mm. The variation in the length of the alveolar space in the females overlaps that of the males, the length of the lower molar series ranging from 145 to 158 mm., and that of the upper molar series from 136 to 152 mm. It thus appears that in respect to the size of the teeth the sexual difference is not very great, — far less than that between other parts of the skull and skeleton.

The individual variation in respect to the horns themselves, in size and direction of curvature, is well worthy of special notice. Of two males of nearly corresponding ages, one has horn-cores measuring 220 mm. in length, the other only 146 mm. The variation in the circumference at the base ranges from 235 to 300 mm. In respect to curvature, the horns are sometimes gently curved the whole length, and sometimes abruptly bent upward at the end of the basal third, as shown in Plates V, VI, and VII. They also vary greatly in size in individuals of corresponding ages. The difference in these respects between different individuals of *Bison americanus* is hence much greater than the average difference between *B. americanus* and *B. bonasus*.

The variation in the size and shape of the horns resulting from differences of age is shown by the series of figures in Plate VIII, where the horn of a male of the first autumn, the horn of a yearling male, of a male of four or five years, and of a male of twelve to fourteen years, is represented, and also two specimens differing greatly in size from about equally aged old bulls.

Synonymy and Nomenclature. — The first systematic name applied to the American bison under the binomial system of nomenclature was *Bos americanus*, given it by Gmelin in 1788, the specific name being evidently adopted from Catesby, who in 1754 called it *Bison americanus*, as did also Brisson two years later. By this specific name, coupled with the generic appellation of either *Bos* or *Bison*, it has since been almost universally known, a few very conservative naturalists having always regarded it as either merely a variety of the aurochs or as absolutely identical with it. It hence forms almost the only exception among North American mammals of a species that has never had a prominent synonym. Hernandez refers to it under the name of *Taurus mexicanus*, but Hernandez wrote long prior to the establishment of the binomial system of nomenclature, as did also Nieremburg, who called it *Taurus quivirensis*, so that these names have never been regarded as having a claim to priority.

To the Spanish colonists the American bison was commonly known under the name of *Cibola*, but some Spanish writers speak of it under the name *Bisonte*, while De Laët and others called it *Armenta*. *Bœuf sauvage* was the name given it by Du Pratz, though often also called *Buffle*, *Vache sauvage*, and sometimes *Bison d'Amérique*, by the early French colonists, while the Canadian *voyageurs* are said to term it simply *le bœuf*. Kalm spoke of the American bisons as *Wilde Ochsen und Kühe*, while the early English explorers also often referred to this animal under the same English equivalent, and also used for it the names *Buffle* and *Bœuf sauvage*. These two last-mentioned names were also applied, by both the early French and the early English explorers, to the Moose (*Alces malchis*) and the elk (*Cervus canadensis*). Charlevoix called the bison the *Bœuf du Canada*. Marquette called it the *Pisikious*, adopting the name then current among the Illinois Indians, while Hennepin called it *Taureau sauvage*. Lawson and Bricknell used the name *Buffelo*, which name, modified to *Buffalo*, was employed by Catesby and was early adopted by the English colonists. According to Richardson it is called *Peecheek* by the Algonquins, *Adgiddah* by the Chepewyans, and *Moostoosh* by the Crees.

In the United States this animal has generally borne the name of *buffalo*, though discriminating writers persist that the name is erroneous, and that it should be called the *American bison*. The latter is undoubtedly its correct English cognomen, but probably among the people generally the name *buffalo* will never be supplanted. The term *American buffalo* is doubtless defensible for those who prefer it, and even *buffalo* is no more a misnomer than scores of the names of our common mammals and birds. The name *Robin*, as applied to *Turdus migratorius*, is even more objectionable than that of *buffalo* as applied to the American bison. The name *buffalo* is of course strictly applicable only to the genus *Bubalus*, embracing the true African and Indian buffaloes.

Figures of the American Bison. — The first figure of the bison ever published is doubtless that given by Thevet in 1558,* three years after the publication of Vaca's "Journal," in which occurs the earliest description of the American bison. This is an extremely rude figure, having but little resemblance to the bison. In 1633 De Laët † published another equally faulty. Nieremburg,‡ in 1635, and Hernandez,§ in 1651, published others, which so much resemble Thevet's that they seem to be merely enlarged, slightly modified

* Les Singularitez de la France Antarctique, p. 145.

† Amer., p. 303. ‡ Hist. Nat., p. 181. § Mex., p. 587.

copies of it. Hernandez's figure, however, has been repeatedly referred to as the first published figure of the American bison. Towards the end of the seventeenth century a somewhat similar figure was published by Hennepin.* During the eighteenth century others were added by Du Pratz, Lawson (in his "History of Carolina †), Catesby,‡ Buffon,§ and others, Catesby's and Buffon's being very fair representations of the animal intended, and are the first that attained a tolerable degree of accuracy.

The first good figures are those given by F. Cuvier and Geoffroy,‖ consisting of a series of three, drawn from specimens living in the Menagerie at Paris. The first is that of a young male in summer pelage, the second that of a young female, and the third that of a calf a few weeks old. These are all very fine, especially in respect to color, in which they excel all others, those of Catlin and Audubon being of too dark a tint.

Catlin, in his "North American Indians" (Vol. I), devotes a series of fourteen spirited plates to the illustration of the American bison. The male is represented in plate vii of this work; the female in plate viii; in plate ix is depicted a collision of a bull and a horse during a chase, and in plate x a wounded bull is represented. In plate cv is figured a herd in the rutting season; in plate cvi a herd at rest, with an old bull wallowing in the foreground; plates cvii to cxii form a series illustrating the hunting of the buffalo by the Indians; plates cxiii and cxiv represent buffaloes attacked by wolves.

Besides Audubon's¶ well-known figures, among those worthy of special notice are those in Schoolcraft's great work on the Indians,** in which in plate viii is given a comparative view of the buffalo and domestic cow; in plate ix, a view of a buffalo chase; in plate x, buffalo hunting in winter; in plate xi, a view of a large herd of buffaloes; in plate xii, another view of a large herd with an old bull in the foreground; plate xiii, buffalo skinning.

The earlier figures are of course noteworthy only as being the first attempts at delineating the American bison. Those by Catlin, on the other hand, truthfully and vividly depict scenes which, though formerly character-

* Discovery of a Vast Country, etc., p. 90.

† Fig. 115.

‡ Nat. Hist. of Carolina, etc., pl. xx.

§ Hist. Nat., Suppl., III, pl. v.

‖ Hist. Nat. des Mam., Tome I, livr. xii (young male); Tome II, livr. xxxii (young female); Tome III, livr. xlix (calf a few weeks old).

¶ Quad. North America, Vol. II, pls. lvi, lvii.

** Hist. Prosp. & Cond. Indian Tribes of North America, Vol. IV, pls. viii - xiii.

istic of our plains, will soon be known only in history, and are well worthy of consultation by any one interested in the subjects he there delineates. Audubon's illustrations are faithful likenesses, and the scenes and figures given in Schoolcraft's work may also be examined with profit; the most accurate figures, however, are those given by Cuvier and Geoffroy.

Fossil Remains. — The remains of the American bison in a fossil or semi-fossil condition have been found sparingly over a wide area, but no instance is at present known of their discovery beyond the known limits of its range at the time of the earliest explorations of the continent. In the National Museum at Washington are semifossil remains from Colorado, collected by Major Powell, and from Kansas, collected by Dr. Hayden. I have found a fossil tooth of this species in Central Iowa, and have received from Mr. Orestes H. St. John a fossil astragalus from the banks of the Big Blue River in Kansas. Professor Wyman has reported its remains from the mounds of the Lead Region in Wisconsin and Iowa; Dr. Leidy has figured a tooth from the Lead crevices of Jo Daviess County, Illinois, and also from the Ashley River, South Carolina.* Professor Baird has reported the existence of its fossil remains in the caverns of Central Pennsylvania. The alleged occurrence of its remains at Gardner, Maine, proves, however, to be probably erroneous, as will be shown further on.†

Its bones have also been found in large quantities about the Salt Licks of the Ohio Valley, especially at Big-bone Lick, Kentucky. The accumulations at the last-named locality date back to remote times, since in the lower strata of these bone-deposits are found the bones of *Mastodon americanus*, *Megalonyx*, *Elephas*, an extinct species of *Equus*, and an extinct species of *Ovibos*, but, according to Professor Shaler, the bones of *Bison americanus* occur only in the more superficial strata, which are composed almost solely of the remains of this animal. These remains differ, as before stated (p. 33), in no appreciable respect, in form or in size, from those of the recent bison of the Plains.‡ The only difference of note consists in the very different manner of the wearing of the molar teeth. In the recent

* In both instances doubtfully referred by Dr. Leidy to *Bison latifrons*.

† See the chapter on the Geographical Distribution of the American Bison.

‡ A skull from Big-bone Lick (No. 2047, M. C. Z.) presents the greatest convexity of the forehead (see Plate V, figs. 5, 6) of any I have met with, but does not differ in other respects from ordinary examples. On the other hand, other Big-bone Lick skulls exhibit the usual degree of flatness. No 2050 has unusually large horn-cores, but is not in other respects distinguishable from average recent examples.

bison of the Plains, the crowns of the teeth present a nearly even surface, every part of the tooth being worn to nearly the same level. In the remains from Big-bone Lick, however, the crown surface wears into a series of deep transverse serrations, the ridges of which often rise a fourth of an inch above the intervening hollows. The difference between the two in this respect is strikingly great (see Plate IX *), and evidently relates to the different character of the food obtainable in the two districts. The bison of the Plains necessarily feeds wholly upon short, fine grasses, which rarely attain a height of more than a few inches, and are consequently at times more or less sprinkled with sand and dust. The Ohio Valley, on the contrary, is a region of rank herbage, and tall succulent grasses. The Plains bison must take with its food more or less gritty material,† which tends not only to wear the teeth down evenly, but far more rapidly than was the case in the Ohio Valley, the teeth in the Plains bisons generally being very much worn even in middle-aged animals, while in very old animals the teeth are often worn down to the fangs. Even the temporary set become wholly worn out before they give place to the permanent series. Nothing of this kind has been observed in specimens from Big-bone Lick, even in the oldest individuals.

Geographical Distribution. — Since the geographical distribution of the American bison, past and present, is treated at length in a subsequent chapter devoted especially to the subject, a few words only on this point will suffice in the present connection. The habitat of the bison (see Map I) formerly extended from Great Slave Lake on the north, in latitude about 62°, to the north-eastern provinces of Mexico, as far south as latitude 25°. Its range in British North America extended from the Rocky Mountains on the west to the wooded highlands about six hundred miles west of Hudson's Bay, or about to a line running southeastward from the Great Slave Lake to the Lake of the Woods. Its range in the United States formerly embraced a considerable area west of the Rocky Mountains, its recent remains having been found in Oregon as far west as the Blue Mountains, and further south it occupied the Great Salt Lake Basin, extending westward even to the Sierra Nevada Mountains, while less than fifty years since it existed over the head-waters of the Green and Grand Rivers, and other sources of the Colorado. East of the Rocky Mountains its range extended southward far beyond the Rio Grande, and

* This Plate also contains figures of the milk-dentition.

† In the teeth of specimens from the Plains I have found sharp angular particles of quartz sand wedged into the cavities of the teeth.

eastward throughout the region drained by the Ohio River and its tributaries. Its northern limit east of the Mississippi was the Great Lakes, along which it extended eastward to near the eastern end of Lake Erie. It appears not to have occurred south of the Tennessee River, and only to a limited extent east of the Alleghanies, chiefly in the upper districts of North and South Carolina.

Its present range embraces two distinct and comparatively small areas. The southern is chiefly limited to Western Kansas, a part of the Indian Territory, and Northwestern Texas, — in all together embracing a region about equal in size to the present State of Kansas. The northern district extends from the sources of the principal southern tributaries of the Yellowstone northward into the British Possessions, embracing an area not much greater than the present Territory of Montana. Over these regions, however, it is rapidly disappearing, and at its present rate of decrease will certainly become wholly extinct during the next quarter of a century.

Habits. — The American bison is, as is well known, pre-eminently a gregarious animal. At times herds have been met with of immense size, numbering thousands, and even millions, of individuals. The accounts given by thoroughly veracious travellers respecting their size sound almost like exaggerations. Herds were formerly often met with extending for many miles in every direction, so that the expression "so numerous as to blacken the plains as far as the eye can reach" has become a hackneyed description of their abundance. Some writers speak of travelling for days together without ever being out of sight of buffaloes, while it is stated that emigrant trains were formerly sometimes detained for hours by the passage of dense herds across their routes. In the early history of the Kansas Pacific Railway it repeatedly happened that trains were stopped by the same cause. Such statements as these seem like exaggerations, but no facts are perhaps better attested. I must myself confess to slight misgivings in respect to their thorough truthfulness until I had, in 1871, an opportunity of seeing the moving multitudes of these animals covering the landscape on the plains of Kansas, when I was convinced of the possibility of the seemingly most extravagant reports being true. Only when demoralized and broken up by constant persecution from hunters do the herds become scattered. At other times only the old bulls, lean and partly disabled from age, leave the herds and wander as stragglers.

The organization and composition of the herds, though wholly simple and natural, has been the subject of much romancing on the part of a few fanciful writers. Generally the cows with their calves are found towards the middle and on the front of the herds, the cows being at all times more watchful than the bulls, and also more active. The cows are hence the first to detect danger, and generally take the initiative in the movements of the herd. The younger animals of both sexes mingle with the cows, as do also to a greater or less extent the younger and middle-aged bulls. The older bulls are generally found nearer the outside of the herd, while last of all the old patriarchs of the flock bring up the rear. Some of the latter are often found far out on the outskirts, miles away from the main herd, occurring singly or in small parties of three or four to a dozen individuals. These are usually the superannuated members of the community, which lag behind from listlessness or sheer weakness. This simple grouping of the different individuals of the herds has given rise to exaggerated accounts of the sagacity of the buffalo, and much fine writing has at times been expended in describing the supposed regularity and almost military precision of their movements. The sluggish, partly disabled old males constitute the lordly sentinels of such tales, who are supposed to watch with fatherly care over the welfare of the flock, and to give early warning of the approach of danger. On the contrary, these supposed alert protectors are the most easily approached of any members of the flock, the experienced hunter finding no trouble in creeping past within a few yards of them in endeavoring to reach the more desirable game beyond them.* They are slower, too, to recognize danger when it is observed. The timidity and watchfulness of the cows, accustomed as they are to the care of their offspring, lead them to take the initiative in the movements of the herd, and this, as already stated, keeps them near the front, especially when the herd is moving. The popular belief that the bulls keep the cows and the young in the middle of the herd, and form themselves, as it were, into a protecting phalanx, has some apparent basis; but the theory that the old bulls, the least watchful of all the members of the herd, are sentinels posted on the outskirts to give notice of any approaching enemy, is wholly a myth, as is also the supposition that the herds consist of small harems.

The rutting season begins in July, but is not at its height till the following month. Rarely is more than a single calf produced at a birth. The period of pregnancy being about nine months, the calves are born from the begin-

* See the chapter beyond devoted to an account of the different methods of hunting the buffalo.

ning of March till the end of June, and follow the mother for nearly a year. Generally, also, the yearlings and two and three year olds are found associated with the cows and younger bulls. During no part of the year do the sexes form separate herds, but are found mingled together nearly in the manner already described.* It has been asserted, however, that the bulls select their partners and keep near them till the cows are about to calve, when for a time they leave them.† During the rutting season the bulls often wage fierce battles, but they are believed never to result fatally. The actions of the combatants are not much unlike those of domestic cattle under similar circumstances, they pawing the ground and bellowing, blustering loudly before engaging in actual combat. Their short horns are not apparently very dangerous weapons, and the stunning effect of the heavy shocks that must follow the violent collisions of these monsters when fighting is doubtless partly broken by the immense thickness of hair with which their

* Since the above was written I have met with the following remarks from the pen of Colonel R. I. Dodge: "When the calves are young they are kept always in the centre of each small herd, the cows with them, while the bulls dispose themselves on the outside. When feeding the herd is more or less scattered, but on the approach of danger it closes and rounds into a tolerably compact circular mass.

"The small herds, which compose the great herd, have each generally more bulls than cows, seeming all on the very best terms with each other. The old bulls do undoubtedly leave the herd and wander off as advance or rear guards and flankers, but I am disposed to believe this due to a misanthropic abnegation of society on the part of these old fellows, to whom female companionship no longer possesses its charm, rather than to their being driven out by the younger bulls, as is generally believed. This habitual separation of the large herd into numerous smaller herds seems to be an instinctive act, probably for more perfect mutual protection. It has been thought, said, and written by many persons that each small herd is a sort of community, the harem and retainers of some specially powerful bull, who keeps proper order and subjection among them. Nothing is further from the truth. The association is not only purely instinctive, voluntary, free from domination of power, of sexual appetite, or individual preferences, but is most undoubtedly entirely accidental as to individual components. I have, when unobserved, carefully watched herds while feeding. I have seen two or more small herds merge into one, or one larger herd separate into two, or more. This is done quietly, gradually, and, as it were, accidentally, in the act of feeding, each buffalo seeming only intent on getting his full share of the best grass. I have already said that the cows and calves are always in the centre, the bulls on the outside. When feeding herds approach each other and merge into one, the only perceptible change — and this is so gradual as scarcely to be noticeable — is that the bulls on the sides of contact work themselves out toward the new circumference, which is to inclose the whole; and when a larger herd breaks, by the same gradual process, into smaller ones, the bulls instinctively place themselves on the outside of each. When pursued the herds rush together in one compact, plunging mass. As soon as the pursuit is over, and the buffaloes are sufficiently recovered from their fright to begin feeding, those on the outside of the mass gradually detach themselves, breaking into smaller herds, until the whole large herd is in its normal condition. If each dominant bull had on such occasions to run through the herd to look up his lost wives, children, and dependents, this life would not only be a very unhappy, but also a very busy one." — *Chicago Inter-Ocean* (newspaper) of August 5, 1875.

† See Audubon and Bachman's Quad. N. America, Vol. II, p. 37.

foreheads are protected. At this season the bulls become lean, but regain their flesh again in autumn, when they are usually in the best condition. The cows, on the other hand, as well as the yearlings and two-year-olds, are generally fattest in June.

In respect to the degree of maternal affection possessed by the buffalo cow there seems to be a wide range of opinion among observers. Some deny that the mother has any affection for its offspring, stating that when frightened the buffalo cow will abandon her calf without the slightest hesitation. On the other hand, others report her as being not only constantly vigilant in the care of her young, but bold in its defence. Colonel Dodge, indeed, states that the duty of protecting the calves devolves wholly upon the bulls. He says: "I have seen evidences of this many times, but the most remarkable instance I have ever heard of was related to me by an army surgeon, who was an eyewitness. He was one evening returning to camp, after a day's hunt, when his attention was attracted by the curious action of a little knot of six or eight buffaloes. Approaching sufficiently near to see clearly, he discovered that this little knot were all bulls, standing in a close circle with their heads outward, while in a concentric circle at some twelve or fifteen paces distant sat licking their chops in impatient expectancy, at least a dozen large gray wolves, excepting man, the most dangerous enemy of the buffalo. The Doctor determined to watch the performance. After a few moments the knot broke up, still keeping in a compact mass, and started on a trot for the main herd, some half a mile off. To his very great astonishment the Doctor now saw that the central and controlling figure of this mass was a poor little calf, so newly born as scarcely to be able to walk. After going fifty or a hundred yards the calf lay down. The bulls disposed themselves in a circle as before, and the wolves, who had trotted along on each flank of their retreating supper, sat down and licked their chops again. This was repeated again and again, and although the Doctor did not see the *finale* (it being late, and the camp distant), he had no doubt that the noble fathers did their whole duty by their offspring, and carried it safely to the herd."*

Audubon states, on the contrary, that the cow does not at such times desert its young, but tries to defend it,† which statement is confirmed by many plainsmen and hunters who are thoroughly conversant with the habits of the buffalo.

* *Chicago Inter-Ocean*, August 5, 1875.

† Quad. N. Am., Vol. II, p. 37.

The moulting of the buffaloes begins quite early in the season, their skins being in prime condition for robes during only about three months of the year. They are in their best estate for this purpose in December, though they are in fair condition in November and January, and are indeed pretty fully haired in the months preceding and following these. The long hair on the legs, neck, and head is not annually shed, but the soft short woolly covering of the body is usually renewed each year. The short soft hair begins to loosen in February, and during the following months gradually falls, so that by May or June the body of the animal, especially the posterior part, becomes quite naked, and remains so for several weeks. Gradually the dark-colored new hair begins to appear, covering the animal's body with a fine soft velvety coat. During the period of moulting the animal presents a very ragged and uncouth appearance, the woolly hair hanging here and there in matted loosened masses with intervening naked spaces. During this period the animals search for trees, bushes, rocks, or banks of earth against which they may rub to free themselves from the loosened hair, often also rolling on the ground for the same purpose. The hair on the hump, which is thicker and longer than that on the other parts of the body, is last shed, and in very old animals is not always annually renewed. The moulting of the pelage takes place later in the old and lean animals than in the others, and nearly a month later in the cows than in the bulls, so that in June, while the greater part are smooth and dark, a few are conspicuous among the others from still retaining their old and faded coats of the previous year.

The buffalo is quite nomadic in its habits, the same individuals roaming, in the course of the year, over vast areas of country. Their wanderings, however, are generally in search of food or water, or result from the persecutions of human foes. The fires that annually sweep over immense tracks of the grassy plains, sometimes destroying the herbaceous vegetation over thousands of square miles in continuous area, often force the buffaloes, besides inspiring them with terror, to make long journeys in search of food. Occasionally the ravages of the grasshoppers cause similar migrations, these pests leaving large sections of country as bare of vegetation as it is when swept by a prairie fire. The habit of the buffaloes, too, of keeping together in immense herds renders a slow but constant movement necessary in order to find food, that of a single locality soon becoming exhausted. They are also accustomed to make frequent shorter journeys to obtain water. The streams throughout the range of the buffalo run mainly in an east and west direction, and the buffaloes, in passing constantly from the broad grassy divides to the streams, soon form well-worn trails, which, running at right angles to the general course of the streams, have a nearly north and south trend. These paths have been regarded as indicating a very general north and south annual migration of these animals. It is, indeed, a wide-spread belief among the hunters and plainsmen that the buffaloes formerly performed regularly very extended migrations, going south in autumn and north in spring. I have even been assured by former agents of the American Fur Company that, before the great overland emigration to California (about 1849 and later) divided the buffaloes into two bands, the buffaloes that were found in summer on the plains of the Saskatchewan and Red River of the North spent the winter in Texas, and *vice versa*. The early Jesuit explorers reported a similar annual migration among the buffaloes east of the Mississippi River, and scores of travellers have since repeated the same statement in respect to those of the Plains. That there are local migrations of an annual character seems in fact to be well substantiated, especially at the southward, where the buffaloes are reported to have formerly, in great measure, abandoned the plains of Texas in summer for those further north, revisiting them again in winter. Before their range was intersected by railroads, or by the great trans-continental emigrant route by way of the South Pass, the movements of the herds were, doubtless, much more regular than at present. North of the United States, as late as 1858, according to Hind,* they still performed very extended migrations, as this author reports the Red River bands as leaving the plains of the Red River in spring, moving first westward to the Grand Coteau de Missouri, then northward and eastward to the Little Souris River, and thence southward again to the Red River plains.

As already stated, a slight movement northward in summer and southward in winter is well attested as formerly occurring in Texas; the hunters report the same thing as having taken place on the plains of Kansas; further north the buffaloes still visit the valley of the Yellowstone in summer from their winter quarters to the southward; along the 49th parallel they also pass north in summer and south in winter; there is abundant evidence also of a similar north and south migration on the Saskatchewan plains. Yet it is very improbable that the buffaloes of the Saskatchewan plains ever wintered on the plains of Texas; and absolutely certain that for twenty-five years they have not passed as far south even as the valley of the Platte.

* Canadian Exploring Expeditions, etc., Vol. II, p. 108.

Doubtless the same individuals never moved more than a few hundred miles in a north and south direction, the annual migration being doubtless merely a moderate swaying northward and southward of the whole mass with the changes of the seasons. We certainly know that buffaloes have been accustomed to remain in winter as far north as their habitat extends. North of the Saskatchewan they are described as merely leaving the more exposed portions of the plains during the deepest snows and severest periods of cold to take shelter in the open woods that border the plains. We have, for instance, numerous attestations of their former abundance in winter at Carleton House, in latitude 53°, as well as at other of the Hudson's Bay Company's posts.

The local movements of the buffaloes are said to have been formerly very regular, and the hunters conversant with their habits knew very well at what points they were most likely to find them at the different seasons of the year. Of late, however, the buffaloes have become much more erratic, owing to the constant persecutions to which they have been for so long a time subjected. In Northern Kansas the old trails show that their movements were formerly in the usual north and south direction, the trails all having that course. Since the construction of the Kansas Pacific Railway, however, their habits have considerably changed, an east and west migration having recently prevailed to such an extent that a new set of trails, running at right angles to the earlier, have been deeply worn. Until recently the buffaloes ranged eastward in summer to Fort Harker, but retired westward in winter, few being found at this season east of Fort Hays. In summer and early autumn, hunting-parties, as late as 1872, made their headquarters at Hays City; later in the season at Ellis and Park's Fort; while in midwinter they had to move their camps as far west as Coyote, Grinnell, and Wallace, or to a distance of one hundred to one hundred and fifty miles west of their fall camps, in consequence of the westward winter migration of the buffaloes. Two reasons may be assigned for this change of habit: first, their reluctance to cross the railroad, and secondly, the greater mildness of the winters to the westward of Ellis as compared with the region east of this point. During the winter of 1871-72 I found that for a period of several weeks, in December and January, the country east of Ellis was covered with ice and encrusted snow sufficiently deep to bury the grass below the reach of either the buffaloes or the domestic cattle. In the vicinity of Ellis the amount of snow and ice began rapidly to diminish, while a little further westward the ground was almost wholly bare. I was informed, furthermore, that this was the usual distribution of the snow in this region whenever any fell there. Although occasionally the snow does not accumulate in sufficient quantity to render grazing difficult over any of the country west of Fossil Creek, the buffaloes regularly abandon this region in winter for the country further west, where snow is of more exceptional occurrence.

The wanderings of the buffaloes often render it necessary for them to cross large streams, which they seem to do with reckless fearlessness and at almost any season of the year, though frequently at the cost of the lives of many of the old and feeble as well as of the young. Lewis and Clarke speak of their crossing the Upper Missouri in such numbers as to delay their boat, the river being filled with them as thick as they could swim for the distance of a mile.* Other Western travellers mention similar scenes.† Bad landing-places, such as bluffy banks or miry shores, often prove fatal to the half-exhausted creature after reaching the shore.‡ In winter they boldly cross the rivers on the ice; towards spring, however, after the ice has become weakened by melting, and even occasionally at other times, in consequence of their crowding too thickly together, the ice breaks beneath their weight and great numbers are drowned. In spring they often cross amid the floating ice, at which times they are sometimes set upon by the Indians, to whom they then fall an easy prey. According to Audubon, small herds occasionally find themselves adrift on masses of floating ice, where the majority perish from cold and lack of food rather than trust themselves to the icy, turbulent waters.§

The behavior and movements of the buffalo are in general very much like those of domestic cattle, but their speed and endurance seem to be far

* Lewis and Clarke's Exped., Vol. II, p. 395.

† Catlin, North Am. Indians, Vol. II, p. 13; Fremont, Explorations, etc., p. 23.

‡ The following incident in point is related by Colonel Dodge: "Late in the summer of 1867 a herd of probably four thousand buffaloes attempted to cross the South Platte near Plum Creek. The river was rapidly subsiding, being nowhere over a foot or two in depth, and the channels in the bed were filled or filling with loose quicksand. The buffaloes in front were hopelessly stuck. Those immediately behind, urged on by the horns and pressure of those yet further in the rear, trampled over their struggling companions to be themselves ingulfed in the devouring sand. This was continued until the bed of the river, nearly half a mile broad, was covered with dead or dying buffaloes. Only a comparative few actually crossed the river, and these were soon driven back by hunters. It was estimated that considerably more than half the herd, or over two thousand buffaloes, paid for this attempt with their lives." — *Chicago Inter-Ocean*, August 5, 1875.

§ Audubon and Bachman, Quad. N. Am., Vol. II, p. 38.

greater. When well under way, and with a good start, it takes a fleet horse to overtake them, their speed being much greater than one would suppose from simply watching their movements from a distance, their gait being a rather clumsy, lumbering gallop. When pursued, or when urged on by thirst, rough ground and a tumble now and then seem to scarcely retard their progress, they plunging headlong down the steep sides of ravines and resuming their course up the opposite slope as if they had found the ravine no obstacle to their progress. When thirsty, in order to get at streams or springs, they will often leap down vertical banks where it would be impossible to urge a horse, and will even descend precipitous rocky bluffs by paths where a man could only climb down with difficulty, and where it would seem almost impossible for a beast of their size and structure to pass except at the cost of broken limbs or a broken neck. On the bluffs of the Musselshell River I found places where they had leaped down bare ledges three or four feet in height with nothing but ledges of rocks for a landing-place; sometimes, too, through passages between high rocks but little wider than the thickness of their own bodies, with also a continuous precipitous descent for many feet below. Nothing in their history ever surprised me more than this revelation of their expertness and fearlessness in climbing.* Ordinarily, however, the buffalo shows commendable sagacity in respect to his choice of routes, usually choosing the easiest grades and the most direct courses, so that a buffalo trail can be depended upon as affording the most feasible road possible through the region it traverses.

When moving in large bands across the plains their course is often plainly marked by the column of dust they raise, even when the animals themselves are far beyond sight, the scene calling to mind the passage of a distant troop of cavalry at full speed, or a heavy train of army wagons. The presence of a herd to the windward of the observer, even if a mile or two distant, can usually be detected by the peculiar odor that arises from it, especially during the rutting season. At this time, too, the roaring of the bulls can often be heard when the animals are miles away, and hidden, perchance, by intervening swells of the prairie, particularly at night, or when the air is still. Few things make a more vivid or lasting impression — and one that at the time is often far from agreeable — upon the mind of the traveller, encamped far out on the open prairie, than the roar and tramp of an approaching herd of buffaloes, especially at night-time. Nothing, again, is more pleasantly

* On this point see further Dr. Coues's communication given in Part II.

exhilarating, or gives one a stronger sense of being really amid nature's untamed wilds, than, when encamped on the outskirts of a quiescent herd, to be awakened on a fresh June morning by their distant bellowing, and to see them, as daylight advances, quietly grazing over a vast expanse of the green prairie.

As may be well imagined, not only the movements but the habits of the buffaloes, in their undisturbed daily lives, are in general not far different from those of grazing herds of domestic cattle. They indulge in similar gambols, and, when belligerent, in similar blustering demonstrations. When approached by man they will often assume an aspect so threatening that a novice at buffalo-hunting might easily be appalled by the fierce demonstrations indulged in by the boastful but cowardly old bulls. Bold at first, and apparently challenging attack, the old bulls, with the head lowered and the tail erect, will pace uneasily to and fro, threateningly pawing the earth, or face the approaching enemy with a sullen and most determined air only to take to their heels the very next moment. The bulls are at all times excessively fond of pawing the ground, and of throwing up the earth with their horns, thrusting them into banks when such are at hand, or into the bare level ground, which they accomplish by lowering themselves upon one knee. To such an extent do they pursue this pastime that the horns of the older bulls become very much worn and splintered, in occasional instances the horny covering of the more exposed part being worn very thin, and in rare instances entirely through to the bony core. Particularly bovine, also, is the satisfaction they take in rubbing themselves against whatever will oppose resistance, whether it be rocks, trees, bushes, or a clay-bluff; the telegraph-poles, however, erected along the railroads that cross their range, afforded them especial delight as scratching-posts, and soon became as well smoothed and covered with tufts of hair and grease from their unctuous hides as are the posts about a farmer's cattle-yard. What is very unlike anything in the habits of domestic cattle, however, is their propensity to roll themselves on the ground, which, notwithstanding their seemingly inconvenient form, they do with the greatest ease, rolling over as completely as a horse, and apparently with far less exertion. But their especial delight is to roll in the mud, or in "wallowing," as it is termed, from which exercise they arise looking more like an animated mass of mud than their former selves. The object of these peculiar ablutions is doubtless to cool their heated bodies and to free themselves from troublesome insects. When not finding a muddy pool ready at hand, an old bull proceeds to prepare one. Finding in the low parts of the prairies, says Catlin, who has described the process with considerable detail,* a little stagnant water amongst the grass, and the ground underneath soft and saturated with moisture, an old bull lowers himself upon one knee, plunges his horns into the ground, throwing up the earth and soon making an excavation into which the water trickles, forming for him in a short time a cool and comfortable bath, in which he wallows "like a hog in the mire." In this "delectable laver" he throws himself flat upon his side, and then, forcing himself violently around with his horns, his feet, and his huge hump, ploughs up the ground still more, thus enlarging his pool till he at length becomes nearly immersed. Besmeared with a coating of the pasty mixture, he at length rises, changed into "a monster of mud and ugliness," with the black mud dripping from his shaggy mane and thick woolly coat. The mud soon drying upon his body forms a covering that insures him immunity for hours from the attacks of insects. Others follow in succession, having waited their turns to enjoy the luxury; each rolls and wallows in a similar way, adding a little to the dimensions of the hole, and carrying away a share of the adhesive mud. By this means an excavation is eventually made having a diameter of fifteen or twenty feet, and two feet in depth. These wallows thus become characteristic marks of a buffalo country, outlasting even the ordinary trails, while their effect upon the country is much more marked, rank vegetation growing about their borders and serving to indicate their positions when quite distant.

The buffaloes, however, do not always choose moist places in which to roll, and are quite content with wallowing in the dust when mud-and-water wallows are not conveniently at hand; wherever, in short, large herds have grazed, hollows formed by their indulgence in this propensity are of very frequent occurrence. These circular depressions, which are also usually called "wallows," are of smaller size than the water wallows, being eight to ten or twelve feet or more in diameter, and a few inches to upwards of a foot in depth. These also are not effaced by natural agencies for many years, and hence remain as lasting evidence of the former existence of populous herds of buffaloes at the localities where these old "wallows" are found. Owing to the impervious nature of the clayey soil that generally characterizes the Plains, these hollows temporarily retain the water that collects in

* North American Indians, Vol. I, p. 241.

them during falls of rain, affording grateful supplies of this important element to the various animals of the region, as well as often to man, these pools usually lasting for several days, or until slowly evaporated by the sun.

The American bison, like the other species of the bovine group, is characterized by a rather sluggish disposition, and is by no means remarkable for alertness or sagacity, being not only unwieldy in bulk, but also "the stupidest animal of the plains." As Colonel Dodge has remarked, "his enormous bulk, shaggy mane, vicious eye, and sullen demeanor give him an appearance of ferocity very foreign to his nature. Dangerous as he looks, he is, in truth, a very mild, inoffensive beast, timid and fearful, and rarely attacking but in the last hopeless effort of self-defence. The domestic cattle of Texas, miscalled 'tame,' are fifty times more dangerous to footmen than the fiercest buffalo. . . . . Endowed with the smallest possible amount of instinct, the little he has seems adapted rather for getting him into difficulties than out of them. If not alarmed at sight or smell of a foe, he will stand stupidly gazing at his companions in their death-throes, until the whole herd is shot down. He will walk unconsciously into a quicksand or quagmire already choked with struggling, dying victims. Having made up his mind to go a certain way, it is almost impossible to swerve him from his purpose. . . . . When travelling nothing in his front stops him, but an unusual object in his rear will send him to the about at the top of his speed." *

In illustration of this curious habit of the buffalo to rush into the most apparent danger, Colonel Dodge relates the following: "The winter of 1871–72 was unusually severe in Arkansas. The ponds and smaller streams to the north were all frozen solid, and the buffalo were forced to the rivers for water. The Atchison, Topeka, and Santa Fé Railroad was then in process of construction, and nowhere could this peculiarity of the buffalo of which I am speaking be better studied than from its trains. If a herd was on the north side of the track it would stand stupidly gazing and without symptom of alarm though the locomotive passed within a hundred yards. If on the south side of the track, even though at a distance of one or two miles from it, the passage of a train set the whole herd in the wildest commotion. At its full speed, and utterly regardless of consequences, it would make for the track, on its line of retreat. If the train happened not to be in its path it crossed the track, and stopped satisfied. If the train was in the way, each individual buffalo went at it with the desperation of despair, plunging against

* *Chicago Inter-Ocean*, August 5, 1875.

or between locomotive and cars, just as the blind madness chanced to take them. Numbers were killed, but numbers still pressed on to stop and stare as soon as the obstacle was passed. After having trains ditched twice in one week, conductors learned to have a very decided respect for the idiosyncrasies of the buffalo, and when there was a possibility of striking a herd 'on the rampage' for the north side of the track, the train was slowed up, and sometimes stopped entirely." *

The sluggish nature and in some respects intense stupidity of the buffalo hence tend greatly to place this animal wholly at the mercy of its enemies, chief among whom is man, whether civilized or in the savage state. An account of the various devices for their destruction practised by man, and of the results that have followed the reckless, exterminating slaughter he has waged upon this inoffensive and helpless animal, being given in subsequent portions of this memoir, it is unnecessary to refer at length to these matters here. Let it suffice, then, in this connection, to say that their unwariness renders them an easy prey to the hunter, who, by keeping to the leeward of the herd, finds no difficulty in approaching these animals sufficiently near for their easy destruction, even when he is unmounted, while their pursuit on horseback has ever been one of the favorite pastimes of the sportsman. Fortunately for the buffaloes, they possess few other enemies, the wolves being their only other formidable foe. These have now become so reduced in numbers over most of the present range of the buffalo that they no longer form a very serious check upon its increase. Formerly they everywhere harassed the buffalo, destroying many of the young, and even worrying and finally killing and devouring the aged, the feeble, and the wounded. Thirty years since the wolves, next to the Indians, were the great scourge of the buffaloes, and had no small degree of influence in effecting their decrease. The earlier explorers of the plains often speak of finding a solitary buffalo, disabled by accident or by age, surrounded by a pack of hungry wolves, who would tease and wound him day and night till he finally fell a prey to their ravenous appetites. Catlin and other writers have often referred to this matter at length, Catlin having also given a series of paintings of these encounters between the bison and his hungry tormentors.† Says Catlin, in his graphic account of one of these attacks, "During my travels in these regions [Upper Missouri country], I have several times come across such a gang of these

* *Chicago Inter-Ocean*, August 5, 1875.

† North American Indians, Vol. I, p. 257, pls. cxlii, cxlv.

animals surrounding an old or wounded bull, where it would seem, from appearances, that they had been for several days in attendance, and at intervals desperately engaged in the effort to take his life. But a short time since, as one of my hunting companions and myself were returning to our encampment with our horses loaded with meat, we discovered at a distance a huge bull, encircled with a gang of white wolves; we rode up as near as we could without driving them away, and, being within pistol-shot, we had a remarkably good view, where I sat for a few moments and made a sketch in my note-book (plate cxiv); after which we rode up and gave the signal for them to disperse, which they instantly did, withdrawing themselves to the distance of fifty or sixty rods, when we found, to our great surprise, that the animal had made desperate resistance, his eyes being entirely eaten out of his head, the gristle of his nose mostly gone, his tongue half eaten off, and the skin and flesh of his legs torn almost literally into strings. In this tattered and torn condition, the poor old veteran stood bracing up in the midst of his devourers, who had ceased hostilities for a few minutes to enjoy a sort of parley, recovering strength and preparing to resume the attack in a few moments again. In this group, some were reclining to gain breath, whilst others were sneaking about and licking their chops in anxiety for a renewal of the attack; and others, less lucky, had been crushed to death by the feet or the horns of the bull. I rode nearer to the pitiable object as he stood bleeding and trembling before me, and said to him, 'Now is your time, old fellow, and you had better be off.' Though blind and nearly destroyed, there seemed evidently to be a recognition of a friend in me, as he straightened up, and, trembling with excitement, dashed off at full speed upon the prairie, in a straight line. We turned our horses and resumed our march, and when we had advanced a mile or more we looked back, and on our left, where we saw again the ill-fated animal surrounded by his tormentors, to whose insatiable voracity he unquestionably soon fell a victim."

The buffalo, when taken young, is easily tamed, and soon becomes thoroughly domesticated. With this fact so well known, it seems remarkable that this animal should not have long since been added to our list of domesticated and useful animals. The few experiments that have been made seem to have met with encouraging results, as will be shown in a later portion of the present memoir,* and to have failed simply through lack of interest and persistency. Through crossing them with domestic cattle they have even

* See the chapter on "The Domestication of the Buffalo."

given promise of improved breeds, and an attempt to propagate them in confinement by an enterprising stock-raiser, either as pure stock or as a mixed race, would undoubtedly prove remunerative. In the vicinity of the present range of the buffalo, tame individuals are frequently met with, which are reared and kept simply as pets or objects of curiosity, just as occasional specimens of the deer, elk, or pronghorn are kept. A young buffalo that was owned by the sutler at Fort Hays in 1871, then about two years old, proved to be a most eccentric and amusing beast. Through the attentions of visitors he acquired, among his other accomplishments, a great fondness for beer, of which he would sometimes partake to excess, when he would occasionally perform rather strange antics. He was usually inoffensive in his manners, though latterly his behavior to strangers was rather too familiar to be always agreeable, and gradually he became somewhat irritable in consequence of constant teasing. But on these occasions of inebriety he sometimes took it into his head to clear the so-called "officers' room" at the sutler's, to which he was often admitted, of its occupants. On one of these occasions he is reported to have mounted a billiard-table, from which he was not easily dislodged; at another time he is said to have ascended the stairs leading to the second story, and was with great difficulty induced to descend again. His excesses, lack of proper care, and unnatural diet at length seemed to seriously impair his health, as he soon grew thin, and did not long survive.

The herds of cattle that are driven from Texas to Wyoming and other Northern territories are sometimes accompanied by one or two young tamed buffaloes. Two two-year-old buffaloes thus reached Percy, Carbon County, Wyoming, in December, 1871, *en route* for Utah. One of them, however, was killed by some hunters near Percy, who claimed to have mistaken it for a wild animal, — a fate which not unfrequently befalls the tamed buffaloes of the frontier. The other was shipped westward by rail with the rest of the herd. These individuals mixed as freely with the domestic cattle as any other members of the herd, and were as easily managed, and had no greater fear of man than the others.

The very young buffalo calf, when separated from its mother, often evinces the utmost stupidity and lack of discernment; sometimes thrusting its nose into a tuft of herbage, it seems to imagine itself wholly hidden from view, and, in its fancied security, will stand and allow itself to be captured. A horse seems to possess for it a strange fascination, and it is very apt, when one is lost from the herd, to follow one whenever opportunity for it offers. In this way buffalo calves have frequently been known to follow a horse and its rider into the nearest military or trading post, miles from the herd. Catlin speaks of several that he sent down the Missouri by steamers to friends in St. Louis, which had unwittingly in this way made themselves prisoners.

It may here be added, however, that the stupidity of the buffalo, as well as its sagacity, has been by some writers greatly overstated. A herd of buffaloes certainly possesses, in an eminent degree, the sheep-like propensity of blindly following its leaders, whenever a large affrighted herd is fleeing from some real or fancied danger. It certainly seems a stupid thing for a whole herd to rush into destruction instead of turning aside and avoiding the danger. A little reflection, however, will show that in such instances as the rushing of a herd over a precipice, or into a pound prepared especially to entrap them, the act is not wholly one of stupidity, but comparable to that of a panic-stricken crowd of human beings rushing pell-mell from a public building when an alarm of fire is given, at the cost of limbs and lives, when more deliberate action would avoid such accidents. In the case of the buffalo, the individuals in the front ranks of a herd, rushing to the verge of a precipice or into a pound, discover the danger too late to be able to turn aside if they would, owing to the irresistible pressure of the mass behind, who are not in position to be aware of the danger towards which they are moving. Their crowding together on weak ice may result in disasters they can be hardly expected to foresee. Their crowding forward into quicksands is presumably the blind action of more or less excited herds, — a rashness a single animal or a few together would avoid.

Many other details respecting the habits of the buffalo might be appropriately added to the present account, especially in relation to their behavior in captivity, and when pursued or attacked by their human foes; but as most of these points will be noticed quite fully incidentally in subsequent portions of this memoir, it is perhaps unnecessary to refer to them further in the present connection.

PART II.

1. — Geographical Distribution, past and present, of Bison americanus.

The fate of none of our larger mammals is more interesting than is that of the bison, since total extermination is eventually surer to none than to this former "monarch of the prairies." Since Europeans first came to this continent all the larger ruminants and carnivores have become greatly reduced in number throughout its vast extent, and many species have already become extinct over extensive areas where they were formerly the most characteristic animals. The moose and the caribou have a far less extended range, particularly to the southward, now than formerly; the common deer, once abundant throughout Eastern North America, is now confined to the least settled parts of the country, having totally disappeared over three fourths of the region it formerly occupied; the elk, formerly existing over nearly the whole continent, now scarcely survives east of the Mississippi River, though less than half a century ago it ranged in large bands over the fertile prairies of Illinois, Wisconsin, Iowa, and Minnesota, and was of occasional occurrence in the mountainous parts of even the Atlantic States; the bear, the wolf, and the panther, formerly so numerous as to be, if not dangerous, at least a source of great annoyance to the early settlers, are now found, east of the Great Plains, only in the least settled and more broken wooded portions of the country. The bison, at once the largest and the most important animal to the aboriginal tribes of this continent, as it was also the most numerous over the immense region it frequented, still occurs in almost numberless bands, but it has become so circumscribed in its habitat, and is so constantly persecuted by professional hunters, that its total extermination seems to be fast approaching.

The precise limits of the range of the buffalo at the time when the first

Europeans visited America is still a matter of uncertainty, yet reliable data are sufficiently abundant to establish the boundaries of its habitat at that time with tolerable exactness. These data exist in the form of incidental memoranda in the narratives of the earlier explorers, rather than in formal statements bearing directly upon the subject, and though often unsatisfactorily vague in respect to dates and localities, they enable us to trace approximately the eastern and southern boundary of its habitat at a date as early at least as the beginning of the seventeenth century. It was beyond doubt almost exclusively an animal of the prairies and the woodless plains, ranging only to a limited extent into the forested districts east of the Mississippi River, and never occurring as a regular inhabitant of the denser woodlands. The opinion most prevalent in respect to its primitive range, as expressed by authors who have given most attention to the subject, is, that it for a long time inhabited the whole of that part of North America east of the Rocky Mountains between the parallels of 30° and 60°; some, however, make the Alleghanies the eastern limit of its eastward extension. To the westward some have considered its habitat as embracing a considerable part of that portion of the western slope of the Rocky Mountains contained within the United States. The purpose of the present article is not only to determine, as definitely as can now be done, its former extreme limit of distribution, but to give also a detailed history of its extermination over the area from which it has disappeared. Although hundreds of volumes and distinct papers relating to the early exploration and settlement of the country embraced within the former range of this animal have been consulted in the preparation of this paper, there probably still exist many important facts, incidentally recorded in little-known documents and in works in which such facts would hardly be expected to occur, which have been overlooked, and which will ultimately serve to indicate still more definitely the date of its extinction at particular localities, though little probably that will materially affect the general results herewith presented.

Probable Extent of its Former Habitat.—The boundaries of the former habitat of the buffalo appear to have been about as follows: Beginning with the region east of the Mississippi River, its extension to the northward was limited by the Great Lakes, while the Alleghanies may be taken as its general eastern limit, its occurrence in the mountainous and more elevated parts of the Carolinas being due rather to the occasional wandering of small bands through the mountains from the immense herds that formerly inhabited the valleys of

West Virginia and the adjacent parts of Kentucky and Tennessee, than to this region having been regularly embraced within its habitat. To the southward it seems never to have been met with south of the Tennessee River. It is well known to have ranged over Northern and Western Arkansas, and thence southward over the greater part of Texas, and across the Rio Grande into Mexico. Westward it extended over Northern New Mexico and thence westward and northward throughout the Great Salt Lake Basin, and probably to the Sierra Nevada Mountains in California and the Blue Mountains in Oregon. North of the United States, its western boundary seems to have been formed by the main chain of the Rocky Mountains, among the foot-hills of which it has been found as far north as the sources of the Mackenzie River. Its most northern limit appears to have been the northern shore of the Great Slave Lake in about latitude 62° to 64°. In the British Possessions its range to the eastward did not extend beyond the plains west of the Hudson's Bay highlands. Thence southward it occupied the valleys of the Saskatchewan and its tributaries to Lake Winnipeg and the valley of the Red River of the North. It ranged thence southward over the head-waters of the Mississippi, extending eastward nearly to the western shore of Lake Michigan, and thence still eastward over the prairies of Northern Indiana, and along the southern shore of Lake Erie into Western Pennsylvania, where, as already stated, the Alleghanies formed its eastern limit. It was hence wholly absent from the region immediately north of the Great Lakes, and consequently from every portion of the present Canadas; its existence on the Atlantic slope of the continent being also confined to the highlands of North and South Carolina. With this preliminary statement respecting the extent of its former habitat, we will pass now to the details of the subject, presenting not only the evidence on which this general statement rests, but also investigating the numerous supposed references to its occurrence outside of these boundaries.

The evidence bearing upon the general subject is of course resolvable into two kinds: first, that of a positive character, or direct statements touching the points at issue; secondly, inferential evidence, mainly of a negative character. The first explorers of the different parts of the continent, being largely dependent for sustenance upon the chase, have naturally recorded in the narratives of their explorations the wild animals they met with. In the case of an animal so important as the buffalo, it is presumable that they would usually state where it was first encountered, and that they would refer frequently to its presence or absence, as the case might be, at subsequent periods of their journeys. When no reference whatever is made to the buffalo in the narratives of different travellers who passed at different times over the same region, it has been assumed, in the total absence also of all other evidence to the contrary, that the buffalo did not, during that period at least, exist over the special area in question.

The use of the term *vaches sauvages* by many of the early French Jesuit writers, and that of *wild cows* by some of the early English explorers, and also the terms *buffe*, *buffle*, and *bœuf sauvage*, for the designation of the moose (*Alces malchis*) and the elk (*Cervus canadensis*) as well as the buffalo, has resulted in erroneous conclusions in respect to the former range of the buffalo. Difficulties have also often arisen in respect to the identification of localities from the fact that the names of rivers, lakes, etc., were often differently applied by different writers, and were frequently entirely different from those now employed to designate the same landmarks. Care, however, has been taken to trace out, in such cases, the modern equivalents of the older geographical names.

For convenience of treatment the former supposed habitat of the buffalo is divided into several districts, which are treated separately in what has seemed to be their most natural order.

THE EASTERN BOUNDARY OF THE FORMER HABITAT OF THE BUFFALO CONSIDERED, INCLUDING AN EXAMINATION OF THE ALLEGED EVIDENCE OF ITS OCCURRENCE IN NEW ENGLAND, THE CANADAS, THE MARITIME PARTS OF THE MIDDLE STATES, VIRGINIA, THE CAROLINAS, AND FLORIDA.

As already stated, many prominent authorities have regarded the range of the buffalo as formerly extending eastward to the Atlantic Coast, including the Middle States, and even portions of New England and the Canadas, while others seem to have had no doubt of its former existence from New York along the seaboard to Florida. Its former occurrence in the western parts of North and South Carolina, Georgia, Virginia, and Pennsylvania, is established beyond question; but its presence elsewhere on the Atlantic slope is highly questionable. Dr. Richardson, writing in 1829, says: "At the period when Europeans began to form settlements in North America this animal was occasionally met with on the Atlantic Coast," etc.* De Kay, writing in 1842,

* Richardson, Faun. Bor. Americana, Vol. I, p. 279, 1829.

also leaves it to be inferred that the buffalo existed generally along the Atlantic slope south of New York. He says: "The bison, or American buffalo, has long since been extirpated from this State [New York]; and although it is not at present found east of the Mississippi, yet there is abundant testimony from various writers to show that this animal was formerly numerous along the Atlantic coast, from New York to Mexico." * Unfortunately, however, he gives no reference to any of this "abundant testimony." Captain R. B. Marcy, writing in 1853, says: "Formerly, buffaloes were found in countless herds over almost the entire northern continent of America, from the twenty-eighth to the fiftieth degree of north latitude, and from the shores of Lake Champlain to the Rocky Mountains," † and also cites a number of supposed references to its occurrence in Newfoundland, New England, and Virginia. Professor Baird, as late as 1857, also states as follows: "The American buffalo was formerly found throughout the entire eastern portion of the United States to the Atlantic Ocean, and as far south as Florida." ‡

Region North of North Carolina. — Various writers during the last part of the sixteenth and the early part of the seventeenth centuries speak also of its occurrence in Canada, New England, Virginia, the Carolinas, and Florida; but some of these countries then embraced regions of indefinite extent to the westward, and thus often (as in the case of Canada and Florida, certainly), did in those early times include a portion of the range of the buffalo. But upon careful examination of the writings of these authors I have failed to find a single mention of the occurrence of this animal within the present limits of New York, New England, Canada, or Florida that will bear a critical examination. On the other hand, in a score or more distinct enumerations of the animals of Virginia and New England, made prior to 1650, not a single allusion is made to the buffalo as existing on the Atlantic slope, north of the Carolinas, although all the other larger mammals are mentioned, and here and there described with sufficient detail to render them unquestionably recognizable. § Furthermore, no remains

* Zoölogy of New York, Vol. I, p. 110, 1842.

† Marcy's Exploration of the Red River, p. 103, 1853.

‡ Mammals of N. America, p. 684. See also Patent-Office Report, Agricultural, 1851–52, p. 124, 1852.

§ A few of these general notices, taken from a variety of sources, but largely from Hakluyt's and Purchas's collections of voyages, are appended as examples of their general character: —

James Cartier, or Jacques Carthier, in 1534, reported "great store of wilde beasts, as Fannes, Stags, Beares, Marternes, Hares and Foxes, with divers other sorte," on the St. Lawrence, but mentions no other

of the buffalo have as yet been found in the Indian shell-mounds of the Atlantic coast,* while the bones of elk, deer, caribou, bear, and other large mammals and birds occur with greater or less frequency at different localities.†

large animals — nothing like the buffalo — in his several distinct enumerations of the "beasts." — HAKLUYT, *Voyages*, Vol. III, pp. 231–290.

Sir Francis Roberval, in his account of his voyage up the St. Lawrence in 1542, says of the Indians: "They feed also of Stagges, wild Bores, Bugles, Porkespynes, and store of other wild beastes." — HAKLUYT, Vol. III, p. 290.

In Hariot's account of Virginia, written in 1587, he enumerates among the beasts, "Deere," "Conies," "Saquenuckot, and Maquowoc, two kinds of small beasts, greater than Conies which are very good meat," "Squirels" and "Beares," and adds: "I have the names of eight and twenty severall sorts of beasts, which I have heard of to be here and there dispersed in the countrey, especially in the maine: of which there are only twelve kinds that we have yet discovered, and of those that be good meat we know only them before mentioned." — HAKLUYT, Vol. III, p. 333.

In the Report of Gosnold's Voyage (1602) to Northern Virginia are enumerated "Deere in great store, very great and large: Beares, Luzernes, blacke Foxes, Beavers, Otters, Wilde-cats, very large and great, Dogs like Foxes, blacke and sharpe-nosed; Conies." — PURCHAS, *Pilgrims*, Vol. IV, p. 1653.

Martin Pring, in the account of his voyage (made in 1603), speaks of the "Beasts" of Northern Virginia, as follows: "We saw here also sundry sorts of Beasts, as Stags, Deere, Beares, Wolves, Foxes, Luzernes, and Dogges with sharpe noses." Again, he says: "The Beasts here are Stags, fallow Deere in abundance, Beares, Wolves, Foxes, Luzernes [Raccoons], and (some say) Tygres, Porcupines and Dogges with sharpe and long noses, with many other sorts of wild beasts, whose Cases and Furres being hereafter purchased by exchange may yeeld no small gaine to us." — PURCHAS, Vol. IV, pp. 1654, 1656.

In James Rosier's account of a voyage made by Captain George Waymouth, in 1605, to Virginia, we find, in his enumeration of the products of the country, the following: "*Beasts.* Deere red and fallow, Beare, Wolfe, Beaver, Otter, Conie, Marterns, Sables, Hogs, Porkespines, Polcats, Cats, wild great, Dogs some like Foxes, some like our other beasts the Savages signe unto us with hornes and broad eares, which we take to be Olkes or Loshes." (PURCHAS, Vol. IV, p. 1667.) The locality here referred to more particularly was the mouth of the St. Lawrence River, Virginia at this time including the northern portion of the Atlantic coast as far as it had been explored.

Captain John Smith, in his Description of Virginia, published in 1606, says: "Of Beasts, the chiefe are Deare, nothing differing from ours. In the Desarts, towards the heads of the Rivers, there are many, but amongst the Rivers, few. There is a beast they call *Aroughcun*, much like a Badger, but useth to live on trees as Squirrels doe. Their squirrels, some are neere as great as our smallest sort of wilde Rabbets, some blackish or blacke and white, but the most are gray. A small beast they have, they call *Assapanick*, but wee call them flying Squirrels, because spreading thier legs, and so stretching the largenes of their skinnes, that they have been seen to flie thirtie or fortie yards. An Opassam hath a head like a Swine, and a taile like a Rat, and is of the bignesse of a Cat. Under her belly she hath a bag, wherein she lodgeth, carrieth, and sucketh her young. Mussascus, is a beast of the forme and nature of our water Rats, but

* I have been assured of this fact by the late Professor J. Wyman, and by Mr. F. W. Putnam, and others who have made these prehistoric remains of the aborigines a special study.

† See Wyman's Account of some Kjøkenmøddings, or Shell-heaps, in Maine and Massachusetts. — *Amer. Naturalist*, Vol. I, pp. 561–584, 1868.

Professor Baird, however, refers to the occurrence of their bones "in the alluvial deposits of rivers, bogs, and caves," near Carlisle, in Pennsylvania.*

Among the more important references to the supposed occurrence of the

many of them smell exceeding strongly of Musk. Their Hares are no bigger than our Conies, and few of them to be found.

"Their Beares are very little in comparison of those of *Muscovia* and *Tartaria*. The Beaver is as big as an ordinarie great Dog, but his legs exceeding short. His fore feet like a Dogs, his hinder feet like a Swans. His taile somewhat like the forme of a Racket bare without haire, which to eate the Savages esteeme a great delicate. They have many Otters, which as the Beavers they take with snares, and esteeme the skins great ornaments, and of all those beasts they use to feede when they catch them.

"There is also a beast *Vetchunquoyes*, in the forme of a wilde Cat, their Foxes are like our silver haired Conies of a small proportion, and not smelling like those in *England*. Their Dogs of that Countrey are like thier Wolves, and cannot barke but howle; and their Wolves not much bigger than our *English* Foxes. Martins, Powlecats, Weesels and Minks we know they have, because we have seene many of their skins, though very seldome any of them alive. But one thing is strange, that wee could never perceive their vermine destroy our Hens, Egges, nor Chickens, nor doe any hurt, nor their Flyes nor Serpents any way pernitious, where in the South parts of *America* they are alwaies dangerous and often deadly." — PURCHAS, Vol. IV, pp. 1695, 1696.

In Hakluyt's "Description of Florida," compiled from the French authors, he says, under the head of "The Beastes of Florida:" "The Beastes best known in this Countrey are Stagges, Hindes, Goates, Deere, Leopards [Lynxes], Ounces, Luzernes, divers sorts of Wolves, wilde Dogs, Hares, Cunnies, and a certaine kinde of Beast that differeth little from the Lyon of Africa." — HAKLUYT, Vol. III, p. 369.

In a "True Declaration of the estate of the Colonie in Virginia," printed in 1610, we read: "The Beasts of the Countrie, as Deere, red, and fallow, do answere in multitude (people for people considered) to our proportion of Oxen, which appeareth by these experiences. First the people of the Countrie are apparelled in the skinnes of these beasts; Next, hard by the fort, two hundred in one heard have been usually observed. Further, our men have seen 4000. of these skins pyled up in one wardrobe of *Powhaton*; Lastly, infinite store have been presented to *Captaine Newport* upon sundry occurrents: such a plentie of Cattell, as all the Spaniards found not in the whole kingdome of *Mexico*, when all thier presents were but hennes, and ginycocks, and the bread of Maize, and Cently. There are *Aracouns*, and *Apossouns*, in shape like to pigges, shrouded in hollow roots of trees; There are Hares and Conies, and other beasts proper to the Countrie in plentifull manner." — FORCE's *Coll. Hist. Tracts*, Vol. III, No. 1, p. 13.

Captain John Smith, in his "Description of New England," printed in 1616, thus enumerates the "beasts": "Moos, a beast bigger than a Stagge; Deere, red, and Fallow; Bevers, Wolves, Foxes, both blacke and other; Aroughconds [raccoons], Wild-cats, Beares, Otters, Martins, Fitches, Musquassus, and diverse sorts of vermine, whose names I know not." — FORCE's *Coll. Hist. Tracts*, Vol. II, No. 1, p. 17.

William Strachey, in his "Historie of Travaile into Virginia Britannia," written before 1620, says: ". . . . the people [about the Chesapeake Bay] breed up tame turkies about their howses, and take apes in the mountaines," on the authority of an Indian named Machumps. Again he says: "Martins, polecatts, weesells, and monkeys we knowe they have, because we have seene many of their skynns, though very seldom any of them alive." — *Hakluyt Society's Publications*, Vol. for 1849, pp. 26, 125.

In "New England's Plantation" (London, 1630), it is said: "For Beasts there are some Beares, and

* Patent-Office Report, Agricultural, 1851 – 52, p. 124.

buffalo on the Atlantic slope, north of the Potomac, are the following. One often quoted is that contained in a letter from Mr. Anthonie Parkhurst to Richard Hakluyt, dated 1578, concerning the "true state and commodities of

they say some Lyons also; for they have been seen at Cape Anne. Also here are severall sorts of Deere, some whereof bring three or four young ones at once, which is not ordinarie in *England*. Also Wolves, Foxes, Beavers, Otters, Martins, great wild Cats, and a great Beast called a Molke [moose] as bigge as an Oxe. I have seen the skins of all these Beasts since I came to this Plantation, excepting Lyons. Also here are great store of Squerrels, some greater, and some smaller and lesser; there are some of the lesser sort, they tell me, that by a certaine Skin will fly from Tree to Tree though they stand farre distant." — FORCE's *Coll. Hist. Tracts*, Vol. I, No. 12, p. 8.

Thomas Morton, in his "New English Canaan," printed in 1632, devotes six pages to a description of the "beasts," giving very quaint and curious descriptions of all the more important, but makes no reference to any animal like the buffalo.

Father Andrew White, in describing Maryland in 1632, says, "But so great is the abundance of swine and deer that they are rather troublesome than advantageous. Cows also are innumerable, and oxen suitable for bearing burdens or for food; besides five other kinds of large beasts unknown to us, which our neighbors admit to their table. Sheep will have to be taken hence or from the Canaries; asses also, and mules and horses. The neighboring forests are full of wild bulls and heifers, of which five hundred or six hundred thousand are annually carried to Saville from that part which lies towards New Mexico. As many deer as you wish can be obtained from the neighboring people. Add to this muskrats, rabbits, beavers, badgers, and martens, not however destructive, as with us, to eggs and hens.' — *A Relation of the Colony of the Lord Baron of Baltimore, in Maryland, near Virginia*, etc. (FORCE's *Coll. Hist. Tracts*, Vol. IV, No. 12, pp. 6, 7.)

In "A Perfect Description of Virginia," printed in London in 1649, is given a list of the "*Beasts* great and small as followeth: above 20 severall kinds," including all the larger species, but no reference is made to the buffalo. — FORCE's *Coll. Hist. Tracts*, Vol. II, No. 8, p. 14.

In an "Account of *Virginia* in Generall, but particularly *Carolana*, which comprehends *Roanoak* and the Southern parts of *Virginia*," printed in 1650, it is said, "Nor is the Land any lesse provided of native Flesh, Elkes bigger then Oxen, whose hide is admirable Buffe, flesh excellent, and may be made, if kept domesticke, as usefull for draught and carriage, as Oxen. There in a numerous abundance, and delicate Venison, Racoones, Hares, Conyes, Bevers, Squirrell, Beares, all of a delightfull nourishment for food, and their Furres rich, warme, and convenient for clothing and Merchandise." — FORCE's *Coll. Hist. Tracts*, Vol. III, No. 11, pp. 11, 12.

Clayton, in his very detailed account of the natural products of Virginia, written in 1688, says, "There were neither Horses, Bulls, Cows, Sheep, or Swine, in all the Country, before the coming of the *English*, as I have heard, and have much reason to believe. . . . . *Wild Bulls* and *Cows* there are now in the uninhabited Parts, but such only as have been bred from some that have strayed, and become wild, and have propagated their kind, and are difficult to be shot, having a great Acuteness of Smelling." — FORCE's *Coll. Hist. Tracts*, Vol. III, No. 12, p. 35.

This leads to the inference that the frequent allusions to *wild bulls* and *wild cows* in the early accounts of Virginia, etc., often really refer to domestic cattle that had run wild.

Many citations of a similar character might be added, containing curious and interesting descriptions of the "beasts," but none of the enumerations include the buffalo. As these descriptions of the country and its products were mostly prepared for the purpose of encouraging emigration, it is not presumable that so important an animal as the buffalo would have been omitted if these early writers had ever heard of it as existing in any part of the countries they describe.

Newfoundland." Parkhurst writes: "Nowe againe, for Venison plentie, especially to the North about the grand baie, and in the South neere Cape Race and Plesance: there are many other kinds of beasts, as Luzarnes, and other mighty beastes like to camels in greatnesse, and their feete cloven, I did see them farre off not able to discerne them perfectly, but their steps shewed that their feete were cloven, and bigger than the feete of Camels, I suppose them to bee a kind of Buffes which I read to be in the countreyes adjacent, and very many in the firme lande."* Though it is supposed by some that the musk ox may have been referred to in this allusion to a "kind of Buffes," there is apparently little reason to doubt that these "Buffes" were the moose, which the early voyagers found on the adjacent mainland in great numbers; yet Marcy † and others have supposed this to be a possible reference to the buffalo, probably from the occurrence of the word "Buffes."

Another similar reference to the occurrence of an animal like an ox in Newfoundland is contained in the report of Sir Humphrey Gilbert's voyage to this island in 1583. In an enumeration of the "commodities thereof" are mentioned "Beasts of sundry kindes, red deare, buffles or a beast, as it seemeth by the tract & foote very large, in maner of an oxe." ‡ In the account of the "first voyage made to the coast of America" by Captains Philip Amadas and Arthur Barlowe, in 1584, it is said that they treated with the Indians for "Chamoys, Buffe and Deere skinnes"; § and Thomas Hariot, in his "briefe and true report of the new found land of Virginia," written in 1587, mentions "Deer skinnes dressed after the manner of Chamoes, or undressed," among the commodities of the country.‖ The same writer speaks later of the "beasts" of Virginia, and says, "I have the names of eight and twenty severall sorts, ... of which there are only twelve kinds that we have yet discovered, and of those that be good meat, we know only them before mentioned," among which there is no mention of any "Buffes," "Buffles," "wild Cattle," or anything that can be regarded as at all like the buffalo.¶

* Hakluyt, Voyages, etc., Vol. III, p. 178, London, 1600. (The Edition of 1810 is the one quoted in this memoir.)

† Exploration of the Red River of Louisiana, p. 104, 1853.

‡ Hakluyt, Voyages, etc., Vol. III, p. 195.

§ Ibid., p. 302.

‖ Ibid., p. 327.

¶ Hakluyt, Voyages, etc., p. 333.

In the narrative of the travels of David Ingram from the Gulf of Mexico to Cape Breton, in Nova Scotia, made in 1568 – 69, are unquestionable references to the buffalo, which have been referred to as possible evidence of its existence on the Atlantic slope, but the whole narrative is full of exaggerations and fanciful descriptions of mythical things and scenes, while the localities are wholly vague. The account speaks, for instance, of "great plentye of Buffes . . . . wch are Beastes as bigge as twoe Oxen in length almost twentye foote, havinge longe eares like a bludde hownde wth long heares about there eares, ther hornes be Crooked like Raines hornes, ther eyes blacke, there heares longe blacke, rough and hagged as a Goate, the Hydes of these Beastes are solde verye deare. These Beastes doe keepe Company only by couples a male and a female and doe always fighte wth others of the same kynde." *

The account also says, "He did alsoe see in that Countrye boathe Elephantes and Unces. He did also see one other straunge Beaste bigger then a Beare, yt had nether heade nor necke, his eyes and mouthe weare in his brest." It also describes "redd Sheepe" which lived in herds of five hundred individuals. Since Ingram's route doubtless took him through a portion of the range of the buffalo, the above-quoted description of "Buffes" may refer to that animal, but there is nothing to show that the locality was on the Atlantic slope.

Champlain, as early as 1604, ascended the St. Lawrence River nearly to Lake Ontario, and although he obtained from the Indians quite distinct accounts of Lakes Ontario and Erie, and of the Copper Mines of Lake Superior, he seems not to have learned anything respecting the buffalo. The animal which he describes as the "Orignac" or "Orignal" is without doubt the moose. He mentions it as an animal "which is like an Ox," † and Purchas, in his marginal notes, adds, "Orignac, a beast like an oxe." He first met with it at the mouth of the Saguenay, and later encountered it among the animals he found at the mouth of the Richelieu, speaking of it as the "Orignac," and Purchas again adds, "Orignas are before said to bee like oxen, perhaps Buffes. *Lescarbot*, [says] that *Orignacs* are *Ellans*," ‡ — the French

* The Land Travels of David Ingram and others in the years 1568 - 69. From the Rio de Minas in the Gulph of Mexico to Cape Breton in Acadia. Edited from the original MS. (Sloane MSS., Mus. Brit., No. 1447, ff. 1 - 18) by P. C. J. Weston, in Doc. connected with the Hist. of S. Carolina. London, 1856, p. 14.

† Purchas, Pilgrims, Vol. IV, p. 1607.

‡ Ibid., p. 1613.

term for the moose. The name "orignac" or "orignal" of the early French explorers appears to have been applied indifferently to both the moose (*Alces malchis*) and the elk (*Cervus canadensis*), but never to the buffalo. Champlain, in speaking of the game he found about Lake Champlain, makes no reference to the buffalo, neither do any of the subsequent writers of the seventeenth century. In regard to the "Ellans," we find in Lescarbot's account the following: "The winter being come, the Savages of the Countrey did assemble themselves from farre to Port *Royall*, for to trucke with the *Frenchmen* for such things as they had, some bringing Beavers skins and Otters . . . . and also *Ellans* or Stagges, whereof good *buffe* be made." * We thus see that the term *buffe* was also applied to the products of the elk and moose. Charlevoix's description of the Orignal, however, is strictly applicable to the moose, and to no other animal. Charlevoix says: "What they here [in Canada] call the Orignal, is what in *Germany*, *Poland*, and *Muscovy* they call the Elk, or Great Beast. . . . . Its Horns are not less long than those of a Hart, and much wider. They are flat and forked like those of a Deer, and are renewed every Year." †

Hennepin ascended the St. Lawrence and crossed the lakes to the prairies of Indiana and Illinois in 1679–80, but Hennepin in his narrative of his travels does not speak of meeting with the buffalo until he had reached the Illinois River in December, 1679.‡ In his account of the productions of Canada, he says, "There are to be had Skins of Elks, or *Orignaux*, as they are called in Canada, of the white Wolf or Lynx, of black Foxes, ... of common Foxes, Otters, Martens, wild Cats, wild Goats, Harts, Porcupines," etc.§ In the account he has given of his travels he describes the buffalo with such particularity ‖ as to leave no doubt that if he had met with or known of the occurrence of the buffalo in what is now known as Canada, he would not have failed to enumerate it among the products of that country.

In 1763 Marquette passed up the St. Lawrence, and through the Great Lakes to the Mississippi Valley, by way of Lake Michigan and the Fox and

* Purchas, Pilgrims, Vol. IV, p. 1613.

† Letters to the Dutchess of Lesdiguières, Goadby's English Ed., London, 1763, p. 64.

‡ New Discovery of a great Country in America, English Ed., 1698, p. 90.

§ Voyage into North America, English Ed., 1679, pp. 136, 137.

‖ New Discovery, etc., p. 91.

Wisconsin Rivers, but he appears not to have met with the buffalo till he reached the Wisconsin River.*

Charlevoix, who traversed the same country in 1720, and who has left us in his letters a full account of his journey up the St. Lawrence, and thence westward through Lakes Ontario and Erie, only heard of their existence on the southern shore of Lake Erie, he himself coasting along the northern shore. Concerning the game of the country bordering Lake Erie he says, "Water-fowl swarmed everywhere: I cannot say there is such Plenty of Game in the Woods, but I know that on the South Side there are vast Herds of wild Cattle." † Again he says, "But at the end of five or six leagues [from Detroit River], inclining towards the Lake *Erié* to the South West, one sees vast Meadows which extend above a hundred Leagues every Way, and which feed a prodigious Number of those Cattle which I have already mentioned several Times." ‡ He gives, however, an account of the "chase" in Canada, in which he describes the method of hunting the buffalo, but the locality is specified as "the Southern and Western Parts of New France, on both Sides of the Mississippi," § which was then generally called Canada.

In the account of the Voyage of Father Simon Le Moine to the country of the "Iroquois Onondagoes" in 1653 – 54 we find what at first sight seems to be indisputable evidence of the existence of the buffalo at the eastern end of Lake Ontario, in both New York and Canada. In this account we find the following: "At the other side of the Rapid ‖ I perceived a herd of *wild cows*, ¶ which were passing at their ease in great state. Five or six hundred are seen sometimes in these regions in one drove." ** In the "Relation de la Nouvelle France en l'Année 1665," we find the following description of the St. Lawrence River: "This is one of the most important rivers that can be seen, whether we regard its beauty or its convenience, for we meet there almost throughout, a vast number of beautiful Islands, some large, others

* An Account of the Discovery of some new Countries and Nations in N. America in 1673. Translation in French's Hist. Coll. La., Part II, pp. 279 – 297.

† Letters, Goadby's English Ed., 1763, p. 170. Dodsley's English Edition says "a prodigious quantity of Buffaloes" (Vol. II, p. 3).

‡ Ibid., p. 178. Dodsley's Translation says again, "those buffaloes" (Vol. II, p. 18).

§ Ibid., p. 68.

‖ This locality is just below St. Ignatius, on the St. Lawrence, not far from Lake Ontario.

¶ "Vaches sauvages," in the original. Relation de la Nouv. France en les Années 1653 - 54, p. 85.

** Documentary Hist. New York, Vol. I, p. 31.

small, but all covered with fine timber and full of deer, bears, *wild cows*,* which supply abundance of provisions necessary for the travellers, who find it everywhere, and sometimes entire herds of fallow deer." †

We have here a term (*vaches sauvages*) employed which was often used by the early French writers to designate the buffalo, and also the account of large herds being seen, which seems still further to imply that the animals were unquestionably buffaloes, yet the locality is one which was frequently passed over by travellers during the previous fifty years, not one of whom mentions the occurrence of the buffalo on the St. Lawrence, nor is any mention of its occurrence there made by subsequent writers. The region is, furthermore, a heavily wooded country, situated several hundred miles from the prairies, and from the most easterly known range of the buffalo. These facts alone tend to render these accounts improbable, but fortunately we are not left in doubt as to the character of the animals here mentioned, for in the sequel of Father Le Moine's Journal the following passages render it certain that the animals referred to were either deer or elk: —

"1st day of Sept. I never saw so many deer, but we had no inclination to hunt. My companion killed three, as if against his will. What a pity! for we left all the venison there, reserving the hides and some of the most delicate morsels.

"2nd of the month. Travelling through vast prairies, we saw in divers quarters immense herds of wild bulls and cows; ‡ *their horns resemble in some respects the antlers of the stag*.

"3d and 4th. Our game does not leave us; it seems that venison and game follow us everywhere. Droves of twenty cows plunge into the water, as if to meet us. Some are killed, for sake of amusement, by blows of an axe." §

From the context we learn that the locality was but a few leagues above Montreal, on the St. Lawrence. These bands of "bulls and cows" were doubtless elks (*Cervus canadensis*). ‖

* "Vaches sauvages." Relation de la Nouv. France en l'année 1665, pp. 49, 50. Mr. J. G. Shea also observes: "The animal called by the Canadian French *vache sauvage* was the American elk, or moose," and cites Boucher (Hist. Nat. du Canada) as authority. "Boucher," says Shea, "expressly states that the buffaloes were found only in the Ottawa country, that is, in the far West, while the *vache sauvage*, or Original and the *ane sauvage*, or Cariboo, were seen in Canada."—*Discovery and Exploration of the Mississippi Valley*, p. 16, footnote.

† Documentary History of New York, Vol. I. p. 62.

‡ The original says, "grand troupeaux de bœufs & de vaches sauvages." — *Rel.* etc., 1653 - 54, p. 90.

§ Ibid., pp. 43, 44. Translated from Relation de la Nouv. France, 1653 - 54, pp. 95, 96.

‖ Hunters, both in Northern New England and in the West, commonly speak of the male moose and elk as "bull moose" and "bull elk," and the females as "cow moose" and "cow elk."

Peter Kalm says: "Wild cattle are" [1749] "abundant in the southern parts of Canada, and have been there from time immemorial. They are plentiful in those parts, particularly where the Illinois Indians live, which are nearly in the latitude of Philadelphia; but further north they are seldom observed." * In respect to this passage it is almost needless to add that the portion of *Canada* here mentioned is the present State of Illinois.

Ogilby says: "Towards the South of New York are many Buffles, Beasts which (according to *Erasmus Stella*) are betwixt a Horse and a Stag: . . . . they have broad branching Horns like a Stag, short Tail, rough Neck, Hair colored according to the several seasons," etc. The animals here called *Buffles* were of course elks, showing again that the use of the term *buffles* does not necessarily imply a reference to the buffalo. The same writer, however, in his description of Maryland, says: "In the upper parts of the Country are *Buffaloes*, *Elks*, *Tygers*, *Bears*, *Wolves*, *Racoons*, and many other sorts of Beasts." † What portion of the country may have been referred to as the "upper parts of the Country" is uncertain, but the preceding narratives of exploration, on which Ogilby's work is based, make no mention of the existence of the buffalo in the region now known as Maryland.

Father Andrew White, in "An Account of the Colony of the Lord Baron of Baltimore, in Maryland, near Virginia," published in 1677, in his account of the animals previously quoted (p. 78, footnote), says: "There are also vast herds of cows and wild oxen, fit for beasts of burden and good to eat. . . . . The nearest woods are full of horses and wild bulls and cows. Five or six thousand of the skins of these animals are carried every year to Saville, from that part of the country which lies westward towards New Mexico." ‡ It is evident that this reference to herds of wild cattle refers not at all to the buffalo, nor even to the region of country now known as Maryland, but to the Spanish Possessions in the southwest, whence the exportation of hides of the domestic cattle to Spain had long before begun. §

Professor E. D. Cope,‖ however, recently says: "Of the Ruminants [of Maryland], the bison (*Bos americanus*) and the elk (*Cervus canadensis*), the

* Kalm's Travels in N. America, Forster's Translation, Vol. III, p. 60.

† Ogilby's America, pp. 172, 186 (London, 1681).

‡ Translation of Father White's "Account," in Force's Coll. Hist. Tracts, Vol. IV, No. 12, pp. 6, 7.

§ See Clavigero's History of Mexico, Cullen's English Translation, Vol. II, p. 308, where Clavigero states, on the authority of Acosta, that in 1587 sixty-four thousand three hundred and fifty ox hides were taken to Spain, so rapidly had the domestic cattle increased in Mexico.

‖ New Top. Map of Maryland, p. 16, 1873.

largest known of the true deer, have been destroyed by human agency," implying their former existence in that State. On inquiry of Professor Cope for the grounds of such an inference he states * that he has found their unfossilized bones in superficial deposits in Virginia, and adds: "I think, but will not now assert, from more northern localities." †

In Salmon's "Present State of Virginia," printed in 1737, we read that Sir William Berkley sent (apparently about 1733) a small party of "about fourteen *English* and as many *Indians*, under the Command of Captain Henry Batt," to explore the country to the westward of the settlements in Virginia. "They set out together," says Salmon, "from *Appomattox*, and in Seven Days March reach'd the Foot of the Mountains. The Mountains they first arriv'd at were not extraordinary high or steep, but after they had pass'd the first Ridge they encounter'd others that seem'd to reach the Clouds, and were so perpendicular and full of Precipices, that sometimes in a whole Day's March they could not travel three miles in a direct Line. In other Places they found large level Plains and fine Savanna's three or four Miles wide, in which were an infinite quantity of Turkies, Deer, Elks, and Buffaloes, so gentle and undisturbed that they had no Fear at the Appearance of the Men, but would suffer them to come almost within Reach of their Hands." ‡ This account shows that buffaloes were not seen by the explorers till they entered the mountains and encountered the herds that extended eastward from the valleys of West Virginia.

Another reference to the supposed occurrence of the buffalo on the eastern slope of the Alleghanies is the discovery by Sir Samuel Argoll of "Shag-haired Oxen" in Virginia. In his letter to "Master Nicholas Hawes (written "June, 1613"), as given by Purchas, Sir Samuel says: . . . . "[I] returned my self with the ship into *Pembrook* River, and so discovered *to the head of it*, which is about 65. leagues into the Land, and navigable for any ship. *And then marching into the Countrie*, I found great store of Cattle as big as Kine, of which, the Indians that were my guides, killed a couple which wee found to be very good and wholesome meate, and are very easie to be killed, in regard they are heavy, slow, and not so wild as other beasts of the Wilder-

* In a letter dated December 22, 1875.

† In this connection I may add that I have examined remains from the banks of the Susquehanna, and other localities in Maryland, some partly fossilized and others nearly unchanged, which though collected for bison remains proved to be those of domestic cattle.

‡ Salmon (T.), The Present State of Virginia, p. 14, (London, 1737).

nesse."* Purchas also says, in his "*Virginias* Verger, or Discourse on Virginia," in enumerating the animals of Virginia, "I might adde Shag-haired oxen, seen by Sir Samuel Argoll."

The "Pembrook," or "Penbrooke" mentioned in Argoll's account has generally been considered as the "Patowomeck," or one of its affluents, but it was, I think, unquestionably the James.† The region visited by Captain Batt must have also been somewhere on the head-waters of the James. There is still traditional evidence that buffaloes formerly passed eastward from the head-waters of the Great Kanawha in West Virginia to this region. Professor Shaler, being aware of the existence of such names as "Buffalo Springs" and "Buffalo Ford," in the region of Amherst, Bath, and Pocahontas Counties, Virginia, has made successful effort to ascertain whether they indicated the former presence there of buffaloes. In answer to his inquiries respecting the matter, Mr. C. W. Pritchett has kindly sent him the following important information. Mr. Pritchett says that the "old men" of that country affirm "that the Buffalo Springs were so named from a Salt Lick near by of that name, to which their fathers were guided by the buffalo trails. The tradition is abundant and easily verified, that buffalo and elk were numerous in that part of Virginia within a period comparatively recent. These traditions are especially abundant in Bath and Pocahontas Counties, lying between the Blue Ridge and the Alleghanies. On the Cow Pasture River (which with the Jackson forms the James), in Bath County, a few miles below the Blowing Cave and Wallawhatoola Springs (Indian namė for Crooked River), is a salt lick, near which they still show the deep-worn trail of the buffalo, at the point where they crossed the river, still called Buffalo Ford. . . . . There are men still living there whose fathers and grandfathers saw the buffalo, and even, *in one instance*, caught and domesticated them."‡ In corroboration of the above

* Purchas, Vol. IV, p. 1765.

† The "Patowomeck" mentioned by Argoll (or Argall) is evidently the Indian chief of that name, and not the river "Patowomeck." Purchas, in his marginal notes to Argoll's letter, says, "His first Voyage to *Patawomec* and *Penbrooke* River," not *Rivers*; and again, "The second voyage to *Penbrooke* River." Argoll himself speaks of going to "fetch Corne from *Patowomeck*," for which purpose he "entered into *Pembrooke* River," and after obtaining his cargo of corn he "hasted to *James* Towne," and later arrived at Point Comfort. After distributing the corn he returned again "into *Pembrook* River," and made the discovery of a "great store of Cattle as big as Kine." Whilst engaged "in this business" he conceived the idea of going to the "great King *Patowomeck*" for the purpose of obtaining possession by "stratagem" of the "Great *Powhatans* Daughter *Pokahuntis*."

‡ Letter to Professor Shaler, dated Glasgow, Mo., July 31, 1875.

important statements, Mr. Pritchett refers to a number of the descendants of the first settlers of the region in question as being ready to vouch for his statements. The localities he mentions are all well up in the mountains, beyond the Blue Ridge, Pocahontas County being wholly west of the divide, on the Greenbrier River. Bath County adjoins it on the east, and embraces the extreme upper tributaries of the James. These counties are the ones referred to by Mr. Pritchett as those where the evidence of the former presence of the buffalo is still "abundant." Amherst County is some distance lower down the James, and if the name "Buffalo Springs" in that county is to be considered as satisfactory evidence of the former existence there of the buffalo, these animals must have at times wandered to some distance down the James, as far at least as the Blue Ridge.

The only reasons for supposing that buffaloes at times crossed through the low valleys of the Alleghanies in Central Pennsylvania to the Atlantic slope are Professor Baird's report of the occurrence of its bones in the superficial deposits and caves of that State,* and the traditional evidence afforded by the occurrence of such names as "Buffalo Creek" and "Buffalo Valley" in Union County, near Lewisburg. The last-mentioned locality, though of course on the Atlantic slope, is west of the Blue Ridge, which here forms the principal chain of the Alleghany Mountains.

The foregoing historical evidence is sufficient apparently to show the improbability of the occurrence of the buffalo, at the time of the first exploration of the country by Europeans, either north of the great lakes or over that part of the Atlantic slope adjacent to the sea-coast *north of North Carolina*; in other words, within the present limits of Canada, New England, or the maritime part of the eastern slope of the Appalachian Highlands, northward of the present southern boundary of Virginia. On the contrary, it seems to me that the evidence of its absence at that time over these regions is almost conclusive, for had it occurred there, there is every reason to believe that proof of the fact would not be wanting in the early records of the country, in which its products, and especially its larger animals, are so often minutely enumerated. We have also seen that the use of such terms as *buffes*, *buffles*, *wild bulls*, *wild cows*, *wild cattle*, and *vaches sauvages*, not only do not necessarily imply the presence of buffaloes, but, on the contrary, have been repeatedly employed as the designation of both the moose and the elk. If we

* The locality, though not stated, is probably Cumberland County.

accept these terms as implying the presence of buffaloes in the region under consideration, we must allow, on similar evidence, that *wild goats* were found in the seventeenth century along the whole length of the St. Lawrence, throughout the Mississippi Valley and in Florida;* that *wild swine* were found in Canada at the mouth of the Saguenay River, and in the Middle States;† also *wild horses* in Newfoundland prior to the year 1600; *monkeys* and *apes* in Virginia;‡ and that *wild lemons* formerly grew in Southern Michigan.§ Goat Island, at the Falls of Niagara, probably derives its name from the custom of calling the deer that frequented it wild goats. The name of Buffalo River (*Rivière aux Bœufs*) in New York,‖ and the name of the city on Lake Erie now called Buffalo, are not necessarily, though probably, traditional evidences¶ of the occurrence of the buffalo at those localities, since it is not very improbable, as will be shown later, that the buffalo formerly ranged along the southern shore of Lake Erie to its eastern end.

As previously stated, there is good reason also for assuming that the buffalo was not found in New England, nor along the coast of the Middle States, *during a long period antedating the exploration of the continent by Europeans*, or during the period of the formation of the Indian shell mounds of the North Atlantic coast, which contain no traces of the remains of the buffalo, as they probably would do if it had existed here at the time of their formation, since they do contain the bones of all the larger mammals found here by the earliest European travellers. There still remains to be examined, however, one supposed evidence of its existence in New England in prehistoric times.

Shortly before the second visit of Sir Charles Lyell to the United States, some teeth of a species of the ox tribe were found in a clay-bank at Gardiner,

* See the various accounts of the voyages of De Soto, La Salle, Hennepin, Marquette, and others, where the term *wild goat* is probably used for deer, but sometimes as though it referred to a distinct animal, both wild goats, stags, and deer being mentioned in the same sentence.

† That bears were mistaken for swine, in the following account, is of course evident: "Wee might see in some places where Deere and Hares had beene, and by the rooting of the Ground, we supposed wilde Hogs had ranged there, but we could discerne no Beast, because our Noise still chased them away from us." — *George Weymouth's Voyage*, 1605, in Purchas, Pilgrims, Vol. IV, p. 1665.

‡ See Strachey's Historie of Travaile into Virginia, p. 26; Hakluyt Society, Volume for 1849.

§ "There also grow in the Strait [Detroit River] Lemon-Trees in the natural Soil, the Fruit of which have the Shape and Colour of those of *Portugal*, but they are smaller, and of a flat Taste. They are excellent in conserve." — CHARLEVOIX, *Letters*, p. 178.

‖ Supposed to be the present Oak Orchard Creek, Orleans Co., N. Y. See Doc. Coll. Hist. N. Y., Vol. IX, p. 886.

¶ Schoolcraft, Hist. Cond. and Prospects of the Indian Tribes of the United States, Part IV, p. 92.

Maine. The late Mrs. Frederic Allen, of Gardiner, secured these teeth for her cabinet, where they were seen by Sir Charles Lyell, who took with him some of them to England for determination. Respecting these specimens, and others contained in Mrs. Allen's cabinet, Sir Charles speaks as follows: "At Mrs. Allen's I examined, with much interest, a collection of fossil shells and crustacea, made by Mrs. Allen, from the drift, or 'glacial' deposits of the same age as those of Portsmouth, already described. Among other remains I recognized the tooth of a walrus, similar to one procured by me in Martha's Vineyard, and other teeth, since determined by Professor Owen as belonging to the buffalo, or American bison. These are, I believe, the first examples of land quadrupeds discovered in beds of this age in the United States. The accompanying shells consisted of the common mussel (*Mytilus edulis*), *Saxicava rugosa*, *Mya arenaria*, *Pecten islandicus*, and species of the genera *Astarte*, *Nucula*, etc." *

These specimens of supposed bison's teeth having assumed a considerable degree of importance, I wrote, in January, 1873, to Professor Owen, to obtain, if possible, further information respecting them. In his reply, dated Cairo, Egypt, February 6, 1873, he says: "I do not recall the circumstance to which you refer, and no teeth of ruminants from the locality you name were in the Palæontological Department of the British Museum when the state of my health obliged me to winter here. I should be unwilling to accept the responsibility of any determination which I have not myself published, after the care requisite for such a step."

Upon the death of Mrs. Frederic Allen, her collection passed into the possession of her daughter, Mrs. Romeo Elton, now residing in Dorchester, Mass. Through Mrs. Elton's kindness I have been able to obtain the full history of the specimens in question, and to examine the three teeth still remaining in her collection, and which were figured by Dr. A. S. Packard, Jr., in his memoir on the Glacial Phenomena of Labrador and Maine, etc.† There is also a specimen from the original lot of four, in the Museum of the Boston Society of Natural History, presented to the Society by Dr. C T. Jackson, with a collection of Maine tertiary fossils.

The circumstances of the finding of the teeth are fully set forth in a written statement, or deposition, made at the time by the person who collected the specimens. Through the kindness of Mrs. Elton, I have before me the

* Second Visit to the United States of North America, Vol. I, pp. 43, 44, 1849.

† Mem. Boston Soc. Nat. Hist., Vol. I, plate vii, fig. 18.

original document, which represents the teeth as occurring in a solid clay bank, fifteen feet below the surface.* In respect to the character of the locality, and its present condition, I have the following additional information from Dr. A. S. Packard, Jr., in answer to special inquiries on this point. In a letter dated Salem, Mass., December 31, 1872, Dr. Packard writes: "In answer to your other query, I have examined hastily the locality, but many years after Lyell visited this country,—about twenty,—and great changes may have occurred in the locality, as when I was there the high clay-bank was being dug away to supply a brickyard." † Referring to a suspicion I had communicated to him that they would probably prove to be the teeth of a domestic ox, he adds further: "The teeth in question may have fallen over the embankment, and got mixed up in the beds. The beds containing the shells lie below, in a vertical section, where the beds containing the supposed bison's teeth would have been, but the shell-bearing beds graduate into those situated fifteen feet below the surface." One of the teeth remaining in Mrs. Elton's collection was, at the time I saw it, still firmly imbedded in its original matrix of blue clay, of the same character as that enclosing the shells.

From the above it appears that the teeth were not taken from the clay-beds by Sir Charles Lyell, as some have supposed, nor by either a geologist or a scientific collector; that they could not have been associated with the fossil shells, but came from beds considerably above them; and that it is not at all improbable that they rolled down from the surface, and became firmly imbedded in the clay. Furthermore, the teeth are in a remarkably perfect state of preservation, looking as fresh and recent as a tooth would which had had but a short period of exposure to atmospheric or any other decomposing influences, having undergone, indeed, scarcely any perceptible change.

In the structural character of the teeth themselves there is nothing that positively settles the question of their identity, though the evidence favors the assumption of their being the teeth of the domestic ox. My first com-

* The following is a literal transcription of the document: "The teeth that I dug out of the clay-bank about fifteen feet below the surface; was a solid bank of blue clay, so firm that it was impossible for anything to have got in there, there were no cracks or fissures that it could have fallen into as it was perfectly solid; there were four lying very nearly together in the solid clay and required such exertion to get them out that they could not at such a depth have got in by ordinary means.

"GEORGE SOULE of Avon. 1837."

† Mrs. Elton informs me that now the original bank has been wholly removed.

parison of them with the teeth of the buffalo and of the common ox seemed to leave no doubt of their identity with the latter, as I had no difficulty in exactly matching them in every particular, and especially in respect to the character of the folds of the enamel, in the teeth of the domestic ox, while there was a constant variation in several points from those of the buffalo. Later I have found so much variation in the teeth, not only of the domestic species but also of the buffalo, that this test of their identity fails to be a valid one, as I have also found buffalo teeth that closely resemble those from Gardiner. The weight of evidence on this ground, however, is decidedly in favor of their identity with those of the domestic ox. In order to give the evidence impartially, I intended to present in Plate XI first, a series of figures of the teeth of the bison and the domestic ox, for the double purpose of showing not only the range of structural variation in the teeth of the undomesticated bison, and the slight reliance that can safely be placed on single teeth in determining specific differences, but also to figure the four teeth found in the Gardiner clays in order to show their similarity to those of the domestic ox. This, however, circumstances beyond my control have prevented me from doing, only a single tooth from Gardiner, belonging to the Boston Society of Natural History, being represented on the Plate.* Upon the settlement of the question of the identity or non-identity of these teeth with those of the bison hinges the validity of the only supposed evidence we have respecting the former existence of the bison in New England, or anywhere east of the Great Lakes.

In addition to the original notice already quoted from Lyell, respecting the occurrence of bison's teeth in Maine, Dr. A. S. Packard, Jr., refers to it in the American Naturalist,† and in the Memoirs of the Boston Society of Natural History.‡ In each case, however, the authority is the same, that of Lyell, who is, however, represented as having himself discovered the specimens in the clay-beds. Dr. Packard, indeed, speaks of the "intermingling of the bones [teeth] of the walrus and the bison in the same beds," but there is no record showing that they were actually thus associated.§

* A few months since the teeth, with Mrs. Elton's general collection of the tertiary fossils of Gardiner, Maine, were presented by her to Bowdoin College, Brunswick, Maine. My subsequent request for the loan of the teeth to figure the Curator of the Museum declined to grant.

† Vol. I, p. 268, 1867; Vol. VI, p. 98, 1872.

‡ Vol. I, pp. 243, 246, pl. vii, fig. 18, 1867.

§ Says Dr. Packard: "The deposits of Gardiner possess great interest, owing to their unusual thickness, and the rich assemblage of marine invertebrates which occur from the lowest to the highest strata, and

Region South of Virginia. — As already remarked, the only well-authenticated instances of the occurrence of buffaloes east of the Blue Ridge is the apparently casual passage of small bands through the mountains from West Virginia, Kentucky, and Tennessee, into the upper parts of North and South Carolina, by way of the New, Holston and French Broad Rivers.* Audubon and Bachman state that "the Bison formerly existed in South Carolina, *on the sea-board*, and we are informed," say these authors, "that from the last seen in that State two were killed in the vicinity of Columbia."† But they have neglected to add the date of the capture, or the authority on which the statement is made. They state, however, that "Lawson speaks of two buffaloes that were killed on Cape Fear River, in North Carolina." Lawson's statement in full is as follows: "This day [Sunday, February 1, 1700], the King sent out all his able Hunters, to kill Game for a great Feast, that was to be kept at their Departure, from the Town. . . . . This Evening [same day] came down some *Toteros*, tall, likely Men, having great Plenty of Buffeloes, Elks, and Bears, with other sort of Deer amongst them."‡ "The *Toteros*," he says, "a neighboring Nation came down from the Westward Mountains to the *Saponas*," § etc. Lawson was now on the "Sapona River," in or near the mountains,‖ which was apparently one of the sources of the Cape Fear

from the occurrence of the teeth of the bison and of the walrus, which were dug out of the beds at a distance of fifteen feet from the top of the clay, during Sir Charles Lyell's second visit to this country. . . . . The intermingling of the bones of the walrus and bison in the same beds shows the great range both of Arctic and Temperate forms during this period." — *Mem. Bost. Soc. Nat. Hist.*, Vol. I, p. 243.

Again he says: "Teeth of the Walrus and the Bison were discovered by Sir Charles Lyell in the clay-beds of Gardiner, Maine. These are still preserved in a private collection. The association in the glacial clays of the remains of the Bison with those of the Walrus, and the mingling of the arctic animals and plants with those now confined to British North America and New England, show that the climate, during the glacial period, was a little warmer than that of Southern Greenland at present." — *Am. Nat.* Vol. I, p. 268, footnote.

* Gallatin says: "The gap through which they [the buffaloes] passed to the Atlantic rivers is undoubtedly that of moderate elevation and gentle ascent, which divides a northeastern source of the Roanoke from the great Kenawha, called the New River, and through which the State of Virginia is now attempting to open a communication from James River to the Ohio." — *Trans. Am. Ethnological Soc.*, Vol. II, p. li.

† Quadrupeds North America, Vol. II, p. 55.

‡ History of Carolina, p. 46 (London, 1718).

§ Ibid., p. 47.

‖ A rude map of North and South Carolina accompanies his journal, but on the map the word *Saponas* does not occur. The context, however, shows that he was in the northeastern part of the present State of North Carolina, on the sources of the Cape Fear River. Brickell says, however, in his Natural History of North Carolina, published in 1737: "The Sapona Indians live at the West branch of the Cape Fear, or

River. The journey here described commenced at Charleston. He travelled near the coast till he reached the Santee River, and then ascended that river as far, apparently, as Columbia, then turning northeastward, he kept in the highlands, crossing the sources of the Cape Fear, and thence eastward to the "Pamticough" River and the English settlements. In his preface he says: "Having spent most of my Time, during my eight Years Abode in *Carolina*, in travelling; I not only survey'd the Sea-Coast, and those Parts which are already inhabited by the Christians, but likewise view'd a spatious Tract of Land lying betwixt the Inhabitants and the Ledges of Mountains, from whence our noblest Rivers have their Rise, running towards the Ocean, where they water as pleasant a Country as any in *Europe*; the Discovery of which being never yet made publick, I have, in the following Sheets, given you a faithful Account thereof, wherein I have laid down every thing with Impartiality and Truth." But in the narrative of his travels he makes no further allusion to the buffalo, and does not appear to have found the Indians in possession of either its skins or meat. He speaks, however, of the various kinds of game he daily met with, and especially of the abundance of turkeys. In his chapter on the "Natural History of Carolina," concerning which he says, "I have been very exact, and for Method's Sake rang'd each Species under its distinct and proper Head," he again speaks of the buffalo, as follows: "The Buffalo is a wild Beast of *America*, which has a Bunch on his Back, as the Cattle of *St. Laurence* are said to have. He seldom appears amongst the *English* Inhabitants, his chief Haunt being in the Land of *Messiasippi*, which is, for the most part, a plain Country; yet I have known some killed on the hilly Part of *Cape Fair* River, they passing the Ledges of vast Mountains from the said *Messiasippi*, before they can come near us." *

From Lawson's eight years' residence, and extensive travels in the Carolinas, about the year 1700, and from his mentioning only the instance of its capture by the Indians above cited, it was evidently not at that time numerous in the Carolinas.† A few years after the publication of Lawson's work, this same region was visited by John Brickell, who passed through nearly the same districts as those traversed by Lawson. Brickell wrote concerning

Clarendon River, which is very beautiful and has good land about it," etc. (p. 343). He also says: "The Toteras are neighboring Indians to the Saponas, and live Westward in the Mountains" (p. 343).

* History of Carolina, p. 115.

† Yet in the history of Long's Expedition to the Source of St. Peter's River (Vol. II, p. 26), it is stated that "from Lawson we find that great plenty of buffaloes, elkes &c. existed near Cape Fear river and its tributaries!"

the buffalo as follows: "The *Buffelo*, or *wild Beef*, is one of the largest wild Beasts that is yet known in these parts of *America*; it hath a Bunch upon it's Back, and thick short Horns, bending forward. . . . . This Monster of the Woods seldom appears amongst the *European* Inhabitants, it's chiefest haunts being in the *Savannas* near the Mountains, or Heads of the great Rivers. . . . . And it is conjectur'd, that these Buffelo's being mix'd, and breeding with our tame Cattle, would much improve the Species for largeness and Milk; for these Monsters (as I have been inform'd) weigh from 1600 to 2400 pounds Weight. They are a very fierce Creature, and much larger than an Ox. . . . . There were two of the Calves of this Creature taken alive in the Year 1730, by some of the Planters living near *New* River, but whether they transported them to *Europe*, or what other uses they made of them, I know not, having occasion to leave that Country soon after." *

Catesby, who visited South Carolina and Georgia some fifty years later, describes the buffalo quite minutely in his Natural History of Carolina, published in 1754, showing most unquestionably that he was personally familiar with it. He says: "They frequent the remote parts of the country near the mountains, and are rarely seen within the settlements. They range in droves, feeding in open savannas morning and evening; and in the sultry time of the day, they retire to shady rivulets of clear water, glistening through thickets of tall cane, which though a hidden retreat, yet their heavy bodies causing a deep impression of their feet in the moist land, they are often trac'd, and shot by the artful *Indians*." † Catesby tells us in his preface that he spent the first year of his sojourn in America in Carolina, in the settled district near the sea-shore, and passed thence to the "Upper uninhabited Parts of the Country, and continued at and about *Fort Moore*, a small Fortress on the Banks of the River *Savanna*, which runs from thence a Course of 300 Miles down to the Sea, and is about the same Distance from its Source, in the Mountains." This region, he says, "afforded not only a Succession of new vegetable Appearances, but most delightful Prospects imaginable, besides the Diversion of Hunting Buffalo's, Bears, Panthers and other wild Beasts." ‡

Bartram also speaks of the existence of a "Great Buffalo Lick, on the Great Ridges which separate the waters of the Savanna and Alatamaha,

* Natural History of North Carolina, 1737, pp. 107, 108.

† Nat. Hist. Carol., Fla., etc., 1754, Vol. I, Appendix, p. xxvii.

‡ Ibid., p. viii of preface.

about eighty miles distant from Augusta."* Again, in speaking of the middle region of the Carolinas, he says: "The buffalo (*Urus*), once so very numerous, is not at this date [1773] to be seen in this part of the country."†

Hewit, also, in his "Historical Account of the Rise and Progress of the Colonies of South Carolina," published originally in London in 1779, thus refers to the buffalo in enumerating the natural productions of "Carolina," in his description of its condition about the year 1674: "Numbers of deer, timorous and wild, ranged through the trees, and herds of buffaloes were found grazing in the savannas."‡ Keating also says, on the authority of Colhoun: "And we know that some of those who first settled the Abbeville district in South Carolina, in 1756, found the buffalo there."§

Further evidence of the existence of the buffalo in the western parts of North and South Carolina is furnished by maps of these States, prepared about 1771-1775,‖ on which a tributary of Coldwater River, in what is now Cabarrus County, North Carolina, is called Buffalo Creek; while two of the upper tributaries of the Broad River bear the names respectively of Buffalo Creek and Bullock Creek. In South Carolina, on the sources of the Saluda River, in the present County of Abbeville, a swamp is laid down as Buffalo Swamp. I fail to find, however, any of these names preserved on recent maps.

Peter Kalm, in his "Travels in North America," under date of November, 1748, also thus alludes to their existence "in Carolina." "The *wild oxen* have their abode principally in the woods of *Carolina*, which are far up in the country. The inhabitants frequently hunt them and salt them like common beef, which is eaten by servants and the lower class of people. But the hide is of little use, having too large pores to be made use of for shoes. However, the poorer people in *Carolina* spread their hides on the ground instead of beds."¶ Again he speaks of "the wild *Cows* and *Oxen* . . . . which are to be met with in *Carolina*, and other provinces to the south of *Pennsylvania*. . . . . This *American* species of oxen," he says, "is *Linnæus's Bos Bison*, β."**

* Travels through North and South Carolina, Georgia, East and West Florida, etc., 1773-75, pp. 35, 46.

† Ibid., p. 46.

‡ Carroll's Hist. Coll. S. Car., Vol. I, p. 78.

§ Long's Expedition to the Source of the St. Peter's River, etc., 1823, Vol. II, p. 26.

‖ A map of North and South Carolina. Accurately compiled from the old maps of James Cook, published in 1771, and of Henry Mouzon, in 1775. Carroll's Hist. Coll. South Carolina, 1836, Vol. I.

¶ Travels into North America, Forster's Translation, Vol. I, p. 287.

** Ibid., Vol. I, p. 207.

In the verbal relation, reported by Hakluyt, of "Nicholas Burgoignon, aliâs Holy," who spent six years "in Florida" prior to 1586, Burgoignon states that "the Spaniards, entring 50. leagues up Saint Helena, found Indians wearing golde rings at their nostrels and eares. They found also Oxen, but lesse than ours." * The St. Helena here mentioned was in the present State of South Carolina, and must have been either the Combahee or the Edisto River, though most probably the latter, the name St. Helena being still retained for the bay at the mouths of these rivers. It hence seems very probable that the locality referred to was the Abbeville district of South Carolina, where buffaloes at that time doubtless existed.

Governor Oglethorpe, in his "New and Accurate Account of the Provinces of South Carolina and Georgia," published in 1733, makes the following single reference to the buffalo: "The wild beasts are deer, elks, bears, wolves, buffaloes, wild boars, and abundance of hares and rabbits: they have also a catamountain, or small leopard; but this is not the dangerous species of the East Indies." †

Francis Moore, writing in 1744, referring to the absence of the buffalo from St. Simon's Island, adds that "there are large herds there upon the Main." ‡

Governor Glen, in his "Description of Carolina," published in 1761, enumerates "Buffaloes" in his list of the "Wild Beasts, etc., of the Forest." § Drayton, writing in 1802, also enumerates the buffalo as one of the animals formerly existing in South Carolina. He says, "The buffalo and cat-a-mount are entirely exterminated on the eastern side of our mountains." ‖

While the former occurrence of the buffalo in the "upper parts" of the Carolinas "near the mountains" is a well-established fact of history, its absence at the same time from the low country near the coast seems equally certain. As early as 1562, Jean Ribault (or Ribaut) landed at Port Royal, and explored to some distance into the interior ¶ without meeting with buffaloes, as did also Hilton, ** in 1663, and numerous other travellers

* Hakluyt, Voyages, etc., Vol. III, p. 433.

† Collections of the Georgia Historical Society, Vol. I, p. 51.

‡ A Voyage to Georgia, etc., p. 55.

§ Description of Carolina, p. 68.

‖ Drayton (John), View of South Carolina, p. 88.

¶ See Laudonnière's narrative in Hakluyt's Voyages, Vol. III, pp. 367–427.

** Hilton (William), A Relation of a Discovery lately made on the Coast of Florida, etc., London, 1664 (Force's Coll. Hist. Tracts, Vol. IV, No. 2, p. 8).

later, many of whom have given detailed enumerations of the animals they met with. While every species of mammal now known to exist there, from the squirrel to the deer, is mentioned, the buffalo is absent from them all.* It was also absent from this region at the time when Lawson, Brickell, and Catesby explored the Carolinas with special reference to their natural products.

The Buffalo not found within the present limits of Florida. — The buffalo is also believed by some to have been found within the present limits of Florida, and throughout the Gulf States down to the Gulf of Mexico. This, however, is a mistake, mainly arising, probably, from the former vast extent of Florida as compared with its present limits.†

These writers are Forbes,‡ who as recently as 1821 wrote, "The buffalo is said to be among the number of wild beasts, but not commonly seen"! Davis also says, on the authority of Romans, that "their tracks have been seen as far south and southeast as the Withlacoochee River."§ But from the context of Romans's work, and from the known range of the buffalo at the time he wrote (1776), he must have been mistaken in respect to the identity of the tracks. Romans says: ". . . . at the junction of Flint River and the river in the south extreme of this division is the head of *Manatee* River, between which and the *Amazura* I saw a vast number of deer, and the marks

* Among the authors here referred to are Robert Horn (Briefe Description of the Province of Carolina on the Coasts of Florida, etc., 1666); Samuel Wilson (An Account of the Province of Carolina, in America, etc., 1682); "T. A." [Thomas Ash] (Carolina; or a Description of the Present State of that Country and the Natural Excellencies thereof, etc., by T. A., Gent., 1682); and John Archdale (A New Description of that fertile and pleasant Province of Carolina, etc., 1707). Reprinted in Carroll's Hist. Coll. of S. Car., Vol. II. See also Hakluyt, Voyages, etc., Vol. IV, for these papers.

† As is well known, for many years subsequent to the disastrous expedition of De Soto, Florida, as claimed by Spain, embraced all the Atlantic coast as far north as the Gulf of St. Lawrence, and for more than a century after, or till 1651, extended northward to the present southern boundary of Virginia, and comprised an immense unexplored region in the interior. Not until 1721 was its western boundary restricted to its present limits. In 1764, the year following its acquisition by the British crown, its western boundary was again temporarily extended to the Mississippi River. — *Monette's Hist. of the Valley of the Mississippi*, Vol. I, pp. 65 – 77.

In 1745 the British possessions in North America embraced only that portion of the United States north of the present limits of Florida, east of the Alleghanies, exclusive, however, of those portions of New York and Vermont north of the 44th parallel. The whole vast interior belonged to the French, and while almost the whole basin of the Mississippi was denominated *Louisiana*, or the *Province of Louis*, the northeastern part, including not only the present Canadas, but nearly all the territory north of the Ohio, was called Canada, or New France. — *Ibid.*, Vol. I, map.

‡ Sketches, Historical and Topographical, of the Floridas; more especially of East Florida, p. 67.

§ Conquest of New Mexico, 1869, p. 67, footnote.

of many of the hunting-camps of the savages. We found the footsteps of six or eight buffaloes hereabouts, so plain as to be convinced of the track being made by those animals."* Professor Baird, in 1852, says, "Theuet, in the very rare work entitled 'Les Singularitez de la France antarctique,' Paris, 1557 [1558], gives (p. 147), in a representation of a curious beast of West Florida, a readily recognizable figure of the buffalo."† The figure bears some resemblance to a bison, and the description seems to clearly indicate this animal. The locality, too, is near Palm River, south of Tampa Bay. Thevet's work, however, is merely a compilation, abounding with the grossest exaggerations. He cites no authority for the presence of "*une espece de grands toureaux*" at this locality, where certainly no bison has ever been found. Maynard, writing in 1872, says, "The historians of De Soto's travels speak of herds of wild cattle being found in Florida. They probably refer to the buffalo (*Bos americanus*), which without doubt extended its range to the prairies of the west coast."‡ None of the references to the buffalo contained in these writings relate, however, to the present region of Florida,§ De Soto not apparently hearing of the existence of this animal until he had reached the Mississippi, except in the single instance soon to be noticed in another connection.

The late Professor Wyman, in a posthumous paper, also says, "The buffalo was an inhabitant of Florida, and it could have been no other than this animal which the French met with in their ill-fated retreat from Fort Caroline"; and he adds in a footnote: "De Challeux, the carpenter of Ribaut's expedition, says, 'near the break of day we saw a great beast, like a deer, at fifty paces from us, who had a great head, eyes flaming, the ears hanging, and the huger parts elevated. It seemed to us monstrous because of its gleaming eyes, wonderfully large, but it did not come near us to do us any harm.' There is no other animal," adds Professor Wyman, "which corresponds with this animal but the buffalo, though that animal is as unlike 'a deer' as possible."‖ It seems to me, however, that the reference is in no way applicable to the buffalo, and if not really a deer, the beast here described must have

* A Concise Natural History of East and West Florida, pp. 280, 281.

† Patent Off. Rep., Agricult., 1851-52, Part II, p. 124.

‡ Bull. Essex Institute, Vol IV, p. 149.

§ Schoolcraft says that the distinction between the former and present boundaries of Florida "is overlooked, in reference to the buffalo in Florida, by the translator of De Soto's first letter." — *History, Condition, and Prospects of the Indian Tribes*, etc., Part V, p. 68, footnote.

‖ Fresh-Water Shell Mounds of the St. John's River, Florida, p. 80, and footnote, December, 1875.

been a creation of the excited imagination of the much terrified Frenchman, having no more real foundation than the accounts of other strange creatures found in the narratives of numerous other early explorers of America, — a supposition borne out by the general character of De Challeux's account of that night's experiences.

In the detailed account by M. Réné Laudonnière of Ribaut's attempt to plant a colony on the St. John's River in Florida, however, no mention of this incident reported by the carpenter is mentioned. Laudonnière says the only game found was deer, leopards, bears, etc., while in his "description of the West Indies in generall, but chiefly and particularly of Florida," as translated by Hakluyt,* he says, "The Beastes best known in this Countrey are Stagges, Hindes, Goates, Deere, Leopards, Ounces, Lucerns, divers sortes of Wolves, wilde Dogs, Hares, Cunnies, and a certain kinde of beast that differeth little from the Lyon of Africa."† No allusion is made to the existence of any animal like a buffalo in Laudonnière's whole narrative of the fortunes of the French in Florida during the period embracing the founding and abandonment of Fort Caroline, covering a period of five years and quite extended explorations along the St. John's River.

Professor Wyman also quotes Buckingham Smith as saying, in a note to his (Smith's) translation of the "Memoir of Fontaneda respecting Florida" (p. 49), "The bison appears to have ranged in considerable numbers through Middle Florida a hundred and fifty years ago. It was considered in 1718 that the Spanish garrison at Fort San Marco, on a failure of stores, might subsist on the meat of the buffalo." The text in Fontaneda's Memoir (written about 1575), to which this note refers, contains the following: "The men of Abalachi go naked, and the women have waistbands of the straw that grows from the trees, which is like wool, of which I have given some account before; they eat deer, wolves, *woolly cattle*, and many other animals." ‡ Smith in his commentary on this passage cites Barcia as authority for making this passage a reference to the buffalo. But I find nothing in Barcia that seems to refer to the occurrence of the buffalo within the region embraced by the present boundaries of Florida.

Professor Wyman further cites Stow ("p. 10") as saying, "The buffalo is found in the savannahs, or natural meadows of the interior parts," but as no title is given of Stow's work I have been unable to find it in order to ascer-

* Voyages, etc., Vol. III, pp. 368–384.

† Ibid., p. 369.

‡ Smith's Fontaneda, p. 27.

tain on what authority he based his statement. Wyman further quotes Baird as authority for the occurrence of the buffalo in Florida, but Professor Baird, as previously noticed, only makes the general statement that it "was formerly found throughout the eastern portion of the United States to the Atlantic Ocean, *and as far south as Florida*." *

The first explorers not only did not meet with the buffalo in any part of the present States of Florida or Georgia, but probably had not at this time even heard of its existence anywhere. Among these are Ponce de Leon, who visited Florida in 1512, landing near the present site of St. Augustine, and Vasquez de Ayllon, who landed, it is supposed, on the coast of Georgia, in 1520, and again in 1525; but neither of them made extended excursions into the interior, and make no reference to the buffalo.

In 1528 Pamphilo de Narvaez marched from Tampa Bay northwardly into the interior, to the source of the Suwanee River, in Southern Georgia, without, however, either meeting or hearing of the buffalo. De Soto, on the occasion of his journey through Florida, disembarked at Tampa Bay, from which point he made his long journey into the interior, finally crossing the Mississippi and reaching the edge of the plains beyond. His course was first northward through Central Florida, and thence northwestward nearly to the site of the present town of Tallahassee, and then northeastward across Central Georgia to the Savannah River. From this point his course was again northwestward to the mountains of Northern Georgia. In all this long journey he obtained no information of any animal resembling the buffalo, only hearing of it later on sending out soldiers to the northward from his camp in the extreme northern parts of Georgia, to search for gold, who returned at length with the report that they had seen in the possession of the Indians ox-hides an inch in thickness, which were undoubtedly skins of the buffalo.† These

* Mam. N. Amer., p. 684.

† Irving's account of this expedition is as follows: He says two fearless soldiers were sent northward from the village of Ichiaha, which is supposed to have been near the site of the modern town of Rome, Ga. "After an absence of ten days they returned to the camp and made their report. Their route had lain part of the way through excellent land for grain and pasturage, where they had been well received and feasted by the natives. They had found among them a buffalo hide *an inch in thickness*, with hair as soft as the wool of a sheep, which, as usual, they mistook for the hide of a beef. In the course of their journey they had crossed mountains [supposed to be the Lookout Mountains] so rugged and precipitous that it would be impossible for the army to traverse them." — IRVING (THOMAS), *Conquest of Florida*, p. 244.

The Gentleman of Elvas says (Hakluyt's translation), they "brought an oxe hide, which the Indians gave them, *as thinne as a calves skinne*, and the haire like a soft wooll, betweene the course and fine wooll of sheepe." — *Discovery and Conquest of Terra Florida* (Hakluyt Society), p. 66.

facts certainly show that the buffalo was absent both from Florida and Georgia during the early part of the sixteenth century, and I have found no writers who claim to have ever seen the living buffalo at any time in any part of Florida, or of Southern and Eastern Georgia. In the many enumerations of the natural productions of Florida (as at present restricted) made prior to the beginning of the present century, *based on personal observations*, the buffalo is absent from all. Romans, it is true, supposed he saw its tracks, but this, in the light of other contemporaneous history of the region, seems wholly improbable. Roberts, writing a few years before Romans wrote, says, "The wild animals found in this country are the panther, bear, catamountain, stag, goat, hare, rabbit, beaver, otter, fox, raccoon, and squirrel." *

Had the buffalo formerly inhabited Florida, it seems probable that its remains would occur in the shell-mounds of that State; but Professor Wyman specializes the buffalo as one of the animals whose remains he had *not* found in the mounds of Florida, although he had obtained the bones of most of the other large species of Florida mammals from them, among which he enumerates those of the bear, raccoon, hare, deer, otter, and opossum, together with those of the turkey and alligator, and of several different species of turtles and fishes.†

Southern Boundary of the Range of the Buffalo East of the Mississippi.

As already shown, the buffalo was never met with in the present States of Florida and Georgia, except over a small area west of the Savannah River adjoining the Abbeville District in South Carolina. It was apparently also altogether absent from the rest of the Gulf States east of the Mississippi. Certainly it was not met with by De Soto in his journey across this region in 1540–41, during which journey he explored the Coosa River from its source to its junction with the Alabama, and descended the latter to its union with the Tombigbee. He thus crossed the State of Alabama diagonally from northeast to southwest, and afterwards traversed what is now

* Roberts (Wm.), An Account of the First Discovery and Natural History of Florida, 1763, p. 4.

† Mem. Peabody Acad. Sciences, Vol. I, pp. 78, 80.

the State of Mississippi, also diagonally, from the southeast to the northwest.* De Soto learned nothing respecting the buffalo, save the report brought him by the soldiers whom he sent northward from Northern Georgia into the present State of Tennessee, till after he crossed the Mississippi.

Du Pratz states (in a work published in 1758) that the Indians of Lower Louisiana leave that country in winter to hunt the buffalo, as this animal, he says, cannot come thither on account of the thickness of the forest.† Adair, who spent several years in this region prior to 1770, and who describes with considerable minuteness all the low country bordering the Gulf Coast east of the Mississippi River,‡ makes no mention of the existence there of the buffalo, although he gives a general account of the game animals, and speaks especially of the abundance of the deer, bears, and turkeys. Gallatin § gives the Tennessee River as their southern limit, and I have found no positive reference to their occurrence south of that boundary. On an old map,‖ published originally in 1718, and reproduced in *facsimile* in French's "Historical Collections of Louisiana" (Vol. II), the region between the Cumberland and Ohio Rivers is marked as follows: "*Desert de six vint lieues detendue ou les Ilinois font la Chasse des bœufs.*" They are well known to have been formerly abundant in the region about Nashville, and they probably extended southward nearly or quite to the Tennessee, as a stream called Buffalo River forms one of the tributaries of Duck River, itself one of the principal tributaries of the Tennessee from the eastward.

* For authorities on the Route of De Soto, see Biedma's Narrative, and that of the Gentleman of Elvas, in French's Historical Collection of Louisiana, Vol. II, and in the Hakluyt Society's publications (1851), with an Introduction, Notes, and a Map by W. B. Rye; McCulloch's Researches; Gallatin's Synopsis of the Indian Tribes (Archæologia Americana, Vol. II); Pickett's History of Alabama, etc.; Nuttall's Journal of Travels into the Arkansas Territory; Meek's Sketches of the History of Alabama (Southron Monthly Magazine and Review, 1839); Monette's History of the Discovery and Settlement of the Valley of the Mississippi; Bancroft's History U. S.; Irving's Conquest of Florida; Schoolcraft's History, Condition, and Prospects of the Indian Tribes of the United States, Part III, pp. 37–50, pl. xliv; etc., etc.

† History of Louisiana, Engl. ed., pp. 254, 255.

‡ History of the American Indians (London, 1775), pp. 223 - 375.

§ "Colonies of the buffaloes had traversed the Mississippi, and were at one time abundant in the forest country between the lakes and the Tennessee River, south of which I do not believe they were ever seen." — *Trans. Am. Ethnological Soc.*, Vol. II, p. l.

‖ Carte de la Louisiane et du Cours du Mississippi. Dressée sur un grand nombre de Memoires entrau tres ceux sur de Mr. le Maire par GUILLAUME DE L'ISLE de l'Academie Rle des Sciences.

THE EXTENT OF THE REGION EAST OF THE MISSISSIPPI FORMERLY INHABITED BY THE BUFFALO, WITH A HISTORY OF ITS EXTIRPATION THEREFROM.

The accounts of the first exploration of the region between the Alleghany Mountains and the Mississippi River show that the buffalo, early in the seventeenth century, existed in vast herds not only on the prairies bordering the Mississippi, but throughout nearly the whole of the more open portions of the area drained by the Ohio River and its tributaries. Its range eastward extended nearly or quite to the eastern end of Lake Erie, and throughout the valleys among the mountains of Western Pennsylvania, West Virginia, Eastern Kentucky, and Eastern Tennessee. It also inhabited the region drained by the Illinois River, and by some of the lesser upper eastern tributaries of the Mississippi. The country between the Ohio and the Great Lakes was quite generally occupied by them, as was that south of the Ohio, between this river and the Tennessee. There is less certainty in regard to their former occupation of Southern Michigan and Wisconsin, though it is probable that they also at times roamed over most of this region also, notwithstanding the fact that they were not found there by the first Europeans who visited this section of the country. Considerable documentary evidence relating to their former presence over the region between the Mississippi and the Alleghanies, together with many references to their extermination there, has been brought together in the following pages, and is presented generally in the words of the original narrators. Beginning with the northwestern portion of the region in question, we shall pass thence southward and eastward, giving the facts bearing upon particular localities somewhat in a chronological order.

On the eastern side of the Mississippi River buffaloes were found by the early Jesuit explorers occupying the country from the sources of the Mississippi almost uninterruptedly southward nearly to the mouth of the Ohio River. Hennepin, as early as 1680, met with them in considerable numbers in the vicinity of the St. Francis River, above the Falls of St. Anthony, where they were also seen later by other explorers. In 1766 Jonathan Carver found them on the plains around Lake Pepin, he speaking of them as "the largest buffaloes of any in America." * Pike, in ascending the Mississippi in the autumn of 1804, met with the first signs of this animal about two hun-

* Travels, p. 56.

dred miles above the Falls of St. Anthony;* and Schoolcraft reports their existence in the same vicinity as late as 1820. On the map accompanying Schoolcraft's narrative of his expedition to the sources of the Mississippi River, he has marked the plains above the Falls of St. Anthony as the "Buffalo Plains"; and in the text he says: "Here also [mouth of De Corbeau River] the Buffalo Plains commence, and continue down on both sides of the river to the Falls of St. Anthony."† The buffaloes may never have existed in Northeastern Wisconsin, though they probably ranged over the prairies of the western and southern portions of the State. They were not met with, however, even there by the first European explorers of that region.

Father Marquette does not appear to have met with them in crossing from Green Bay to the Wisconsin River, in 1673, nor did he see them in his subsequent descent of that river.‡ La Hontan, in 1687, also found none on either the Fox or Wisconsin Rivers, first meeting with them on the Mississippi not far above the mouth of the Wisconsin.§ Marquette first found them on the Mississippi River, in latitude "41° 28'," in July, 1673. "Having descended the River," he says, "as far as 41° 28', we find that turkeys have taken the place of game, and the *Pisikious* that of other beasts. We call the Pisikious wild buffaloes, because they very much resemble our domestic oxen."‖ Following this is a description of the "pisikious," or buffaloes, and the uses made of them by the Indians; and he adds, "they graze upon the banks of rivers, and I have seen four hundred in a herd together."¶ Hennepin, Marest, Gravier, Charlevoix, and other Jesuit missionaries appear not to have met with it on the St. Joseph's River, nor anywhere in Southern

* Expedition to the Sources of the Mississippi, etc., Pt. I, App. p. 58.

† Narrative Journal of Travel to the Sources of the Mississippi, etc., p. 275.

‡ In an English translation of Marquette's narrative of his discoveries (French's Hist. Coll. of Louisiana, Part II, p. 284), we find the following passage: in speaking of the Wisconsin ("Mesconsin") he says: "'The country through which it flows is beautiful; the groves are so dispersed in the prairies that it makes a noble prospect"; and he adds: "We saw neither game nor fish, but roebuck and *buffaloes* in great numbers." Mr. J. G. Shea says: "The French word here is *vaches*, which has generally been translated bison or buffalo." In this instance, Mr. Shea says, it is clearly a mistake, as Marquette and his party had not yet reached the buffalo grounds, and the missionary afterwards describes the animal when he meets it. — *Discoveries and Explorations in the Mississippi Valley*, p. 16.

§ La Hontan, Voyages, Eng. ed., Vol. I, pp. 111, 112.

‖ As Henderson has remarked, "Father Marquette was doubtless the first white man who penetrated to the habitat of the buffalo by way of the Great Lakes, although, according to Marquette, their skins had been previously exported to Europe." — *Am. Naturalist*, Vol. VI, p. 82.

¶ French's Historical Collection of Louisiana, Part II, p. 285.

Michigan,* although they found it abundant on the Kaskaskia, and further southward.† Marquette, in his description of the Illinois River, says: "I never saw a more beautiful country than we found on this river. The prairies are covered with buffaloes, stags, goats, and the rivers and lakes with swans, ducks, geese, parrots, and beavers." ‡

That buffaloes were formerly abundant over the greater part of Illinois is well attested. Father Hennepin, in describing the journey he made from Fort Miamis, at the mouth of the Chicago River, to the village of the Illinois, on the Illinois River, "one hundred and thirty leagues from Fort Miamis," in December, 1679, says: "There must be an innumerable quantity of wild Bulls in that Country, since the Earth is covered with their Horns. The *Miami's* hunt them towards the latter end of *Autumn*." Again he says: "We suffer'd very much on this Passage; for the Savages having set the Herbs of the Plain on fire, the wild Bulls were fled away, and so we could kill but one and some Turkey-Cocks." "They change their Country," he adds, "according to the Seasons of the Year; for upon the approach of the Winter, they leave the North, and go to the Southern Parts. They follow one another, so that you may see a Drove of them for above a League together, and stop all at the same place. . . . . Their Ways are as beaten as our great Roads, and no Herb grows therein. They swim over the Rivers they meet in their Way, to go and graze in other Meadows." §

Father Marest, in passing from the southern end of Lake Michigan to the Kankakee, in 1712, by way of the St. Joseph's River, says, in his narrative of the journey: "At last [after having passed the portage, and embarked on the Kankakee] we perceived our own agreeable country, the wild buffaloes, and herds of stags, wandering on the border of the river," etc.‖ Charlevoix, in 1721, in crossing over from the St. Joseph's River to the "Theakiki" (Kankakee) soon found them in abundance. About fifty leagues from the source of the Kankakee, he says: "The country begins to be fine: The

* Schoolcraft says, but I know not on what authority: "It not only ranged over the prairies of Illinois and Indiana, but spread to Southern Michigan, and the western skirts of Ohio. *Tradition* says it was sometimes seen on the borders of Lake Erie." — *History, Condition, and Prospects of the Indian Tribes*, Vol. IV, p. 92. It would, however, be quite strange if it had not at times extended its range over the prairie portions of both Michigan and Wisconsin.

† J. G. Shea, Discoveries and Explorations of the Mississippi, pp. 18, 20.

‡ French's Hist. Coll. of Louisiana, Part II, p. 297.

§ A New Discovery of a vast Country in America, etc., pp. 90, 91, 92.

‖ Kip's Jesuit Missions, p. 224.

Meadows here extend beyond Sight, in which the Buffalo go in Herds of 2 or 3 hundred." * In describing the country bordering the Illinois River, below the junction of the Kankakee, he says: "In this Route we see only vast Meadows, with little Clusters of Trees here and there, which seem to have been planted by the Hand; the Grass grows so high in them, that one might lose one's self amongst it; but everywhere we meet with Paths that are as beaten as they can be in the most populous Countries; yet nothing passes through them but Buffaloes, and from Time to Time some Herds of Deer, and some Roe-Bucks." Later he writes: "The 6th [of October, 1721] we saw a great Number of Buffaloes crossing the River in a great Hurry"; and adds that they soon provided themselves with food "by killing a Buffalo or Roe-Buck, and of these we had the Choice." †

Vaudreuil alludes to their abundance on Rock River in 1718. From the bluffs along this river, he says, "you behold roaming through the prairie herds of buffalo of Illinois." ‡ Pittman, writing fifty years later, describes the country of the Illinois Indians as abounding with "buffalo, deer, and wild fowl." §

The buffalo seems also to have been abundant over large portions of Indiana. Charlevoix, writing of the Ohio River in 1720, says: "All the Country that is watered by the Ouabache [Ohio], and by the Ohio [Wabash] which runs into it, is very fruitful: It consists of vast Meadows, well-watered, where the wild Buffaloes feed by Thousands." ‖ Vaudreuil, writing at about the same time, says, in his "Memoir on the Indians between Lake Erie and the Mississippi": "Whoever would wish to reach the Mississippi easily would need only to take this Beautiful river [Ohio] or the Sandosquet [Sandusky]; he could travel without any danger of fasting, for all who have been there have repeatedly assured me that there is a vast quantity of Buffalo and of all other animals in the woods along that Beautiful River; they were often obliged to discharge their guns to clear a passage." ¶

There is further evidence also of the former abundance of the buffalo in

* Letters, Goadby's English Edition, pp. 290, 291.

† Letters, Goadby's English Edition, p. 290.

‡ New York Coll. of MSS., Paris Doc. VII, p. 890.

§ Pittman (Captain Philip), Present State of the European Settlements on the Mississippi, p. 51, 1770. The region referred to is described in the context as being enclosed by the Mississippi on the west, the Illinois on the north, the Ohio on the south, and the Wabash (Ouabache) and "Miamis" on the east.

‖ Letters, Goadby's English ed., p. 303.

¶ New York Coll. of MSS., Paris Doc., VII, p. 886.

Ohio, along the southern shore of Lake Erie, particularly towards its western end. La Hontan, in his description of Lake Erie, as he saw it about 1687, says: "I cannot express what quantities of Deer and Turkeys are to be found in these Woods, and in the vast Meads that lye upon the South side of the Lake. At the bottom of the Lake, we find beeves upon the Banks of two pleasant Rivers that disembogue into it, without Cataracts or rapid Currents."* Vaudreuil, describing Lake Erie in 1718, says: "There is no need of fasting on either side of this lake, deer are to be found there in such abundance; buffaloes are found on the south, but not on the north shore." Again he says: "Thirty leagues up the [Maumee] river is a place called La Glaise [now Defiance, Ohio], where buffaloes are always to be found; they eat the clay and wallow in it."† The occurrence of a stream in Western New York called Buffalo Creek, which empties into the eastern end of Lake Erie, is commonly viewed as traditional evidence of its occurrence at this point, but positive testimony to this effect has thus far escaped me. This locality, if it actually came so far eastward, must have formed the eastern limit of its range along the lakes.

I have found only highly questionable allusions to the occurrence of buffaloes along the southern shore of Lake Ontario. Keating,‡ on the authority of Colhoun, however, has cited a passage from Morton's "New English Canaan" as proof of their former existence in the neighborhood of this lake. Morton's statement is based on Indian reports, and the context gives sufficient evidence of the general vagueness of his knowledge of the region of which he was speaking. The passage, printed in 1637, is as follows: "They [the Indians] have also made descriptions of great heards of well growne beasts that live about the parts of this lake [Erocoise], such as the Christian world (untill this discovery) hath not bin made acquainted with. These Beasts are of the bignesse of a Cowe, their flesh being very good foode, their hides good lether, their fleeces very usefull, being a kinde of wolle, as fine almost as the wolle of the Beaver and the Salvages doe make garments thereof. It is tenne yeares since first the relation of these things came to the eares of the English."§ The "beast" to which allusion is here made is unquestionably the buffalo, but the locality of Lake "Erocoise" is

* La Hontan, New Voyages to North America, English ed., Vol. I, p. 217.

† New York Coll. MSS., Paris Documents, VII, pp. 885, 891.

‡ Long's Expedition to the Source of St. Peter's River, etc., Vol. II, p. 25.

§ Morton (Thomas), New English Canaan, p. 98, Amsterdam, 1637.

not so easily settled. Colhoun regards it, and probably correctly, as identical with Lake Ontario, while other writers (among them Marcy) have applied this reference to Lake Champlain.* The context states that this lake is three hundred miles west of Massachusetts Bay, and that it may be reached by the Hudson River, while it is also given as the source of the Potomac.†

The extreme northeastern limit of the former range of the buffalo seems to have been, as above stated, in Western New York, near the eastern end of Lake Erie. That it probably ranged thus far there is fair evidence. As also already noticed, buffaloes may at times have passed over to the eastern slope of the Alleghanies, since near Lewisburg, Union County, is a stream still bearing the name of Buffalo Creek; but the accounts of the exploration and early settlement of this region make no mention of its occurrence there at the time it was first visited by Europeans. The earliest evidence of their former existence in this region is afforded by a map published by Forster, in 1771, accompanying the English translation of Peter Kalm's travels. On this map a marsh called "Buffalo Swamp" is indicated as situated between the Alleghany River and the West Branch of the Susquehanna, near the heads of the Licking and Toby's Creeks (apparently the streams now called Oil Creek and Clarion Creek). The most explicit testimony, however, is that furnished by Mr. Ashe,‡ who has given an account

* Marcy (R. B.) says, "Formerly buffaloes were found in countless herds over almost the entire northern continent of America, from the 28th to the 50th degree of north latitude, and from the shores of Lake Champlain to the Rocky Mountains," and cites this passage from Morton in proof of its existence around Lake Champlain. — *Exploration of the Red River of Louisiana*, pp. 103, 104, 1853.

† "And from this Lake Southwards, trends that goodly River called of the Natives Potomack, which dischargeth herselfe in the parts of Virginea, from whence it is navigable by shipping of great Burthen up to the Falls (which lieth in 41. Degrees, and a halfe of North latitude:) and from the Lake downe to the Falls by a faire current." He adds: "It is well knowne, they [the Dutch] aime at that place, and have a possibility to attaine unto the end of thier desires therein, by meanes, if the River of Mohegan, which of the English is named Hudsons River (where the Dutch have settled: to well fortified plantations already. .... The Salvages make report of 3 great Rivers that issue out of this Lake, 2 of which are to us knowne, the one to be Patomack, the other Canada, and why may not the third be found there likewise, which they describe to trend westward, whichis conceived to discharge herselfe into the South Sea [probably a reference to the Mississippi]." — *New English Canaan*, p. 99; Force's Hist. Tracts, Vol. II, No. 5, p. 67.

‡ Mr. Ashe speaks of the fondness "all the animals of those parts" have for salt, and of their resorting in large numbers to "Onondargo" Lake to drink of its brackish waters, and adds that the best roads to this lake were the "buffalo tracks; so called from having been observed to be made by the buffaloes in their annual visitations to the lake from their pasture-grounds; and though this is a distance of above two hundred miles, the best surveyor could not have chosen a more direct course, or firmer or better ground." The region about Onondaga Lake was thoroughly explored as early as 1670, and settlements were made and a fort erected before 1705. Prior to 1736, lines of communication had been established

not only of their former abundance here, but of their extirpation. The following circumstantial account of their former abundance in this region, and their sudden extermination upon the arrival of the first white settlers, was obtained by him from one of the participants in the work of destruction. "An old man," says Mr. Ashe, "one of the first settlers in this country, built his log-house on the immediate borders of a salt spring. He informed me that for the first several seasons the buffaloes paid him their visits with the utmost regularity; they travelled in single files, always following each other at equal distances, forming droves, on their arrival, of about three hundred each. The first and second years, so unacquainted were these poor brutes with the use of this man's house, or with his nature, that in a few hours they *rubbed* the house completely down; taking delight in turning the logs off with their horns, while he had some difficulty to escape from being trampled under their feet, or crushed to death in his own ruins. At that period he supposed there could not have been less than two thousand in the neighborhood of the spring. They sought for no manner of food, but only bathed and drank three or four times a day, and rolled in the earth, or reposed, with their flanks distended, in the adjacent shades; and on the fifth and sixth days separated into distinct droves, bathed, drank, and departed in single files, according to the exact order of their arrival. They all rolled successively in the same hole, and each thus carried away a coat of mud to preserve the moisture on their skin, and which, when hardened and baked in the sun, would resist stings of millions of insects, that otherwise would persecute these peaceful travellers to madness or even death.

"In the first and second years this old man, with some companions, killed from six to seven hundred of these noble creatures, merely for the sake of their skins, which to them were worth only two shillings each; and after this 'work of death' they were obliged to leave the place till the following season, or till the wolves, bears, panthers, eagles, rooks, ravens, etc., had devoured the carcasses, and abandoned the place for other prey. In the two following years, the same persons killed great numbers out of the first droves that arrived, skinned them, and left their bodies exposed to the sun and air; but they soon had reason to repent of this, for the remaining droves, as they came up in succession, stopped, gazed on the mangled and putrid bodies, sorrowfully moaned or furiously lowed aloud, and returned

between both the Susquehanna and Alleghany Rivers, but not a buffalo is mentioned as having been met with anywhere in the Onondaga region. Hence Mr. Ashe was undoubtedly misinformed in respect to the trail to Onondaga Lake having been made by buffaloes.

instantly to the wilderness in an unusual run, without tasting their favorite spring, or licking the impregnated earth, which was also once their most agreeable occupation; nor did they, nor any of their race, ever revisit the neighborhood.

"The simple history of this spring," he adds, "is that of every other in the settled parts of this Western world; the carnage of beasts was everywhere the same; I met with a man who had killed two thousand buffaloes with his own hand; and others, no doubt, have done the same. In consequence of such proceedings, not one buffalo is at this time [in 1806] to be found east of the Mississippi, except a few, domesticated by the curious, or carried through the country on a public show." *

Warden also refers to the former existence of buffaloes in the western part of Pennsylvania, and to their early extinction there and in Kentucky.† Gallatin says: "The name of Buffalo Creek, between Pittsburg and Wheeling, proves that they had spread thus far eastwardly when that country was first visited by the Anglo-Americans." ‡ Further to the southward, in West Virginia, in the valleys of the Kanawha and its tributaries, as well as thence westward, the former abundance of the buffalo is well attested.

One of the earliest references to the existence of the buffalo in West Virginia is that contained in the journal of the Rev. Daniel Jones, who in 1772 made a journey to the Indian tribes west of the Ohio River. Under date of June 18, 1772, he writes: "Went out to view the land on east side [of the Little Kanawha] to kill provisions. Mr. Owens killed several deer and a stately buffalo bull. The country is here level, and the soil not despicable." § In speaking of that part of the valley of the Ohio near the mouth of the "Great Guiandot," he says, under date of January, 1773: "In this part of the country even in this season, pasturage is so good that creatures are well supplied without any assistance. Here are great abundance of buffalo, which are a species of cattle, as some suppose, left here by former inhabitants." In describing the country about Wheeling ("Weeling"), he says: "The wild beasts met with here are bears, wolves, panthers, wild cats, foxes, raccoons, beavers, otters, and some few squirrels and rabbits; buffaloes, deer, and elks, called by the Delawares *moos*." ‖

* Ashe (Thomas), Travels in America, performed in 1806, for the purpose of exploring the Rivers Allegheny, Monongahela, Ohio, and Mississippi, etc. pp. 47–49. London, 1808.

† Warden (D. B.). Statistical, Political and Historical Account of the United States, Vol. I, p. 250.

‡ Trans. Am. Ethnol. Soc., Vol. II, p. l.

§ Journal of Two Visits, etc., p. 17.

‖ Ibid., pp. 50, 84.

Buffaloes are well-known to have existed on the Monongahela,* and throughout the region between this river and the Ohio, over the area drained by the Little Kanawha, Buffalo, Fishing, Wheeling, and other small tributaries of the Ohio, where is said to have been much interval or open land,† and and thence southward to the Great Kanawha. As already noticed, there is abundant evidence of its former existence on the sources of the Kanawha, extending even to the head of the Greenbrier River, in Pocahontas County, and thence eastward, at times at least, over the sources of the James.

Gallatin states that in his time (1784–1785) "they were abundant on the southern side of the Ohio, between the Great and Little Kenawha. I have," he adds, "during eight months lived principally upon their flesh." ‡ The following additional testimony, contained in a letter written by Dr. Charles McCormick, dated "Fort Gibson, Cherokee Nation, August 18, 1844," is furnished by Dr. Elliott Coues. Dr. McCormick says: "I have just seen Captain [Nathan] Boone, and he promises to write and tell you all about it. In the mean time, he says, he killed his first buffalo somewhere about 1793, on the Kenawha in Virginia. He was then quite a small boy. He has also killed buffalo on New River, and near the Big Sandy in Virginia, in '97 and '98." §

Ample evidence of the former existence of the buffalo in Northern Ohio has already been given; it seems to have been also found abundantly in other parts of the State. Colonel John May met with it on the Muskingum in 1788,‖ and Atwater says, "we had once the bison and the elk in vast numbers all over Ohio." ¶ Hutchins says that in the natural meadows or savannahs, "from twenty to fifty miles in circuit," situated northwestward of the Ohio River, from the mouth of the Kanawha far down the Ohio, the herds of buffalo and deer were innumerable, and also mentions their abundance over the region drained by the Scioto.** Its former occurrence over considerable portions of Kentucky is also most abundantly sub-

* Trans. Amer. Antiq. Soc., Vol. II., pp. 139, 140, footnote.

† Hutchins (Thomas), Topog. Descrip. of Virginia, Pennsylvania, and North Carolina, comprehending the Rivers Ohio, Kanawha, Scioto, Cherokee, Wabash, Illinois, Mississippi, etc. (London, 1778), p. 4.

‡ Trans. Am. Ethnol. Soc., Vol. II, p. l.

§ Amer. Naturalist, Vol. V, p. 720.

‖ Journal and Letters of Colonel John May of Boston, etc., Hist. and Phil. Soc. of Ohio, New Series, Vol. I, pp. 81, 83.

¶ Atwater (Caleb), History of the State of Ohio, Natural and Civil, 1838, p. 67.

** Topog. Descrip. of Virginia, Pennsylvania, etc., pp. 11–15.

stantiated, as the subjoined extracts from reliable authorities sufficiently attest.

M'Clung, in his sketch of Simon Kenton, "taken from a manuscript account, dictated by the venerable pioneer himself," relates the following: "Kenton, with two companions, set out from Cabin Creek, a few miles above Maysville, apparently about 1773 and 1774, to explore the neighboring country. In a short time they reached the vicinity of May's Lick, where they fell in with the great buffalo trace, which in a few hours brought them to the Lower Blue Lick. The flats upon each side of the river were crowded with immense herds of buffalo, that had come down from the interior for the sake of salt; and a number of elk were seen upon the bare ridges which surround the springs. . . . . After remaining a few days at the lick, and killing an immense number of deer and buffalo, they crossed the Licking, and passed through the present counties of Scott, Fayette, Woodford, Clarke, Montgomery, and Bath, where, falling in with another buffalo trace, it conducted them to the Upper Blue Lick, where they again beheld elk and buffalo in immense numbers." *

In an account of the adventures of Colonel Daniel Boone, published by Filson, Boone states that he left his "family and peaceable habitation on the Yadkin River, in North Carolina, the 1st of May, 1769, to wander through the wilderness of America, in quest of the country of Kentucke." Crossing the "mountain wilderness," he and his five companions found themselves on Red River, on the seventh of June following. Here they encamped and began to reconnoitre the country. Boone writes: "We found every where abundance of wild beasts of all sorts, through this vast forest. The buffaloes were more frequent than I have seen cattle in the settlements, browzing on the leaves of the cane, or croping the herbage on those extensive plains, fearless, because ignorant, of the violence of man. Sometimes we saw hundreds in a drove, and the numbers about the salt springs were amazing." † During the severe winter of 1780 and 1781, Boone says that the inhabitants of Kentucky "lived chiefly on the flesh of the buffalo."

Filson says (writing in 1784): "I have heard a hunter assert, he saw above one thousand buffaloes at the Blue Licks at once; so numerous were they before the first settlers had wantonly sported away their lives. There still

* Western Adventures, p. 86.

† Filson (John), Discovery, Settlement, and Present State of Kentucky, 1784, pp. 50, 51.

remain a great number in the exterior parts of the settlement." * Again he says, after describing the salt licks of Kentucky: "To these [the licks] the cattle repair, and reduce high hills rather to valleys than plains. The amazing herds of Buffaloes which resort thither, by their size and number, fill the traveller with amazement and terror, especially when he beholds the prodigious roads they have made from all quarters, as if leading to some populous city; the vast space of land around these springs desolated as if by a ravaging enemy, and hills reduced to plains; for the land near these springs is chiefly hilly." †

Cuming, in describing the salt licks along the Licking and Ohio Rivers, thus refers to the former abundance of the buffalo at these localities: "These licks were much frequented by buffaloes and deer, the former of which have been destroyed or terrified from the country. It is only fourteen or fifteen years since no other except buffalo or bear meat was used by the inhabitants of this country." He was informed by Captain Waller that "buffaloes, bears, and deer were so plenty in the country, even long after it began to be generally settled, and ceased to be frequented as a hunting-ground by the Indians, that little or no bread was used, but that even the children were fed on game, the facility of gaining which prevented the progress of agriculture, until the poor innocent buffaloes were completely extirpated and other wild animals much thinned; and that the principal part of the cultivation of Kentucky had been within the last fifteen years. He said the buffaloes had been so numerous, going in herds of several hundreds together, that, about the salt licks and springs they frequented, they pressed down and destroyed the soil to a depth of three or four feet, as was conspicuous yet in the neighborhood of the Blue Lick, where all the old trees have their roots bare of soil to that depth." ‡

Other references to the abundance of the buffalo in Kentucky, at the time this region was first visited by the white settlers, might be given, but those above cited seem sufficient for the present occasion.

The buffalo seems also to have existed in considerable numbers in portions of Tennessee, particularly about the salt springs on the Cumberland River, as shown by Putnam's "History of Middle Tennessee." § This author gives

* Filson (John), Discovery, Settlement, and Present State of Kentucky, 1784, pp. 27, 28.

† Ibid., pp. 32, 33.

‡ Cuming (John), Sketches of a Tour to the Western Country, etc., 1810, pp. 155, 156.

§ Counties *Davidson*, *Sumner*, *Robertson*, and *Montgomery*.

extracts from the journal of John Donelson, respecting a voyage made by him from Fort Patrick Henry, on the Holston River to the French Salt Springs on the Cumberland River, in December, 1780. Donelson says that he "procured some buffalo meat on the Cumberland, near its mouth," and two days further up this river, he says, "We killed some more buffalo." The next day, he writes: "We are now without bread, and are compelled to hunt the buffalo to preserve life." * Subsequently, in speaking of the salt or sulphur springs on the Cumberland, apparently near the present site of Nashville, we find the following passages: "The open space around and near the sulphur or salt springs, instead of being an 'old field,' as had been supposed by Mr. Mansker, at his visit here in 1769, was thus freed from trees and underbrush by the innumerable herds of buffalo and deer and elk that came to these waters. . . . . Trails, or buffalo paths, were deeply worn in the earth from this to other springs. . . . . All the rich lands were covered with cane-brakes; through these there were paths made by the buffalo and other wild animals." †

Ramsey states that in 1769 and 1770 an exploring party of ten persons passed up the Cumberland, and that "where Nashville now stands they discovered the French Lick, and found around it immense numbers of buffalo and other wild game. The country was crowded with them. Their bellowings sounded from the hills and forest." ‡ According to the same authority, the buffalo was at one time also numerous in the valleys of East Tennessee. He states that in 1764 Daniel Boone left his home on the Yadkin to explore, in company with others, the then unknown country to the westward. "Callaway," says Ramsey, "was at the side of Boone when, approaching the spurs of the Cumberland Mountain, and in view of the vast herds of buffalo grazing in the valleys between them, he exclaimed: 'I am richer than the man mentioned in Scripture, who owned the cattle on a thousand hills, — I own the wild beasts of more than a thousand valleys!'" § Whether or not the buffalo ranged formerly to the Tennessee River, I have been unable to determine, although, as already noticed, there is pretty good evidence that it did not extend beyond this boundary. The existence of a stream named Buffalo River, near the Great Bend of the Tennessee, seems to render it probable that it extended nearly or quite to the Tennessee itself. Gallatin gives the

* Putnam's Middle Tennessee, pp. 74, 75.

† Ibid., p. 81.

‡ The Annals of Tennessee, to the End of the Eighteenth Century, etc., p. 105.

§ Ibid., p. 69.

range of the buffalo east of the Mississippi as being "between the Lakes and the Tennessee River";* but he also says that it formerly ascended the Valley of the Tennessee "to its sources," and adds: "They were but rarely seen south of the ridge which separates that river from the sources of those which empty into the Gulf of Mexico, and nowhere, in the forest country, in herds of more than from fifty to two hundred." † I have found, however, no positive reference to their being found anywhere south of the Tennessee.

As previously stated, the range of the buffalo east of the Mississippi, with the exception of its occasional appearance on the eastern slope of the Alleghanies in North and South Carolina, on the head-waters of the James River in Virginia, and possibly in Union County, Pennsylvania, was restricted to the area drained by the Ohio and Illinois Rivers and their tributaries, and the lesser eastern tributaries of the Mississippi in Northern Wisconsin and Minnesota. It was also absent from the lowlands of the lower portion of the Ohio River. The foregoing citations, however, show it to have been originally very numerous and uniformly distributed over the prairies of Illinois and Indiana, and also throughout the country immediately bordering the Ohio and its upper tributaries, as the Licking, Great and Little Kanawha, and the Alleghany and Monongahela Rivers. It seems to have been somewhat less uniformly and less numerously dispersed over the States of Ohio, the western parts of Pennsylvania, West Virginia, Kentucky, and the northern parts of Tennessee, although it regularly frequented portions of each of these States, and was probably more or less abundant throughout the open woods and "Barrens" of the two last named. Its range was hence restricted to the prairies, the scantily wooded districts, and the narrow belts of open land along the streams. ‡

* Transactions Amer. Ethnological Society, Vol. I, p. I.

† Transactions Amer. Antiquarian Society, Vol. II, p. 139.

‡ The area of wooded and woodless territory is thus given by Gallatin: As is well known, the whole Atlantic slope "was covered with a dense and uninterrupted forest when the European settlers landed in America"; and the country south of the 40th parallel, excepting "the Barrens" of Kentucky, westward to the Mississippi Valley, and north of the Great Lakes as far west as Winnipeg, was similarly forested. Between the 40th parallel and Lake Erie there were areas destitute of wood, or prairies, which increased in size westward, till in Central and Northern Illinois they equalled the timbered areas, while west of the Mississippi the forests were confined to narrow belts along the rivers. — *Trans. Amer. Antiq. Soc.*, Vol. II, pp. 137, 138, 1836.

In respect to the former distribution of forests in the United States, see also Professor W. H. Brewer's map of the distribution of woodland recently published in General Francis A. Walker's "Statistical Atlas of the United States," Plates III and IV (1873).

Its Extirpation.— Upon the establishment of the first permanent white settlements over this region, the extermination of the buffalo progressed with wonderful rapidity. Its history is a shameful record of wasteful and wanton destruction of life, like that which ever marks the contact of man with the larger mammalia. The extermination of the buffalo in Western Pennsylvania, West Virginia, Ohio, Kentucky, and Tennessee, was very rapid, this animal surviving at most points for but a few years after the first permanent settlements were made. In Illinois and Indiana it existed for about a century and a quarter after the country was first explored by the Jesuit missionaries, and for more than half a century seems to have scarcely diminished in numbers. As late as 1773 it was abundant on both sides of the Kaskaskia River, and also along the Illinois, and apparently over all the prairies of the intermediate region.* Later its extermination was more rapid, its disappearance here apparently antedating by several years its extirpation along the upper tributaries of the Ohio. The date of its disappearance from Illinois and Indiana, however, I can give less definitely than that of its extermination at points more to the eastward. In Pennsylvania, according to Mr. Ashe, they were all destroyed within a few years after the arrival of the first settlers, being apparently wholly exterminated prior to the year 1800. It lingered in West Virginia till a few years later, as it did also in portions of Kentucky. Toulmin, writing about 1792, says, "The buffalo are mostly driven out of Kentucky. Some are still found upon the head-waters of Licking Creek, Great Sandy, and the head-waters of Green River."† It appears, according to Audubon, to have lingered here, however, only a few years longer. "In the days of our boyhood and youth," says this author, "buffaloes roamed over the small and beautiful prairies of Indiana and Illinois, and herds of them stalked through the open woods of Kentucky and Tennessee; but they had dwindled down to a few stragglers, which resorted chiefly to the 'Barrens,' towards the years 1808 and 1809, and soon after entirely disappeared."‡ Cuming adds that all had been driven from the salt licks of the Licking and Ohio Rivers before 1807, while Mr. Ashe,§ an apparently reliable authority, affirms that as early as 1806 not one was to

* See Kennedy's Journal of an Expedition from Kaskaskia Village to the Head-waters of the Illinois River, in Hutchins's Topog. Descrip. of Virginia, Pennsylvania, etc., pp. 51–64; also Hutchins's Topog. Descrip., etc., pp. 35, 41, 44.

† Toulmin (Henry), Description of Kentucky, p. 85.

‡ Quadrupeds of North America, Vol. II, p. 36.

§ Travels in America, etc., p. 49.

be found in a wild state east of the Mississippi, referring, doubtless, to the Mississippi below latitude 41°. Brackenridge,* in 1814, says the buffalo may be said to have retired to the northward of the Illinois, and to the westward of the Mississippi, and other writers confirm this statement.†

Schoolcraft, writing in 1821, says that "the only part of the country east of the [Mississippi] river where the buffalo now remains, is that included between the Falls of St. Anthony and Sandy Lake, a range of about six hundred miles." Sibley says that "two individuals were killed in 1832 by the Dacotahs or Sioux Indians, on the Trempe à l'Eau [Trempeleau] River, in Upper Wisconsin," and adds, "They are believed to be the last specimens of the noble bison, which trod, or will ever again tread, the soil of the region lying east of the Mississippi River." ‡

Most writers, in alluding to the extirpation of the buffalo throughout the region east of the Mississippi River, speak of it as having been "driven out" by the encroachment of settlements.§ While a few of the herds may have migrated westward, it seems more probable that it was *exterminated* rather than *driven out*, as it appears to have existed in West Virginia and

* Views of Louisiana, p. 56.

† Ellsworth states, in his "Notes on the Wild Animals of Illinois," published in 1831, that "the buffalo has entirely left us. Before the country was settled, our immense prairies afforded pasturage to large herds of this animal and the traces of them are still remaining in the 'buffalo paths' which are to be seen in several parts of the State. These are well-beaten tracks, leading generally from the prairies in the interior of the State to the margins of the large rivers; showing the course of their migrations as they changed their pastures periodically, from the low marshy alluvion to the dry upland plains. In the heat of summer they would be driven from the latter by prairie flies; in the autumn they would be expelled from the former by the mosquitoes; in the spring, the grass of the plains would afford abundant pasturage, while the herds could enjoy the warmth of the sun, and snuff the breeze that sweeps so freely over them; in the winter the rich cane of the river banks, which is evergreen, would furnish food, while the low grounds thickly covered with brush and forest would afford protection from the bleak winds." — ELLSWORTH (H. L.), *Illinois in 1837*, p. 38. (First published in the Illinois Magazine, July, 1831, and republished in Featherstonhaugh's Monthly American Journal of Geology and Natural Science October, 1831, p. 180.)

‡ Sibley (H. H.) in Schoolcraft's History, Condition, and Prospects of the Indian Tribes, Part IV, p. 94. Major Long states that in 1822 its wanderings down the St. Peter's River did not extend beyond Great Swan Lake (Camp Crescent). — *Exped. to the Sources of the St. Peter's River*, etc., Vol. II, p. 29.

§ Even scientific writers speak of it as having "gradually retired westward in advance of the migrating column of the white race of man." — LEIDY, *Mem. Ext. Sp. Amer. Ox*, 1852.

"At the time of the discovery by the Spaniards, an inhabitant even down to the shores of the Atlantic, it has been beaten back by the westward march of civilization, until, at the present day, it is only after passing the giant Missouri and the head-waters of the Mississippi that we find the American bison or buffalo. Many causes have combined to drive them away from their old haunts: the wholesale and indiscriminate slaughter by the whites, the extension of settlements, the changes of the face of the country; but above all, the mysterious dread of the white man, which pervades animal life in general as a congenital instinct." — BAIRD, *Pat. Off. Rep., Agricult.*, 1851–52, Part II, p. 124.

in Eastern Kentucky to quite as late, or even to a later period, than on the prairies adjoining the Mississippi. The extension of settlements down the Mississippi River would tend to hem the buffalo in on that quarter, and, as will be shown later, it disappeared at nearly the same time over a considerable breadth of country bordering the western shore of this river.

Schoolcraft says that the buffalo "was found in early days to have crossed the Mississippi above the latitude of the mouth of the Ohio, and at certain times to have thronged the present area of Kentucky," etc.; from which it may be inferred that he deemed its presence east of the Mississippi River to have been of comparatively brief continuance. Gallatin also always speaks of it as having "spread from the westward" over the region east of the Mississippi. Professor Shaler has referred to the probability of its having been unknown to the mound-builders,* since they have left nothing indicating that they were acquainted with it, which is not the case with most of the other large mammals of the interior of the continent.† He also states that in his exploration of the salt licks of Kentucky he had found its bones in great abundance "just below the recent mould, in a bed about eighteen inches thick"; but that "in the rich deposits of extinct mammals just beneath, immediately above which traces of worked flint were also found, no buffalo bones were discovered."*

THE FORMER RANGE OF THE BUFFALO WEST OF THE ROCKY MOUNTAINS.

The vast region situated between the Mississippi River and the Rocky Mountains, excepting the lowlands bordering the Lower Mississippi, is well known to have been formerly embraced within the range of the buffalo. So well established is this fact that a special consideration of this region will be deferred till the former boundaries of its range to the westward and southward have been traced.

Although the main chain of the Rocky Mountains has commonly been supposed to form the western limit of the range of the buffalo, there is abundant proof of its former existence over a vast area west of this supposed boundary, including a large part of the so-called Great Basin of Utah, the Green River Plateau, and the Plains of the Columbia. It is probably not yet half a century since it ranged westward to the Blue Mountains of Oregon and the Sierra Nevada Mountains of California.

* Proc. Bost. Soc. Nat. Hist., Vol. XIII, p. 136.

† See further Professor Shaler's note on this point in the Appendix.

Respecting its former occurrence in Eastern Oregon, Professor O. C. Marsh, under date of New Haven, February 7, 1875, writes me as follows: "The most western point at which I have myself observed remains of the buffalo was in 1873, on Willow Creek, Eastern Oregon, among the foot-hills of the eastern side of the Blue Mountains. This is about latitude 44°. The bones were perfectly characteristic, although nearly decomposed."

The former existence of the buffalo in the Great Salt Lake Valley is established by the occurrence of its remains there, in a still good state of preservation, as well as by the testimony of those who have seen them there. Along the railroad leading from Ogden City to Salt Lake City I examined, in September, 1871, numbers of skulls in a nearly perfect state of preservation, which had been exposed in throwing up the road-bed across the marshes, a few miles north of Salt Lake City. I also saw a few on the terraces north and west of Ogden City, but generally in a disintegrated condition, as were all that I saw which had not been buried in the recent deposits about the Great Salt Lake. I was also informed that there is a tradition among the Indians of this region that the buffaloes were almost entirely exterminated by deep snows many years since. Mr. E. D. Mecham, of North Ogden, a reliable and intelligent hunter and trapper of nearly forty years' experience in the Rocky Mountains, and at one time a partner of the celebrated Joseph Bridger, informed me that few had been seen west of the great Wahsatch range of mountains for the last thirty years, but that he had seen their weathered skulls as far west as the Sierra Nevada Mountains.* In 1836, according to Mr. Mecham, there were many buffaloes in Salt Lake Valley, which were nearly all destroyed by deep snow about 1837, when, according to the reports of mountaineers and Indians, the snow fell to the depth of ten feet on a level. The few buffaloes that escaped starvation during this severe winter are said to have soon after disappeared. Mr. Henry Gannet, astronomer of Dr. Hayden's Survey, informs me that the Mormon Danite, "Bill" Hickman, claims to have killed the last buffaloes in Salt Lake Valley about 1838. How long the buffalo inhabited the Basin of the Great Salt Lake, it is of course now impossible to determine, but it seems probable that their occupation must date back to a remote

* I was informed by several persons, whom I met in the Salt Lake Valley, that they had seen skulls of buffaloes as far west as the eastern slope of the Sierra Nevada Mountains. These persons were unknown to each other, and their accounts were wholly distinct in respect to date and locality, and hence seem all the more entitled to credence.

period, since their skulls occur wholly buried in the marshes about the lake, where the deposition appears to have been quite slow. I am also informed by Mr. H. W. Henshaw, the well-known ornithologist of Lieutenant Wheeler's Survey, that their skulls have been found in Utah Lake. Mr. Henshaw, under date of Washington, D. C., March 6, 1875, writes as follows:—

"The only information I have regarding its [the buffalo's] presence in Utah was derived from Mr. Madsen, a Danish fisherman, living on the borders of Utah Lake; and, I may add, I am perfectly convinced of the trustworthiness of his statement. In using the seine in the waters of the lake, he has on several occasions brought up from the bottom the skulls of buffaloes, in a very good state of preservation. Their presence in the lake may perhaps be accounted for on the supposition that, in crossing on the ice, a herd may at some time have broken through, and thus perished. From him I also learned that he had talked with Indians of middle age whose fathers had told them that in their time the buffaloes were numerous, and that they had hunted them near the lake. If this can be accepted as truth, it would place the existence of these animals in Utah back to a not very distant date. I learn from my friend, W. W. Howell, that during the past season he obtained the cranium of a buffalo, which was unearthed by some laborers while digging a mill-race, at a depth of ten feet below the surface. This was in a broad cañon near Gunnison. While, from the fact of its being in a cañon, no very exact estimate can be made of the time of its deposit, there seemed every evidence that the soil above it had remained undisturbed for a long time. The lower portion of the cranium is gone, leaving the part above the orbits, and the horn-cores, intact and in an excellent state of preservation. A comparison of this with a recent specimen of the *B. americanus* shows that in certain characters it exhibits an approach to the *Bison latifrons*, as described by Leidy. In size it varies little from the *B. americanus*, but in all other characteristics is much nearer the *B. latifrons*." *

The buffalo seems, however, to have lingered later on the head-waters of the Colorado than in either the Great Salt Lake Valley, or the valley of Bear River, or on the head-waters of the two main forks of the Columbia. Frémont found them on St. Vrain's Fork of Green River, and on the Vermilion in 1844,† and Stansbury, in 1849, found them on the northern tributaries of

* Its agreement in size with *Bison americanus* is sufficient to indicate its identity with that species.

† First and Second Expeditions, etc., p. 281.

the Yampah, and the upper tributaries of Green River; but the scarcity of water seemed to have forced the greater part of them southward. Respecting their occurrence near Bridger's Fork of the Muddy, Stansbury says: "As long as the water lasted, the whole plain must have been covered with buffalo and antelope, as the profusion of 'sign' abundantly proved; but as this indispensable article was absorbed by the sandy soil, they seemed, from the direction of their trails, to have struck a course for the Vermilion." *

They have, however, long since disappeared from the head-waters of Green River, and, indeed, from all the country drained by the tributaries of the Colorado. Although their bleached skulls are still found throughout the valleys, I was informed by old hunters whom I saw there in the autumn of 1871, that no buffaloes had been seen in this region for more than twenty years.

The best account of their range in recent times, west of the Rocky Mountains, and of their extermination over this vast region, is that given by Frémont, based on his own extensive travels and on the still more extended experience of Mr. Fitzpatrick. Frémont states that in the spring of 1824 "the buffalo were spread in immense numbers over the Green River and Bear River Valleys, and through all the country lying between the Colorado, or Green River of the Gulf of California, and Lewis's Fork of the Columbia River; the meridian of Fort Hall then forming the western limit of their range. The buffalo then remained for many years in that country, and frequently moved down the Valley of the Columbia, on both sides of the river, as far as the *Fishing Falls*. Below this point they never descended in any numbers.† About 1834 or 1835 they began to diminish very rapidly, and continued to decrease until 1838 or 1840, when, with the country we have just described, they entirely abandoned all the waters of the Pacific north of Lewis's Fork of the Columbia. At that time the Flathead Indians were in the habit of finding their buffalo on the heads of Salmon River and other streams of the Columbia, but now [1843] they never meet with them farther west than the three forks of the Missouri or the plains of the Yellowstone River.

"In the course of our journey it will be remarked that the buffalo have not so entirely abandoned the waters of the Pacific, in the Rocky Mountain

* Stansbury's Expedition to the Great Salt Lake, p. 238.

† The locality at which Professor Marsh found the crumbling bones of the buffalo is some two hundred and fifty miles further northwest, or lower down the river. See *antea*, p. 119.

region south of the Sweet Water, as in the country north of the Great Pass. This partial distribution can only be accounted for in the great pastoral beauty of that country, which bears marks of having long been one of their favorite haunts, and by the fact that the white hunters have more frequented the northern than the southern region, — it being north of the South Pass that the hunters, trappers, and traders have had their rendezvous for many years past; and from that section also the greater portion of the beaver and rich furs were taken, although always the most dangerous, as well as the most profitable, hunting-ground.

"In that region lying between the Green or Colorado River and the head-waters of the Rio del Norte, over the *Yampak*, *Kooyah*, *White*, and *Grand* Rivers, — all of which are the waters of the Colorado, — the buffalo never extended so far westward as they did on the waters of the Columbia; and only in one or two instances have they been known to descend as far west as the mouth of White River. In travelling through the country west of the Rocky Mountains, observation readily led me to the impression that the buffalo had for the first time crossed that range to the waters of the Pacific only a few years prior to the period we are considering; and in this opinion I am sustained by Mr. Fitzpatrick, and the older trappers in that country. In the region west of the Rocky Mountains we never meet with any ancient vestiges which, throughout all the country lying upon their eastern waters, are found in the *great highways*, continuous for hundreds of miles, always several inches and sometimes several feet in depth, which the buffalo have made in crossing from one river to another, or in traversing the mountain ranges. The Snake Indians, more particularly those low down upon Lewis's Fork, have always been very grateful to the American trappers for the great kindness (as they frequently expressed it) which they did to them in driving the buffalo so low down the Columbia River." *

It would thus seem to be Frémont's belief that their occupation of the Snake River country was temporary, and that they did not pass west of the mountains till driven thither, at a comparatively recent period, by persecution east of the mountains. That they were absent from this region not long previously appears evident from the fact that Lewis and Clarke, in 1805, met with no buffaloes west of the mountains, nor even on the upper portion of the three forks of the Missouri, although there was evidence of

* Report of the Exploring Expedition to the Rocky Mountains, in the year 1842, and to Oregon and California, in the years 1843 – 44, p. 141.

their former existence in immense herds on the Jefferson Fork. In their enumeration of the animals of the Pacific slope these travellers make no allusion to the buffalo. They also state that the Indians on Clarke's River crossed the mountains in spring to traffic for buffalo robes with the Indians of the eastern slope.*

In 1820 Major Long also states: "They have not yet crossed the entire breadth of the mountains at the head of the Missouri, though they penetrate, in some parts, far within that range, to the most accessible fertile valleys, particularly the valley of Lewis's River. It was there that Mr. Henry and his party of hunters wintered, and subsisted chiefly upon the flesh of these animals, which they saw in considerable herds, but the Indians affirmed that it was unusual for the bisons to visit that neighborhood." This would seem to fix the date of their arrival at the head-waters of the Columbia between 1805, when Lewis and Clarke visited them, and Mr. Henry's visit, about 1817.

From Washington Irving's entertaining narrative of Captain Bonneville's tour across the continent † we learn that Captain Bonneville first met with the buffalo west of the Rocky Mountains on the head-waters of Bear River, in November, 1833.‡ Passing thence northward, they found these animals in abundance on the plains of Portneuf, where the Bannack Indians were engaged in hunting them.§ But in his subsequent long winter march up the Snake River, no buffaloes appear to have been met with. Returning, however, to Bear River Valley, he again encountered large herds. The following summer (July, 1834) they again found them in great numbers on the sources of the Blackfoot River,‖ but in a subsequent long journey northwestward, from the Upper Snake River nearly to Fort Walla Walla and back, they met with none, and rejoiced to find them again "in immense herds" near their old camping-ground on an eastern tributary of the Snake River. Captain Bonneville's party passed the winter of 1834 – 35 in camp on the upper part of Bear River, surrounded by immense herds of buffaloes, which came down to them from the north. "The people upon Snake River," says

* Lewis and Clarke's Expedition to the Sources of the Missouri, and down the Columbia to the Pacific Ocean, Vol. I, p. 469.

† The Rocky Mountains; or, Scenes, Incidents, and Adventures in the Far West, — a Digest of the Journal of Captain B. L. E. Bonneville. 2 vols., 12mo, 1837.

‡ Ibid., Vol. I, pp. 125, 129.

§ Ibid., Vol. II, p 33.

‖ Irving's Rocky Mountains, Vol. II, p. 179.

the narrative, "having chased off the buffalo before the snow had become deep, immense herds now came trooping over the mountains; forming dark masses on their sides, from which their deep-mouthed bellowing sounded like the peals and mutterings from a gathering thunder-cloud. In effect, the cloud broke, and down came the torrent into the valley. It is utterly impossible, according to Captain Bonneville, to convey an idea of the effect produced by the sight of such countless throngs of animals of such bulk and spirit, all rushing forward as if swept on by a whirlwind." * In the autumn of 1835 Parker met with great herds on the east fork of the Salmon River and on other tributaries of the Snake River.†

Dr. J. S. Newberry, writing in 1855, says: "The range of the buffalo does not *now* extend beyond the Rocky Mountains, but there are many Indian hunters who have killed them in great numbers to the west of the mountains, on the head-waters of the Salmon River, one of the tributaries of the Columbia. While I was at the Dalles, the party of Lieutenant Day, U. S. A., came in from an expedition to the Upper Salmon River, and I was assured by the officers that they had not only seen Indians who claimed to have killed buffalo there, but that, in many places, great numbers of buffalo skulls were still lying on the prairie." ‡

Dr. Suckley, writing under date of December, 1853, also says: "Buffalo were formerly in great numbers in this valley [the valley of the Bitter Root, or St. Mary's River, one of the sources of Clarke's Fork of the Columbia], as attested by the number of skulls seen and by the reports of the inhabitants. For a number of years past, none had been seen west of the mountains; but, singular to relate, a buffalo bull was killed at the mouth of the Pend d'Oreille River, on the day I passed it. The Indians were in great joy at this, supposing that the buffalo were coming back to them." § Just east of the mountains separating the sources of the Jefferson and Salmon Rivers, buffaloes still existed in immense numbers. Lieutenant Mullan reports meeting, on December 4, 1853, with several bands of the Nez Percés Indians returning from their hunt east of the mountains, with many animals loaded with

* Irving's Rocky Mountains, pp. 208, 211.

† Parker (Samuel), Journal of an Exploring Tour beyond the Rocky Mountains, pp. 88, 107, 108.

‡ Newberry's Zoölogical Report of Lieutenant Abbot's Report of Explorations for a Railroad Route from the Sacramento Valley to the Colorado River. Pacific R. R. Explor. and Surv., Vol. VI, Zoological Report, p. 72.

§ Suckley (Dr. George), Canoe Voyage from Fort Owen to Fort Vancouver. Pacific R. R. Explor. and Surv., Vol. I, Governor Stevens's Report, p. 297.

meat and furs. "This," he says, "has been a great hunting-season with all the Indians, both east and west of the mountains. Hundreds of thousands of buffalo have been slain, and small game — consisting of antelope, deer, beaver, etc. — has been innumerable." *

It thus appears that the buffalo formerly existed west of the Rocky Mountains, nearly to the northern boundary of the United States, and that they had become completely exterminated there as early, according to Frémont (as above cited), as 1840, although they swarmed there in immense herds as late as 1835. The valleys of the streams in that region are represented as abounding in fertile prairies, and as being generally covered with perennial grasses. As the adjoining country westward is barren and wholly unproductive of grass, it is probable that the buffalo ranged further westward only irregularly, and in straggling bands. Bonneville, at least, failed to meet with any between the sources of Snake River and Fort Walla-Walla in 1834 and 1835, and no other explorer seems to have met with them living so far west. Dr. Hayden informs me that a few still exist in the valley of the Gros Ventres, and in the extreme upper part of the Snake River, — merely straggling old bulls, the last survivors of former populous herds. Professor O. C. Marsh writes me that the last one shot on Henry's Fork was killed in 1844. Professor J. Marcou informs me that a single old buffalo bull made his appearance at Fort Bridger last summer (1875), but that none had been seen there before, according to Dr. Carter, for thirty years. This solitary straggler was probably a wanderer from the remnants of his race still left in the valleys of the Wind River Mountains.

Range westward south of the Thirty-ninth Parallel. — According to Lieutenant Whipple, "there do not seem to be any well-authenticated accounts of the existence of the buffalo west of the Rio Grande." He adds: "On inquiring how far west the buffalo had been seen, a Tegua Indian stated that many years ago his father killed two at Santo Domingo. A Mexican from San Juan de Caballeros added that in 1835 he saw buffalo on the Rio del Norte." Lieutenant Whipple further says that "Father Escalante, in a manuscript journal of a trip from New Mexico to the Great Salt Lake,† in 1776, mentioned having seen signs of their existence on his route; ‡ still, notwithstanding the

* Mullan (Lieutenant John), Report of a Reconnaissance from Bitter Root Valley to Fort Hall, etc., Pacific R. R. Explorations and Surveys, Vol. I, Governor Stevens's Report, p. 325.

† Utah Lake, according to General G. K. Warren (see the next footnote).

‡ According to General G. K. Warren (Pacific R. R. Expl. and Surveys, Vol. XI, p. 35), "Father Escalante, in 1776, travelled from near Santa Fé, New Mexico, in a northwesterly direction to the Great

location of the famed kingdom of Cibola by the early explorers, there do not seem to be any well-authenticated accounts of the existence of these animals west of the Rio Grande."* It appears, however, that two centuries ago these animals were not unknown to the Indians of the Gila and Zuñi Rivers, who obtained their skins from the tribes living several hundred miles to the eastward. Thus Friar Marco de Niça, in 1539, found "ox-hides" in the possession of the Indians living on the tributaries of the Gila, which they had obtained by trading with the people of the kingdom of Cibola;† the ancient pueblo of Cibola being generally supposed to be near the site of the present pueblo of Zuñi, on the river of that name.‡ The people of Cibola at this time not only used the skins as articles of dress, but for shields and other purposes.

From the Yampah and Grand, and other tributaries of the Colorado, the buffalo formerly ranged eastward to the Parks and Great Plains, but I have found no record of their existence in the highlands of New Mexico, or anywhere to the westward or southward of Santa Fé. Coronado, during his great expedition in search of the "Kingdom of Cibola" (1540 to 1543), in marching northward from the western provinces of Mexico across Arizona to the plains east of Santa Fé, met with no buffaloes till he reached a place called Cicuic, situated on the Pecos near the site of the present town of that name,§ "four leagues eastward from which place they met a new kind of oxen, wild and fierce, whereof, the first day, they killed fourscore, which sufficed the army with flesh."

Dr. Elliott Coues, however, in his paper on the "Quadrupeds of Arizona," published in the American Naturalist in 1868,‖ states that "there is abundant evidence that the buffalo (*Bos americanus*) formerly ranged over Arizona, though none exist there now." On requesting recently more detailed information of Dr. Coues respecting this evidence, he writes¶ that he finds

Colorado. . . . . During this journey he was probably in the vicinity of Utah Lake." This route would take him across the range of the buffalo west of the Rocky Mountains, since, as already stated, they at that time existed on the head-waters of the Colorado, and extended as far west as Utah Lake.

* Whipple's Itinerary, Pacific R. R. Explorations and Surveys, Vol. III, Part I, p. 35.

† See Niça's account of his journey as translated by Hakluyt. — *Hakluyt's Voyages*, Vol. III, p. 438.

‡ Davis's Spanish Conquest of New Mexico, pp. 119, 120, footnote.

§ See R. H. Kern's Map of Coronado's route in Schoolcraft's History, Condition, and Prospects of the Indian Tribes of the United States, Part IV, plate lii.

‖ Vol. I, p 540.

¶ Under date of "Washington, D. C., May 5, 1876."

himself now unable to substantiate the statement, but adds, "I distinctly remember being satisfied *at the time* of what I said." I have myself made extensive inquiries of naturalists and army officers who had either passed through Arizona or had been stationed there for a considerable length of time without being able to elicit any corroborative evidence of Dr. Coues's statement.*

Extreme Southwestern Limit. — Respecting the extreme southwestern limit of the former range of the buffalo, Keating, on the authority of Colhoun, wrote, in 1823, as follows: "De Laët says, on the authority of Herrera, that they grazed as far south as the banks of the Yaquimi.† In the same chapter this author states that Martin Perez had, in 1591, estimated the Province of Cinaloa, in which this river runs, to be three hundred leagues from the city of Mexico. This river is supposed to be the same which, on Mr. Tanner's map of North America (Philadelphia, 1822), is named Hiaqui,‡ and situated between the 27th and 28th degrees of north latitude. Perhaps, however, it may be the Rio Gila, which empties itself in latitude 32°." §

On referring to the works cited by Keating, I find that Herrera gives the statement on the authority of Nuña de Guzman, who made a journey to Cinaloa in 1532. According to a map accompanying De Laët's work, the Province of Cinaloa included the parallels of twenty-seven and twenty-eight degrees. Herrera's statement is as follows: "En la ribera de Yaquimi ay algunas vacas, y muy grandes ciervos"; ‖ — simply that many cattle and many deer of very large size were found on the banks of the Yaquimi. In the context, nor in any of the old writings descriptive of this region at the time it was first visited by the Spaniards, do I find any further statements that could by the freest license of translation be rendered bison or buffalo. As the only species of the deer family found in this region is the little *Cervus mexicanus, one of the smallest deer found in North America*, the phrase *muy grandes ciervos* can only refer to this species, and gives at once

* Dr. W. J. Hoffman, under date of "Reading, Penn., June 19, 1875," writes me that he "found no tradition amongst any of the tribes in Arizona, by which we might infer that their ancestors were acquainted with this animal. The tribes visited are located in the northern part of Arizona (Plateau del Colorado), in the Mogollon Mts., Sierra Blanca, and along the Rio Gila and as far eastward as the Rio Colorado-chiquito."

† "Juxta Yaquimi fluminis ripas tauri vaccæque et prægrandes cervi pascuntur." — De Laët, *Americæ Utriusque Descriptio*, Lugd. Batav. Anno 1633, Lib 6, Cap. 6." p 286.

‡ The Rio Yaqui, doubtless, of modern maps.

§ Long's Expedition to the Source of the St. Peter's River, Vol. II, p 28.

‖ Herrera (Antonio de), Historia de las Indias Occidentales, Tomo III, p. 16. (Ed. of 1728.)

sufficient evidence of the exaggerated style of the narrative, — a fault well known to be common to the descriptive writings of those times. This obscure statement does not apparently afford satisfactory ground for doubting what historians have so generally accepted in respect to the buffalo, namely, that it was first met with in its native haunts by Cabeça de Vaca, on the plains of Texas, in 1530, and next by Coronado's expedition in 1542. In rebuttal of this supposed proof of the existence of the buffalo in Western Mexico, on the Yaquimi or Yaqui River during the middle of the sixteenth century, we have the rather weighty evidence that the other early Spanish explorers who traversed this region did not even hear of the buffalo till they reached the Gila, where they found, as before stated, its robes in the possession of the Indians, which the latter had obtained from the tribes living far to the northeastward. In 1539, for example, Friar Marco de Niça set out from the town of San Miguel, in the Province of Culiacan, situated far to the southward of the Rio Yaqui, in search of the famed Kingdom of Cibola. In this journey he reached the Zuñi River, whence he retraced his steps to San Miguel and passed on to Compostella, situated in latitude about 21°. The following year (1540) Coronado, with his large army, passed over nearly the same route, both crossing the Rio Yaqui. Niça, however, saw only the prepared skins of the buffalo, which was also all that Coronado saw till after he had passed Cicuic and reached the Great Plains east of the Rocky Mountains. It is from these explorers and from Cabeça de Vaca that we get the first specific account of the buffalo. It hence follows that there is good reason for supposing the buffalo to have been absent from the western provinces of Mexico, and from that part of the United States west of the Rio Grande del Norte from a period antedating the sixteenth century till the present time. Why it may not during some earlier period have existed throughout this whole region would be hard to say, since, as will be soon shown, its existence on the Yaqui River would not carry its range south of points the buffalo is known to have reached on the Atlantic slope.

Former Range south of the Rio Grande del Norte.

Most writers give the southern limit of the former habitat of the buffalo as latitude 28° to 30°, believing it never to have extended south of the Rio Grande. There is, however, sufficient proof of its former extension over the northeastern provinces of Mexico, including certainly portions of the present States of Tamaulipas, Nuevo Leon, Cohahuila, Chihuahua, and Durango. It thus extended southward to at least the 25th parallel. It seems not, however, to have been abundant over much of this region, and to have been mainly extirpated prior to the beginning of the present century. As late as 1806, however, Pike enumerated the buffalo among the animals of "Cogquilla" * (a province then extending on both sides of the Rio Grande, and embracing a portion of what is now Southwestern Texas), but whether found north or south of the Rio Grande is not stated. The buffalo is not enumerated by Pike in his lists of the animals of any of the other Mexican Provinces situated south of the Rio Grande.†

De Laët ‡ mentions the buffalo (under the name "Armenta"), on the authority of Gomara, as an inhabitant of Quivira, which he describes as a country consisting of plains destitute of trees, and well known as situated far to the northward of the present northern boundary of Mexico. It is to be noticed also that all the references to the buffalo by the older writers on the natural history of Mexico, including Hernandez, Fernandez, and Nieremburg, and even Clavigero, refer to the region of Quivira.

Dr. Berlandier, who was for a long time a resident of the northeastern provinces of Mexico, and who at his death left in MSS. a large work § on the Mammals of Mexico, speaks of the buffalo as formerly ranging far to the southward of the Rio Grande. I am unable to say, however, what are his authorities. In his chapter on this animal, he thus refers to its former range in Mexico: —

"Au Mexique, lorsque les espagnols, toujours avides de richesses, poussaient leurs excursions dans le nord et nord ouest, ils ne tardèrent pas à rencontrer des bisons. En 1602, les moines Franciscains qui découvrirent le Nouveau Leon, rencontrerent dans les environs de Monterey de nombreux troupeaux de ces quadrupèdes. Ils étaient aussi assez répandus dans la Nouvelle

* "*Animals.* — Deer, wild horses, a few buffalo, and wild hogs." — PIKE's (Z. M.) *Western Expeditions*, App. to Part III, p. 28, 1810.

† Catlin in his "North American Indians," Vol. I, gives a map illustrative of the distribution of the Indian tribes in 1833. On this map an attempt is made to also show the range of the buffalo. Although this is done very imperfectly, it may be worthy of mention in this connection that he here represents the buffalo as ranging over the greater part of the above-named provinces of Northeastern Mexico.

‡ America, p. 303.

§ Now in the Smithsonian Institution. For access to this important MS. I am indebted to the kindness of Professor S. F. Baird, Assist. Sec'y of the Smithsonian Institution.

Biscaye (états de Chihuahua et Durango) et s'avançaient quelquefois très au sud de ce pays. Dans le dix-huitième siècle, ils se concentrèrent de plus en plus vers le nord, et restaient encore fort-communs dans les environs du presidio de Bexar. Au commencement du dix-neuvième siècle, on les vit se rapprocher graduellement de l'intérieur des terres à un tel point qu'ils deviennent de jour en jour, de plus en plus rares autour des lieux habités. Ce n'est maintenant que dans leurs émigrations périodiques qu'on les trouve près de Bexar. Chaque année, au printemps en Avril et Mai, ils s'avançent vers le nord, pour de nouveau se rapprocher des régions méridionales en Septembre et en Octobre. Les limites de ces émigrations annuelles sont presque inconnues; il est cependant probable que dans le sud, ils ne dépassent jamais les rives du Rio Bravo, du moins dans l'état de Coahuila et Texas, et dans celui de Tamaulipas. Vers le nord pas même retenus par les courants du Missouri, ils arrivent jusque dans le Michigan, et se trouvent en été sur les territoires et les états internes des États-Unis de l'Amérique Septentrionale. La route que ces animaux suivent dans leurs voyages occupe plusieurs milles de front et devient tellement tracée qu'indépendamment de la verdure détruite, on croirait voir de champs labourés couverts de fiente.

"Ces émigrations ne sont pas générales, car certains troupeaux ne paraissent pas suivre la masse générale de leurs semblables, et restent stationnaires toute l'année dans des prairies couvertes d'une riche végétation sur les rives du Rio de Guadeloupe et du Rio Colorado de Texas, non loin des côtes du golfe, à l'est de la colonie de San Felipe de Austin entre Brazosia et Matagorda, précisément dans le même endroit où La Salle et ses compagnons de voyage les virent, il y a près de deux cents ans. Le R. P. Damian Mansanet les vit aussi, mais de nos jours, les côtes du Texas, couvertes d'habitations, de hameaux, de petites villes et de villages des nouveaux colons, en sont dépourvues quoiqu'en 1828, il y en eut encore. D'après les observations faites à ce sujet, on peut conclure que les Bisons habitent la zone tempérée du nouveau-monde, et qu'ils l'ont habité en tout temps. Au nord, ils ne s'avancent guère au-delà du 48me ou 58me degré de latitude, et au sud, quoiqu'ils soient venus le 25me, maintenant ils ne dépassent plus le 27me ou 28me degré, du moins dans les localités habitées et connues du pays."

FORMER OCCURRENCE OF THE BUFFALO OVER THE REGION BETWEEN THE MISSISSIPPI RIVER AND THE ROCKY MOUNTAINS, AND ITS GRADUAL RESTRICTION TO ITS PRESENT NARROW LIMITS.

For convenience of treatment, this region will be considered as embracing the whole area between the Rio Grande and the British boundary, over nearly the whole of which immense territory the buffalo is well known to have been formerly more or less abundant. It seems to have been absent from only the lowlands of the Lower Mississippi, it formerly ranging throughout nearly all of Texas, the higher prairie-lands of Northwestern Louisiana and Arkansas, and thence uniformly northward and westward to the Rocky Mountains, including also the Parks and the principal valleys within the Rocky Mountains. Beginning at the southward, we find that the earliest allusions to the buffalo refer to this region. Thus Cabeça de Vaca, we are informed, met with the buffalo (he being the first European who saw this animal in its native haunts) in "Florida," in 1530, at which time this name "was given to all that country lying south of Virginia, and extending westward to the Spanish possessions in Mexico." * Davis, in his "Conquest of New Mexico," claims that Vaca was wrecked at some point on the coast of Louisiana west of the Mississippi.† Vaca journeyed thence westward, and in his journal thus speaks of the buffalo, the locality referred to being somewhere in the southeastern part of Texas: "Cattle come as far as this. I have seen them three times and eaten of their meat. I think they are about the size of those of Spain. They have small horns like those of Morocco, and the hair long and flocky like that of the merino. Some are light brown (*pardillas*), and others black. To my judgment the flesh is finer and sweeter than that of this country. The Indians make blankets of those that are not full-grown, and of the larger they make shoes and bucklers. They come as far as the sea-coast of Florida, and in a direction from the North, and range over a district of more than four hundred leagues. In the whole extent of plain over which they roam, the people who live bordering upon it descend and kill them for food, and thus a great many skins are scattered throughout the country." ‡

* French's Historical Coll. of Louisiana, Part II, p. L

† The Spanish Conquest of New Mexico, pp. 41, 42, footnote.

‡ Davis's Translation, in his "Conquest of New Mexico," p. 67. See also the account in Purchas (Pilgrims, Vol. IV, p. 1513), — an "abbreviated" translation from Ramusio.

They were also found in immense herds on the coast of Texas, at the Bay of St. Bernard (Matagorda Bay), and on the lower part of the Colorado (Rio Grande, according to some authorities), by La Salle, in 1685, and thence northward across the Colorado, Brazos, and Trinity Rivers. Joutel says that when in latitude 28° 51′, "the sight of abundance of goats and bullocks, differing in shape from ours, and running along the coast, heightened our earnestness to be ashore."* They afterwards landed in St. Louis Bay (now called Matagorda Bay), where they found buffaloes in such numbers on the Colorado River that they called it La Rivière aux Bœufs. "These bullocks," says the account, "are very like ours; there are thousands of them, but instead of hair they have a very long curled sort of wool." †

In describing the country about their establishment at St. Louis, at the mouth of the Rivière aux Bœufs, M. Joutel says: "We were in about the 27th degree of north latitude, ‡ two leagues up the country, near the bay of St. Louis, § and the bank of the Rivière aux Bœufs, on a little hillock, whence we discovered vast and beautiful plains, extending very far westward, all level, and full of greens, which afford pasture to an infinite number of beeves and other creatures." ‖ Setting out from St. Louis the 12th of January, 1687, they crossed a succession of rivers, between which were "spacious plains" covered with "a multitude of beeves and wild fowl." In crossing the streams, they were often guided by the buffalo paths to the best fords. They crossed the Colorado, called by them *La Maligne*, probably near the present site of Austin, and the Brazos probably somewhat below Fort Graham. Before they reached the Trinity, the country had become more barren, and buffaloes had become scarcer. Here M. de la Salle was assassinated, and a portion of his party under M. Cavelier, his brother, continued their northward march, soon reaching the Trinity River. From the Trinity they took a northeasterly course, crossing the Red River near the mouth of the Sulphur Fork, and bore thence more easterly, crossing the Wachita and reaching the Arkansas, which they struck near its mouth. During this journey from the Trinity to the mouth of the Arkansas, they seem to have

* Joutel's Historical Journal of Monsieur de la Salle's last voyage to discover the Mississippi River, French's Hist. Coll. Louisiana, Part I, p. 98.

† Ibid., p. 116.

‡ The latitude here given is obviously erroneous, as the context and subsequent account of their journey northward clearly shows. The latitude must have been nearly 29° instead of 27°.

§ Later called Bay of St. Bernard, which is the same as the present Matagorda Bay.

‖ Joutel's Journal, French's Hist. Coll. Louisiana, Part I, pp. 120, 121.

met with few buffaloes, and these mainly in the vicinity of the Wachita. Their route was thence somewhat eastward of the great range of the buffalo. The point where M. Cavelier reached the Arkansas is supposed to be only a few miles above its junction with the Mississippi, and in speaking of the surrounding country he says: "The plains on one side [probably to the westward] are stored with beeves, wild goats, deer, turkeys, bustards, swans, teal, and other game," thus showing that the buffalo ranged eastward nearly to the mouth of the Arkansas.

Ferdinando de Soto, during his march from Florida through Northern Alabama and Northern Mississippi into Arkansas, 1539–41,* did not, as previously noticed, enter the habitat of the buffalo until he had crossed the Mississippi and ascended the valley of the Arkansas for some distance. Although they found the Indian tribes well supplied with their robes, none of De Soto's party saw the buffalo alive. A party sent from Pacaha, near the mouth of the Arkansas, to search for "the province of Caluça," did not, in a journey of seven days, get apparently beyond the low grounds, and on their return reported to their chief that from the termination of their journey "thenceforward towards the north the Indians said that the country was very ill inhabited, because it was very cold; and that there was such store of oxen, that they could keep no corn for them; and that the Indians lived upon their flesh." † The Indians of Coligoa, the highest or most northerly point they reached, "reported that five or six leagues from thence toward the north, there were many of these oxen." The "ox-hides" they obtained from the Indians are described as being "very soft and wooled like sheep," showing clearly that what they called ox-hides were the skins of buffaloes. Again it is stated, "Not far from thence, towards the north, were many oxen. The Christians [Spaniards] saw them not, nor came into the country where they were." ‡

Passing from Coligoa across the Washita to the mouth of the Red River, they again (after the death of De Soto, and under the lead of Moscoso) turned westward, and reached the Trinity above the point where La Salle

* See "A Narrative of the Expedition of Hernando de Soto into Florida. By a Gentleman of Elvas. Published at Evora, 1557. Translated from the Portuguese by Richard Hackluyt." London, 1609. Original edition reprinted by the Hakluyt Society in 1851. The edition of 1611 reprinted by French in 1850, in his "Historical Collections of Louisiana," Part II.

† French's Hist. Coll. Louisiana, Part II, p. 175.

‡ Ibid., pp. 177, 181.

crossed it; though they entered the highlands, they turned back before meeting with buffaloes.

It hence appears that at this early date the buffalo frequented none of the lowlands of the Mississippi, nor those of the Washita and the Red Rivers, and only reached the Gulf coast at the mouth of the Guadaloupe and San Antonio Rivers; and that it probably extended thence southward along the coast as far at least as the mouth of the Rio Grande del Norte.

The former existence of the buffalo in the valley of the Pecos seems to be well substantiated. Speaking of Espejo's march down the Pecos River in 1584, Davis says: "They passed down a river they called *Rio de las Vacas*, or the river of oxen [the river Pecos, and the same Cow River that Vaca describes], and was so named because of the great number of buffaloes that fed upon its banks. They travelled down this river the distance of one hundred and twenty leagues, all the way passing through great herds of buffaloes."*

As already noticed, Coronado met with vast herds of buffaloes in 1542 on the plains near Cicuic, on the Upper Pecos River. From Cicuic Coronado marched eastward across the plains of Northern Texas to about the one hundredth meridian, and thence returned again to Quivira,† making a journey of "three hundred leagues." "All that way & plaines are as full of crookebacked oxen, as the mountaine Serena in Spaine is of sheepe."‡

These "crookebacked oxen" Gomara (as translated by Hakluyt) has thus described: "These Oxen are of the bignesse and colour of our Bulles, but their hornes are not so great. They have a great bunch upon their fore shoulders, and more haire on their fore part than on their hinder part: and it is like wooll. They have as it were an horse-mane upon their backe bone, and much haire and very long from the knees downeward. They have great tuffes of haire hanging downe their foreheads, and it seemeth that they have beardes, because of the great store of haire hanging downe at their chinnes and throates. The males have very long tailes, and a great knobbe or flocke at the end: so that in some respect they resemble the Lion, and in some other the Camell. They push with their hornes, they runne, they overtake and kill an horse when they are in their rage and anger. Finally, it is a

* Davis's Spanish Conquest of New Mexico, p. 260. See also Hakluyt, Voyages, Vol. III, p. 472.

† See R. H. Kern's Map of Coronado's route, as before cited.

‡ Hakluyt, Voyages, Vol. III, p. 455. (Translated from Gomara's Historia de las Indias, Cap. 214.)

foule and fierce beast of countenance and forme of bodie. The horses fledde from them, either because of their deformed shape, or else because they had never seene them. Their masters have no other substance: of them they eat, they drinke, they apparel, they shooe themselves." *

According to Davis, Castañeda thus describes the buffalo and the Plains where it was met with by the people of Coronado's Expedition: "The first time we encountered the buffalo, all the horses took to flight on seeing them, for they are horrible to the sight. . . . . They have a broad and short face, eyes two palms from each other, and projecting in such a manner sideways that they can see a pursuer. Their beard is like that of goats, and so long that it drags the ground when they lower the head. They have, on the anterior portion of the body, a frizzled hair like sheep's wool; it is very fine upon the croup, and sleek like a lion's mane. Their horns are very short and thick, and can scarcely be seen through the hair. They always change their hair in May, and at this season they really resemble lions. To make it drop more quickly, for they change it as adders do their skins, they roll among the brush-wood, which they find in the ravines.

"Their tail is very short, and terminates in a great tuft. When they run they carry it in the air like scorpions. When quite young they are tawny, and resemble our calves; but as age increases they change color and form. . . . . Their wool is so fine that handsome clothes would certainly be made of it, but it cannot be died, for it is a tawny red. We were much surprised at sometimes meeting innumerable herds of bulls without a single cow, and other herds of cows without bulls. It would sometimes be forty leagues from one herd to another, and that in a country so level that from a distance the sky was seen between their legs, so that when many were together, they would have been called pines whose foliage united, and if but one was seen his legs had the effect of four pines. When near, then it was impossible by an effort to see the ground beyond, for all this country is so flat that turn which way we will the sky and the grass are alone to be seen.

"Who would believe that a thousand horses, one hundred and fifty cows of Spanish breed, and more than five thousand sheep, and fifteen hundred persons, including Indian servants, would not leave the slightest trace of their passage in the desert, and that it was necessary to raise, from point to point, heaps of stones and buffalo bones, in order that the rear guard might follow

* Hakluyt, Voyages. Vol. III, p. 456.

us, for the grass, short as it was, rose up after having been trodden down, as straight and fresh as ever.

"Another very astonishing thing is that on the eastern margin of one of the salt lakes, towards the south, was found a spot almost half a musket shot long, entirely covered with buffalo bones, to the height of twelve feet, and eighteen feet broad, which is surprising in a desert country, where no one could have brought these bones together. It is pretended that when the lake is troubled by the North winds, it throws upon the opposite shore the bones of all animals which have perished in coming to drink." *

Any one who has seen the buffaloes on their native plains can but recognize the faithfulness of these details, which are remarkable for their minuteness and exact truthfulness. They are further worthy of note from being the first descriptions of the buffalo ever published.

During the exploration of the different portions of the Great Plains, from the time of Lewis and Clarke, Pike, Long, and others, down to the later expeditions of Frémont, Stansbury, Emory, Marcy, Stimpson, Pope, Sitgreaves, and others, and the explorations for "a railroad route from the Mississippi River to the Pacific Ocean" in 1853–55, buffaloes, or recent traces of them, were found everywhere from the Missouri and Upper Mississippi Rivers westward to the remotest valleys of the eastern slope of the Rocky Mountains, from the plains of Texas northward to the 49th parallel. In the further account of this vast territory it is hence necessary to trace only their extirpation over the very large portion from which they have disappeared.

Extirpation in Texas and New Mexico. — Long prior to the time of the later explorations above mentioned, the buffalo had disappeared from the eastern border of the plains south of the Platte River. Even as early as the beginning of the present century the range of the buffalo had begun to be materially restricted, these animals having at that time been apparently wholly exterminated south of the Rio Grande, while they had also disappeared from the adjoining portions of Texas. They appear also to have wholly disappeared in Texas south of the Colorado River prior to the year 1840. Before this date they had also receded far from the coast, and no longer ranged west of the Pecos River, either in Texas or New Mexico; they occupying at this time only a narrow oblique belt through the middle portion of the State, varying from one hundred to two hundred miles in breadth, and widening rapidly as it approached the northern border of the State. From Texas

* Davis's Spanish Conquest of New Mexico, pp. 206, 207, footnote.

northward, however, they still occupied nearly all the Great Plains, from the Rocky Mountains almost to the Mississippi River.

I have as yet met with but few data relating to the extermination of the buffalo, either south of the Rio Grande or in Texas, prior to 1840, but since that period the record is reasonably full. Beginning with the year 1841, we find that at this time Kendall, in travelling north from Austin, Texas, first met with buffaloes seventy-five miles north of Austin, on Little River, a southern tributary of the Brazos, where he found them in immense herds. In speaking of them he says: "There are perhaps larger herds of buffalo at present in Northern Texas than anywhere else on the western prairies, their most formidable enemies, the Indians, not ranging so low down in large parties on account of the whites; but I was told that every year their numbers were gradually decreasing, and their range, owing to the approach of white settlers from the east and south, becoming more and more circumscribed." Kendall also found them numerous on the Brazos, and states that they occasionally took shelter in the Cross Timbers, and that he last met with them, in going westward, on the upper part of the Big Washita, one of the sources of the Red River, near the one hundredth degree of longitude.*

Kennedy, writing in the same year, says, "The bison is still to be met with in the mountainous districts between the Guadeloupe and the Rio Grande."† According to Gregg, however, they had already disappeared *east of the Cross Timbers* as early as 1840.‡

In 1849, in an expedition from Fort Smith, Arkansas, to Santa Fé, Lieutenant J. H. Simpson first saw signs of buffaloes near the 97th meridian, a few miles south of the Canadian, but adds that he saw not more than two buffaloes on the whole journey. In speaking of the game, he says: "In regard to the buffalo, there can be no question that they have been in the habit of infesting the route in places during certain seasons of the year. Indeed, Gregg mentions them as swarming on the plains on his return trip from Santa Fé, in the spring of 1840. During our journey, however, I did not see more than two, from the beginning to the end of the trip, and therefore I am not at liberty to hold them up as any certain source upon which to rely for subsistence." §

* Kendall (G. W.), Narrative of the Texan Santa Fé Expedition, Vol. I, pp. 78, 79.

† Kennedy (Wm.), Texas: The Rise, Progress, and Prospects of the Republic, Vol. I, p. 122.

‡ Commerce of the Prairies, Vol. II, p. 122.

§ Congress. Rep., 31st Congr., 1st Session, Senate Ex. Doc., No. 12, pp 6, 20.

Roemer, in 1849, says that the buffalo was then found only in the hilly parts of the State, far from the coast, and that herds of a thousand together were still seen between the Brazos and Austin.* It would seem, however, that at this time there were very few buffaloes south of the Red River, as during the years 1849, 1850, and 1851 a series of military reconnaissances were made in Texas, forming a network of lines covering a large part of the State, during the running of which no buffaloes seem to have been met with. Lieutenant Michler surveyed a line from Fort Washita southward along the 97th meridian,† from 34° 30′ to about 31°, and thence southwestward to San Antonio. Another line was run from Fort Washita southwestward, in a nearly direct line to the Pecos River, striking it in longitude 103°, and latitude 31° 20′. A line was continued from this point eastward again to the 100th meridian, and thence southeastward to Corpus Christi Bay, in longitude 96°, and latitude 28° 40′. Another line was carried down the Pecos to longitude 101° 40′, and thence to the head-waters of the Nueces, and down this river also to Corpus Christi Bay. The narratives of these explorations make no mention of buffaloes, as they doubtless would if buffaloes had been met with.‡ In 1850 Marcy met with a few stragglers south of the Canadian, near the divide between the Canadian and the Washita Forks of the Red River, and saw their tracks and other indications of their presence there. He reports that the Kiowas and Comanches went north in summer to hunt the buffalo on the plains of the Arkansas, only a few buffaloes crossing at this time to the south of the Canadian.

In 1852, according to the "Topographical Sketches of the Military Posts" in Texas, buffaloes had entirely disappeared from the region about Fort Worth§ (on the west fork of the Trinity, just west of the 97th meridian); they are not mentioned among the animals found at this date about Fort Belknap‖ (on the Brazos, longitude about 98° 30′), neither were they then found about Fort Terret¶ (on the 100th meridian). Very few are said to have been found as far south as Fort Phantom Hill, since 1837.** At Camp Johnston,†† on the Concho River (near the present Fort Concho), one only is reported as having been seen, and the region is said to have been then

* Roemer (Ferdinand), Texas, p. 462.

† The central portion of the wooded belt known as the "Cross Timbers" lies along this meridian.

‡ Congress. Rep., 31st Congr., 1st Session, Sen. Doc. No. 64, and accompanying maps.

§ Med. Statistics U. S. Army, 1839–1854, p. 373.

‖ Ibid., p. 372.

¶ Ibid., p. 395.

** Ibid., p. 376.

†† Ibid., p. 380.

not within their favorite range; but they are at the same time enumerated among the animals met with about Fort McKavett,* situated some fifty miles to the southward of Fort Concho.

Lieutenant Whipple, in his report of the survey of the thirty-fifth parallel, made in 1853, found buffalo bones bleaching near a brackish spring, just west of the Cross Timbers, and nearly on the 99th meridian. A few days later they saw the first living buffalo, and met with a few stragglers on succeeding days, on the sources of the Washita Branch of the Red River. He speaks of seeing buffalo signs as far west as Camp 44, a little east of the 102d meridian. The main herds, however, were north of the Canadian, from which these were merely stragglers.† Professor Jules Marcou, who accompanied Lieutenant Whipple's expedition as geologist, has kindly furnished me with a few additional particulars from his note-books. He informs me that the first bones of the buffalo were met with as far east as the Cross Timbers, or near the 98th meridian; but the region appeared not to have been visited by these animals for ten or twelve years. The first living buffalo was seen between Camps 33 and 34, about 99° 40′, just south of the Canadian. The next day many carcasses were observed, and two days later five old bulls were seen. An old bull was killed between Camps 36 and 37, near the meridian of 100° 25′, but no living buffaloes were seen west of the 101st meridian, and no fresh signs were seen west of the 102d. All the recent indications of buffaloes were thus met with between the meridians of 98° 30′ and 102°. The journey being made in September, the herds had not returned from the north, the individuals met with being only stragglers which had wandered somewhat to the southward of the usual southern limit of the summer range.

Captain (now Major-General) Pope in 1854 surveyed the 32d parallel, from El Paso and Doña Aña, on the Rio Grande, to Preston, on the Red River, passing northerly, and crossing the Pecos and the head-waters of the Colorado, Trinity, and Brazos Rivers. Mr. J. H. Byrne, in his diary of the expedition, reports meeting *bois de vache* "for the first time" at Camp No. 10, near the Ojo del Cuerbo, or Salt Lakes, west of the Guadeloupe Mountains, and in the Valley of the Rio Grande. This is the only allusion to buffalo or buffalo "sign" contained in the narrative, although the kinds and quantity of game

* Med. Statistics, U. S. Army, 1839–1854, p. 301.

† Pacific R. R. Exploration and Surveys, Vol. III, Lieutenant Whipple's Report on the 35th Parallel, Part I, pp. 26, 28, 29, 35.

met with each day appear to be duly chronicled.* We are further led to infer the entire absence at this time of buffaloes in Texas by some remarks made by Captain Pope, in his General Report, respecting the Comanche Indians, whose country was on the head-waters of the Canadian and Red Rivers, in the extreme northern part of Texas. He says: "During the summer months nearly the whole tribe migrates to the north, to hunt buffalo and wild horses on the plains of the Upper Arkansas." †

Captain H. M. Lazelle, 8th U. S. Infantry, informs me that in 1859 there were no buffaloes in New Mexico, nor in Texas west of the 99th meridian, but that there were vast numbers in Northern Texas between the meridians of 99° and 96°; but that they did not extend so far south as Pope's old trail of 1854. ‡

Hence it appears that for quite a number of years the buffaloes nearly abandoned Texas, or visited only its northwestern portions, and were of somewhat uncertain occurrence, in summer at least, as far north as the Canadian. Of late, however, they have again become common over a considerable portion of the northwestern part of the State, occasionally extending southward along the 100th meridian almost to the Rio Grande. Major-General M. C. Meigs, Quartermaster-General of the United States Army, says, in some valuable MS. notes on the buffalo, § that in the winter of 1869–70 he saw their carcasses near Fort Concho, Texas, "showing that the buffalo had been abundant in that neighborhood the previous year." The prairies having been extensively burned that winter about Concho, the buffaloes had not appeared within twenty miles of the post that season. He also says that in the winter of 1871–72 they extended their migrations westward to the Staked Plains.‖

Mr. J. Boll, the well-known entomological collector, also informs me that during the winter of 1874–75 they were still more abundant over quite a large part of Northern Texas, doubtless in consequence of their persecution by the hunters in Southwestern Kansas. Respecting the eastern boundary of

* Pacific R. R. Exploration and Surveys, Vol. II, Pope's Exploration of the 32d Parallel, from the Red River to the Rio Grande, pp. 51–93.

† Ibid., p. 15.

‡ Pope's trail crosses the 96th meridian in about latitude 33° 30', and strikes the Pecos in longitude 103° and latitude 31° 30', at Emigrant Crossing.

§ For access to this interesting paper I am indebted to the kindness of Dr. Elliott Coues, the eminent ornithologist.

‖ MS. Notes on the Buffalo.

their range at the present time (January, 1876), he says: "So viel mir bis jetzt bekannt, so geht der Bison östlich im Texas nicht mehr über die Linie hinaus welche von der Mündung der Little Wichita in den Red River in gerader Richtung fast südlich bis zur Mündung des Pecan Bayou in den River Colorado sich austreckt. Wie sich diese Linie vom Colorado River bis zum Rio Grande gestaltet ist schwer zu sagen, doch glaube ich dass von der Mündung des Pecan Bayou sie mehr eine stark sudwestliche Richtung bis zum 30° nordlich Breite annehmen wird."

Respecting their present southern limit in Texas, a letter written by Mr. J. Stevens in answer to my inquiries on this point, and kindly transmitted to me by Mr. C. E. Aiken, of Colorado Springs, Colorado, states, on the authority of Mr. W. H. Case, who has lived for the last two or three years at Fort Concho, that buffaloes have of late been quite numerous there in winter, and that they were especially so last winter. He says that "after severe storms they come in from the north in large numbers," at which times he has seen larger herds there than anywhere else, not excepting Kansas and the Indian Territory. East of Fort Concho he says they do not go south of the latitude of that post, but that to the westward they go twenty to fifty miles further to the southward, but only occasionally. Mr. Stevens adds that none are found very far to the westward of Fort Concho, and that none have been found for a long time in any part of New Mexico, and that probably none ever will be found there again. From the best information I have been able to obtain, their present western limit seems to be the eastern border of the Staked Plains.

Their Extermination in Arkansas, Missouri, Iowa, and Minnesota. — Passing now to the region north of Texas, the history of the extermination of the buffalo throughout the tier of States adjoining the Mississippi River — namely, Arkansas, Missouri, Iowa, and Minnesota — will be first given, and afterward an account of its extermination over the region between the Platte River and the northern boundary of Texas.

According to Nuttall, the bison was still to be met with in Arkansas as late as 1819, a few then existing near the Arkansas River, in the present county of Conway, not far from the centre of the State.* In a journey from Fort Smith southwestward to the Red River, his party also met with large herds on Riameche Creek, in the present Indian Territory, near the southwestern border of Arkansas.† Major Long found their skulls and other remains at

* Travels into the Arkansas Country, p. 118.

† Ibid., pp. 149, 150.

Massern and Vache Grasse Creeks, in Western Arkansas in 1820, showing that they had existed at that point at a not very remote period.*

Gregg, writing about 1844, says: "Even within thirty years they were abundant over much of the present States of Missouri and Arkansas," or as late as 1815.† In 1820 settlements had extended up the Arkansas nearly to the western border of the State, and probably soon after this date the buffaloes were wholly extirpated throughout the present State of Arkansas.

Beck states that in Missouri, as late as 1823, "immense herds" of buffaloes were "frequently seen covering the extensive plains which stretch along the west part of the State. During the dry seasons," he says, "they remain in the neighborhood of rivers, but they uniformly migrate to the south at the approach of winter." ‡

It thus appears that the buffalo also lingered in Western Missouri till about 1820 to 1825. They probably disappeared from Southern Iowa at about the same period, but they existed for a much longer time in the northern half of the State. In earlier times Charlevoix found "magnificent meadows" in Southeastern Iowa, on the Des Moines River, "quite covered with buffalo, and other wild creatures." § Major Long, in a trip eastward from Council Bluffs in 1819 found "their skulls and other remains on the plains of the Nishnabatona, and in one instance discovered the tracks of a bull; but," he adds, "all the herds of these animals appear to have deserted the country east of Council Bluffs." ‖ According to Assistant Surgeon Charles C. Keeney, the buffalo was sometimes met with on the open prairies a few miles west of Fort Dodge, on the Des Moines River, as late as 1852.¶

M. Belon, an old French *voyageur*, whom I met in 1873 on the Yellowstone, acting as interpreter for the expedition of that year, and who moved to Minnesota in 1837, informed me that buffaloes were abundant within fifty miles of St. Paul as late as 1836, and were common on the head-waters of the Cedar and Des Moines Rivers, on both sides of the Iowa and Minnesota boundary, as late as 1845. They have, however, been for many years extinct throughout the present State of Iowa, with the exception of the occurrence

* Long's Expedition from Pittsburg to the Rocky Mountains, Vol. II, p. 264.

† Gregg, Commerce of the Prairies, Vol. 2, p. 113.

‡ Beck (L. J.), Gazetteer of the States of Illinois and Missouri, p. 167.

§ Letters, Goadby's English ed., p. 295.

‖ Expedition to the Rocky Mountains, Vol. I, p. 421.

¶ Med. Statistics U. S. Army, 1839–1854, p. 55.

of a few stragglers in the extreme western counties. When I was in the western part of the State in 1867, I was informed that a few still remained in that section, and that up to that time one or more had been killed every year as far south as Greene County. They were represented as being more common further north, but that no herds were met with south of the Sioux River, and rarely east of the Missouri. Those found further east were only stragglers from distant herds.* Professor Bessey, of the Iowa Agricultural College, informs me that a few were seen in the bottom-lands below Council Bluffs as late even as about 1869, and also, at about the same time, in the northwestern part of the State, — stragglers, of course, from remote herds.

In Minnesota, west of the Mississippi, buffaloes remained until a recent period. In 1823 Major Long found herds numbering thousands of individuals about the sources of the Red and Minnesota (or St. Peter's) Rivers. He states that in 1822 they did not descend the Minnesota River below Great Swan Lake, and that in 1823 "the gentlemen of the Columbia Fur Company were obliged to travel five days in a northwest direction from Lake Travers before they fell in with the game, but they soon succeeded in killing sixty animals." † The buffaloes are said, however, to have lingered about Fort Ridgely, situated a few miles above Swan Lake, till about 1847, and that as late as 1856 they were found one hundred miles to the northwestward of this point. ‡ As late as 1844 Captain Allen found large herds in the southwestern part of the present State of Minnesota. He says: "Seventy-five miles west of the source of the Des Moines we struck the range of the buffalo, and continued in it to the Big Sioux River, and down that river about eighty-six miles. Below that we did not see any recent signs of them. They were sometimes seen in droves of hundreds. . . . . While among the buffalo we killed as many as we wanted, and without trouble." § Pope states that in 1850 buffaloes were still killed in the immediate vicinity of the settlements at Pembina, and that they existed in great abundance between the Pembina and the Shayenne Rivers,‖ or along the present western boundary of the State. They appear, however, to have

* See Proc. Bost. Soc. Nat. Hist., Vol. XIII., p. 186, 1869.

† Expedition to the Source of the St. Peter's River, etc., Vol. II., pp. 9 - 24, 29.

‡ Assistant Surgeon A. B. Hasson, in Med. Statis. U. S. Army, 1839 - 1854, p. 67.

§ Allen (Captain J.), Congress. Rep., 29th Congr., 1st Session, Doc. No. 168, p. 5.

‖ Pope (General John), Report of an Expedition to the Territory of Minnesota, Congress. Reports, 31st Congr., 1st Session, Sen. Doc. No. 42, p. 27.

very soon after left the whole valley of the Red River, being rapidly slaughtered and pressed westward by the incursions of the Red River half-breed hunters, who are reported to have killed annually, at about this time, twenty thousand buffaloes south of the United States and British Boundary.* A few lingered in the southwestern part of the State till within a very few years, or occurred there rather as stragglers from the herds west of the Big Sioux River, in Southwestern Dakota.

From the foregoing it hence appears that the buffalo was more or less abundant over large portions of the States of Arkansas and Missouri as late as 1812 to 1815, but that few remained in either State later than 1820. At about this date they seem to have also disappeared from Eastern and Southern Iowa, but were quite numerous in the northwestern part of the State, and adjoining parts of Minnesota, as late as 1840 to 1845, where occasionally an old bull was met with as late as 1860. As already stated, they disappeared in Minnesota east of the Mississippi River prior to 1832;† and they appear to have been exterminated over the whole region east of the Red River as early as 1850, and to have survived later elsewhere in the State only in the extreme southwestern counties, where a few lingered till about 1860.

Permanent Division of the Buffalo into two distinct Herds, and their Extermination over the greater Part of the Region between the Northern Boundary of Texas and the Platte River. — As is well known to those who have given much attention to the subject, the great buffalo herd that once extended continuously from the plains of the Saskatchewan to the Rio Grande was divided about 1849 into two bands by the California overland immigration, and that since that time the two herds have never united. The great overland route, as is well known, followed up the Kansas and Platte Rivers, and thence westward by the North Platte, crossing the Rocky Mountains by way of the South Pass. The buffaloes were all soon driven from the vicinity of this line of travel, thousands being annually slaughtered, a large proportion of them being killed wantonly.‡ The increase of travel, and finally the construction of

* Rice (H. M.), Pope's Report (cf.), p. 4.

† See anteà, p. 117.

‡ Respecting the influence of the overland emigration upon the buffalo, we find Captain Stansbury, who passed over the emigrant trail in the summer of 1849, speaking as follows: Under date of June 27, he says, "To-day the hunters killed their first buffalo, but in order to obtain it had to diverge some four or five miles from the road and to pass back of the bluffs, the instinct or experience of these sagacious animals having rendered them shy of approaching the line of travel. This has always been the case, for it is

the Union Pacific Railroad and the consequent opening up of the country to settlement, has effected a wider separation of the herds, the buffaloes retiring every year further and further from their persecutors. None are now found for a long distance to the north of this road, and they approach it from the southward only along that portion situated between Fort Kearney and the Forks of the Platte. In treating of the "Southern Herd," as the southern division is commonly termed, it will be found convenient to trace first its extirpation over the region to the eastward, and afterwards to the westward, of its present range.

As previously stated, Nuttall found buffaloes in 1819 in Southwestern Arkansas and the adjoining portions of the Indian Territory.* Pike, however, in 1806, first met with these animals on the divide between the sources of the Osage River and those of the Neosho Fork of the Arkansas, near the 98th meridian, or near Council Grove in Eastern Kansas, and reports that they were already nearly exterminated over the hunting-grounds of the Osages and Pawnees.† In 1820 Major Long found no large herds east of the mouth of the Little Arkansas, near the 98th meridian. At the Great Bend of the Arkansas, however, he met with them for several days "in vast and almost continuous herds."‡ Catlin's "Outline Map of Indian localities in 1833" § purports to give also the range of the buffalo, but none are represented as occurring between the Kansas and Arkansas Rivers east of the 99th meridian, but in his account of his visit to the Comanche country he speaks of meeting with buffaloes about forty miles east of the junction of the False Washita and Red Rivers, or near the 96th meridian.‖

General Doniphan, during his march in 1846 from Fort Leavenworth to Santa Fé, used *bois de vache* for fuel when passing the head of the Little Arkansas, and first met with herds of buffaloes on the Arkansas at Pawnee Ranch, near the present site of Fort Larned.¶ The previous year Lieuten-

a well-attested fact, that when the emigration first commenced, travelling trains were frequently detained for hours by immense herds crossing their track, and in such numbers that it was impossible to drive through them. In many instances it was quite difficult to prevent their own loose cattle from mingling with the buffaloes, of which they did not seem to be at all afraid." — *Salt Lake Expedition*, p. 34.

* Travels into the Arkansas Country, pp. 149, 150.

† Pike (Z. M.), Expedition to the Sources of the Mississippi, and to the Sources of the Arkansas, Kansas, La Platte, and Pierre Jaune Rivers, etc., in the years 1805, 1806, and 1807.

‡ Long's Exped. from Pittsburg to the Rocky Mts., Vol. II, pp. 204, 207.

§ Catlin (G.), North American Indians, Vol. I, map.

‖ Ibid., Vol. II, p. 46.

¶ Hughes (J. T.), Doniphan's Expedition, pp. 43, 47.

ant J. W. Abert found them as far east as 97° 32'.* Lieutenant Abert reports meeting with them the following year near the 98th meridian, just west of which he found them in immense herds.†

Lewis and Clarke, in ascending the Missouri River in 1804, first met with buffaloes at the mouth of the Kansas River, but state that they did not become common till they reached the Sioux River.‡ Bradbury found them in 1810 at Floyd's Bluff. Audubon says that when he and his party went up the Missouri River in 1843, "the first buffalo were heard of near Fort Leavenworth, some having a short time before been killed within forty miles of that place. We did not, however," he says, "see any of these animals until we had passed Fort Croghan, but above this point we met with them almost daily, either floating dead on the river or gazing at our steamboat from the shore." §

As early as 1834, Murray, in his journey westward from Fort Leavenworth into the Indian country, first met with buffaloes on the Republican,‖ showing that they had already become extinct or of uncertain occurrence in Eastern Kansas. Frémont, in 1842, in marching northwestward from Fort Leavenworth to the Platte River, by way of the Kansas River, came suddenly upon great herds just above Grand Isle, in about longitude 99° 30', or near the present site of Fort Kearney. The following year (1843), in crossing the plains considerably to the southward of his route of the previous year, he first met with the buffalo on the divide between the Solomon and the Republican Forks, also near the 99th meridian.¶ Emory, in 1846, says that the range of the buffalo along the Arkansas was "westward, between the ninety-eighth and the one hundred and first meridians of longitude." ** In 1849 Stansbury saw no buffaloes east of the Forks of the Platte, but found them in abundance to the westward of this point. Captain Stansbury's guide reported to him that not many years before the plains somewhat to the east of Fort Kearney were black with herds of buffaloes "as far as the eye could reach." ††

* Congress. Rep., 29th Congr., 1st Sess., House Ex. Doc. No. 2, p. 217.

† Notes of a Military Reconnaissance from Fort Leavenworth, Mo., to San Diego, Cal. Congress. Rep., 30th Congr., 1st Sess., Sen. Doc. No. 7, p. 11.

‡ Expedition to the Rocky Mountains, Vol. I, pp. 10, 67.

§ Quadrupeds of North America, Vol. II, p. 50.

‖ Travels in North America, Vol. I, pp. 208, 227.

¶ Frémont's Explorations during 1842, '43, and '44, pp. 18, 25, 49, 57, 109, *et seq.*

** Emory (W. H.), Notes of a Military Reconnaissance from Fort Leavenworth to San Diego, California, p. 16.

†† Stansbury's Expedition to the Great Salt Lake, pp. 29, 36.

In July, 1853, Captain Gunnison's party first met with fresh signs of the buffalo on the Saline, and on the Kansas near the mouth of the Saline; their first buffalo was killed on the Little Arkansas; somewhat later, they found themselves in the midst of immense herds on the Republican Fork.*

Dr. Hayden, writing of his journey across the plains in the summer of 1858, says, "Before going into the interior of the Territory [of Kansas] we had expected to find the whole country immediately west of Fort Riley comparatively sterile; on the contrary, however, we were agreeably disappointed at meeting with scarcely any indications of decreasing fertility, as far as our travels extended, which was about sixty miles west of Fort Riley. Here we found the prairies clothed with a luxuriant growth of grass, and literally alive with vast herds of buffalo, that were quietly grazing as far as the eye could reach, in every direction." †

Lieutenant E. S. Godfrey, of the 7th U. S. Cavalry, who has recently spent several years in the Department of the Missouri, informs me that when Fort Harker was established, in 1866, the buffaloes ranged regularly as far east as this point, and even passed beyond it. They were taken here for several years after, but in 1870 had almost wholly retired to points further westward.

Professor B. F. Mudge, of the Kansas State Agricultural College, has given me the following general statement respecting their extermination in Eastern Kansas. Under date of February 7, 1873, in kind response to my inquiries, Professor Mudge wrote as follows: —

"The buffalo ranged to the eastern border of Kansas as recently as 1835. About that time the United States authorities removed the Delaware, Pottawattamie, Kaws, and other tribes of Indians to 'Reservations' in the eastern part of what is now Kansas. These Indians soon drove the buffalo as far west as the Blue River (one hundred miles west of the Missouri River), which was as far as the reservations extended. The buffalo held that range till 1854, when Kansas was made a Territory and whites began to settle here. For fifteen years from that time the buffalo receded, on an average, about ten miles a year. For three years past they have been hunted in summer for their hides for *tanning;* this is exterminating them very rapidly. Now they are not found in Northern Kansas east of 100° of longitude; in Southern

* Beckwith's Report of Captain Gunnison's Exploration of the 38th and 39th Parallels, Pacific R. R. Explorations and Surveys, Vol. II.

† Geological Report of the Exploration of the Yellowstone and Missouri Rivers, p. 172.

Kansas as far easterly as longitude 98°, the western boundary of Kansas being 102°. In a few years I think they will not range north of the Arkansas River."

None of the government expeditions sent across the plains since 1840 seem to have met with the buffalo east of the longitude of Fort Riley, or east of the 97th meridian, from the Platte southward to Texas. In the Indian Territory they have not for a number of years ranged to the eastward of Fort Sill.* It thus appears that the buffaloes were exterminated in Eastern Kansas and in the eastern part of the Indian Territory over a breadth of about four degrees of longitude between 1835 and 1870.

The extermination along the western border of the southern herd has also extended over a considerable area. In 1806 Pike found them throughout his march across the plains from the western edge of Arkansas to the eastern base of the Rocky Mountains, meeting with them in the greatest abundance between the Smoky Hill Fork and the Arkansas.† In 1845 Lieutenant Turner found buffaloes abundant in the valley of the Arkansas from Bent's Fort thence eastward for over two hundred miles.‡ The following year (1846) Dr. Wislizenus reports that on Colonel Doniphan's march across the plains all signs of the buffalo, even including the *bois de vache*, disappeared near the meridian of 101°, between the Arkansas and Cimarron.§

Frémont states that in 1842, at 103° 30', between the two forks of the Platte, they absolutely covered the plains, and were abundant thence westward to St. Vrain's Fort, situated a little to the southward of the present town of Cheyenne. Between the forks of the Platte and along the North Platte to Fort Laramie but few were found, but recent signs of them were abundant. On the Laramie plains westward as far as Laramie River, large herds were constantly met with, but this year none were seen on the North Platte above the junction of Laramie River, the grasshoppers and the dry weather having destroyed every blade of grass.‖

* Captain J. W. Powell, of the 8th United States Infantry, informs me that in 1872 the buffalo did not range as far east as Fort Sill, but occurred fifty miles west of this point in considerable numbers. Lieutenant Godfrey (7th Cavalry) also states that during 1871 and 1872 he met with them throughout that part of the Indian Territory west of Fort Sill.

† Pike (Z. M.), Expedition to the Sources of the Mississippi, and to the Sources of the Arkansas, Kansas, La Platte, and Pierre Jaune Rivers, etc. in the years 1805, 1806, and 1807.

‡ Cong. Rep., 29th Congress, 1st Session, House Ex. Doc. No. 2, p. 217.

§ Wislizenus (Dr. A.), Memoir of a Tour to Northern Mexico in company with Colonel Doniphan's Expedition in 1846–47, Cong. Rep., 30th Congress, 1st Session, Miscel. Doc. No. 26.

‖ Frémont's Explorations during 1842, 1843, and 1844, etc.

In June, 1844, Frémont found them in immense numbers in North, Middle, and South Parks, in the present State of Colorado, as well as on the tributaries of the Green River on the western slope of the mountains, and on the Sweet Water, and the other extreme head-waters of the North Platte, from all of which extensive region they were nearly or quite exterminated during the following twenty years.

When the miners first visited the parks and mountains of Colorado, in the summer of 1859, they found them occupied by small bands of buffaloes, which afforded them an abundance of meat for several years. They have been scarce there, however, for the last ten years, during which time only stragglers have been met with. In the summer of 1871 I found their skulls still frequent in South Park and up the valley of the South Platte to its extreme source. They were very frequent at and above Montgomery, and even on the neighboring mountains above timber-line, showing that not many years ago the buffalo ranged over the grassy slopes of the mountains even to above the limit of the timber. I heard of a single small band of two or three dozen individuals near the southern borders of South Park, in the vicinity of Buffalo Springs, and saw a calf at one of the ranches that was captured in June of that year as the band passed up the valley of the South Platte into the Park.* Mr. Wm. N. Byers. of Denver, Colorado, writes me that a band of twelve were seen in South Park in 1873, and that "occasionally a little band is still seen in the northern edge of Middle Park and in North Park." "About seventy-five wintered on the head of Muddy or Milk River, Middle Park, last winter [1874–75]. Another band was seen on the head-waters of Willow Creek, ranging thence over the divide into North Park. Most of our people call these mountain animals Bisons, and think them smaller than the Plains Buffalo, but they are evidently the same animal, resorting to the mountains of their own choice."

One of these small parties, according to Western newspapers, seems to have recently fallen a prey to the Indians, a Denver paper of a recent date containing the following: "A party of Indians in the northwestern edge of the Middle Park came upon a herd of buffalo the other day, and killed them all, — forty-two in number. All they saved was the skins, leaving the meat to rot. Such waste of the game ought to be stopped, and the sooner the better."

Dr. Hayden informs me that a band of eighteen was seen by one of his

* Bull. Essex Inst., Vol. VI, pp. 54, 55.

parties near Pike's Peak in 1873, and that in 1875 there was a band of about nineteen on the west side of Pike's Peak, and another band of about sixty near Mt. Lincoln in the South Park. Mr. C. E. Aiken, probably referring to these, writes me that he knows of but two bands existing at the present time (February, 1876) in the mountains about South Park, one of which "grazes on the mountains at the head of Tarryall Creek, and is frequently found above timber-line; the other ranges in the rugged mountains south of Pike's Peak, and numbers some thirty or forty individuals."

In 1871 their bleached skulls were still frequent in the valley of the North Platte, in Western Wyoming, as well as on the Laramie Plains, but I was assured that only stragglers had been seen in all this region during the previous ten or fifteen years.* Stansbury reports meeting with them in abundance on Pass Creek and other head-waters of the North Platte in 1849.†

In respect to the extermination of the buffalo along the western edge of the plains in Colorado, and the present western boundary of the Southern Herd, I have been favored with a valuable communication from Mr. William N. Byers, editor and proprietor of the "Rocky Mountain News." In kindly answer to my inquiries he thus refers (writing under date of July 3, 1875) to the gradual extermination of the buffalo along the eastern base of the Rocky Mountains. He says: "Perhaps the best idea I can give you of the shrinkage of the column on this side is gathered from the history of the early trading-posts established here, mainly for barter in their hides. The first trading-post in this [South Platte] valley was built in 1832, six miles below Denver, and about fifteen miles, direct, from the mountain foot. A trader employed here from 1832 to 1836 told me that he thought that he never looked out over the walls of the fort without seeing buffalo, and sometimes they covered the plain. At that time their moving columns surged up against the mountain foot. Five or six years later the next fort was built five or six miles down the river, then a third a few miles below the second, and, about 1840, a fourth, nearly twenty miles below the third, or forty odd miles from the mountains. There the trade was concentrated and the up-river forts were successively abandoned, owing to the decrease of the buffalo in their vicinity. But great herds of buffaloes occasionally ranged over the present site of Denver as late as 1846.

* See Bulletin Essex Institute, Vol. VI, p. 59.

† Salt Lake Expedition, pp. 243 - 247.

"The trading-posts in the valley of the Arkansas possess a similar history. The earliest, built about 1826, was some twenty miles from the mountains. Others succeeded, one after another, until *New Fort Bent*, — afterward Fort Bent, now Fort Lyon, — about eighty miles from the mountains, closed the history of these early trading outposts. They were placed so as to be most convenient to the camps of the hunters, to enable the traders to supply the latter with goods and to buy their skins.

"The present range of the buffalo in Colorado," he says, "is bounded substantially on the west by a line about one hundred miles east of the foot of the mountains, and parallel therewith. The herds are thin on the edge, thickening to the eastward. Small bands occasionally wander ten or twenty miles further west, but the line is quite distinctly marked. In the fall they move gradually but slowly southward, and in late winter and spring return in the same way north; but the eastern edge of Colorado is really occupied all the winter by herds that come from and return to the north. In summer very few remain upon the Colorado range. I have no idea of the relative movement of individual herds north and south during the year, but there seems to be a regular *ebb and flow* once a year. There has been no marked change in the limit of the range westward in the last five years, but the columns have been thinned *fearfully*, — certainly one half."

Influence of the Railroads upon the Decrease of the Buffalo. — Three railroads now enter or pass near the range of the Southern Herd. Their influence, though immense in respect to its decrease, seems not to have very greatly affected the extent of its range. The railroads, of course, primarily affect the buffalo by affording to the hunters easy access to its haunts, and by placing the hunters in communication with ready markets for the products of the chase. They also open up the country they traverse to permanent settlement, thus rendering the extirpation of the buffalo from the country bordering these avenues of travel not only speedy but permanent. Although the buffalo has no little fear of these iron highways and their thundering trains, this alone would not, for a long time at least, seriously influence its range; and the herds have not, except through the thinning of their ranks by the hunters who make these roads the bases of their operations, materially changed their range since the opening of the Union Pacific Railroad in 1869. The buffaloes still range northward to this road between Fort Kearney and the Forks of the Platte, but they appear to have of late rarely passed north of it. At this point the buffalo range is still within easy drive from the line of the road, and is often chosen by Eastern hunting-parties for their field of operations.

The Kansas Pacific Railway, traversing as it does one of the favorite and formerly most populous portions of the range of the great Southern Herd, has given opportunity, since it was opened in 1870, for the destruction of hundreds of thousands of buffaloes. After two or three years the results of this wholesale slaughter began to be apparent in the thinning of the herds and in their erratic movements and changed habits, especially in respect to their migrations.

During the summer of 1871 straggling bands occurred as far eastward in Northern Kansas as Fossil Creek, while the great herds were rarely met with east of the meridian of Fort Hays. In June of that year they blackened the prairies from the Saline River to the Republican Fork. In January, 1872, they had receded several hundred miles to the westward of their summer limit, ranging then over Eastern Colorado. Between the Union Pacific and Kansas Pacific Railroads they at this time migrated eastward in summer and westward in winter, passing with reluctance either of these great highways. At times, however, they swept across the Kansas Pacific Railway in immense herds, obliging the trains to await their passage.* In consequence of this eastward and westward migration they had already worn deep trails running in this direction, and at right angles to the older set made when their migrations were mainly from the north southward in autumn and from the south northward in spring.† From the great persecution they had suffered from the hunters, who swarmed down upon them from all sides, their movements were already less regular than formerly.

The opening of the Atchison, Topeka, and Santa Fé Railroad has had a far greater influence upon the buffalo than either of the other roads, in consequence of the great number of hunters who seized upon it as a favorable basis for the prosecution of their terrible work of destruction. The story of this destruction and the fatal results attending the encroachment of the settlements upon the range of the buffalo is well told in the subjoined letter from Dr. W. S. Tremaine, U. S. A., kindly written in answer to my inquiries

* General Meigs writes that a conductor of the Kansas Pacific Railway informed him in the winter of 1872–73, that "while he had been several times delayed by the crossing of immense herds going south he had never seen any buffalo returning." — *MS. Notes on the Buffalo.*

† See Bulletin Essex Institute, Vol. VI, pp. 46, 47.

respecting this subject, and dated Fort Dodge, Kansas, July 16, 1875: "In regard to the buffalo, I would say that when I first came to this post, in 1869, the buffaloes ranged in almost countless herds from about where the town of Great Bend, on the Atchison, Topeka, and Santa Fé Railroad, now is, to Fort Lyon, Colorado, and from the Platte River to the Red River of Texas. Throughout this range you might travel for days and scarcely ever be out of sight of buffaloes. This condition remained up to the summer and autumn of 1873, when the Atchison, Topeka, and Santa Fé was completed to this point. Buffalo-hunting for their hides then became quite an industry in this neighborhood, and hundreds of thousands were slaughtered in this vicinity, so that at the present time a buffalo is a rare sight within two hundred miles of Fort Dodge." Dr. Tremaine gives the principal range of the Southern Herd of buffaloes as being now south of the Kansas line, between the North Fork of the Canadian and the Red River of Texas, and from about the 100th meridian to the eastern border of New Mexico. "A few small herds," he says, wander northward from the main body as far as the Platte country, passing along near the eastern boundary of Colorado. Some are also found further to the southward between the Red and Pecos Rivers. He speaks of the herds as having become very much restricted in range and as very much "thinned out." He says: "As regards their present numbers, I was told by an officer of cavalry who had scouted last summer and winter through the region I have indicated, that during his wanderings through this part of the country, which is now considered the principal habitat of the Southern Herd, he saw fewer buffaloes than he had seen in a trip from Fort Hays to Fort Dodge (eighty-six miles) in 1872."

Recent reports from Kansas and Colorado agree in respect to the enormous destruction of buffaloes throughout Kansas, incidentally referred to above by Dr. Tremaine. While the range seems not to have been as yet very materially circumscribed during the last four or five years, the reduction in numbers has been immense, and the vast herds existing there five years since are now represented by only scattered remnants, so fearfully have their ranks been depleted.

The incessant persecution of the buffalo along the lines of the two great Kansas railways has had the effect to crowd them southward and southwestward into Western Texas. In this Indian-infested region, too remote from railroads to render it feasible for the hunter to follow them for their hides and meat, the herd is now mainly concentrated where it is temporarily less exposed to persecution than on the more accessible plains of Kansas. The range of the herd thus not only changes with the seasons of the year, but also from year to year, in consequence of attacks upon them at new localities. Unless legal interference, either by the States of Kansas, Colorado, and Texas, or by the general government, be speedily made, and rigorous restrictions most thoroughly enforced, the fate of the buffalo south of the Platte will be a repetition of its history east of the Mississippi River, namely, speedy extermination.

Area now occupied by the Southern Herd.—The region south of the Platte inhabited by the buffalo is already reduced to a very limited area. At the northward their range extends over only the head-waters of the Republican, and thence westward to the South Platte, to the northward of which river they still sometimes appear, their range thus including the small portion of Southwestern Nebraska that lies south of the Union Pacific Railway. They range thence southward throughout Western Kansas and Eastern Colorado, the extreme western part of the Indian Territory, Northern and Western Texas, extending in the latter State southward to the 30th parallel, and from the 98th meridian westward over the northern portion of the Staked Plains nearly to the eastern boundary of New Mexico. In 1873 they ranged westward to within a hundred miles of Santa Fé.*

Region between the Platte River and Parallel of 49°.—Passing to the northward of the Platte River, we will consider first the region situated between the Platte River and the United States and British boundary, or the 49th parallel. The buffalo, as is well known, formerly ranged over the whole country drained by the Missouri and its tributaries, as well as over the plains of the Red River of the North, and those of the Assinniboine and the Saskatchewan. The plains of the Red River, in Northern Minnesota and Dakota, formerly connected the great buffalo range of the Upper Missouri region with that of the Saskatchewan, whilst the Grand Coteau des Prairies was for a long time one of the regions of their greatest abundance. Beginning with Eastern Dakota, or that portion of the Territory east of the Missouri River, embracing the Grand Coteau des Prairies, we shall pass thence to the region between the Missouri River and the 49th parallel, and, lastly, trace their extermination over the vast triangular area bounded by the Missouri and Platte Rivers and the Rocky Mountains.

* H. W. Henshaw, in a letter to the writer, dated March 6, 1875.

Extermination in Eastern Dakota. — As late as 1850 General John Pope stated that the buffalo ranged "in immense herds between the Pembina and Shayenne Rivers," and were "found in great numbers, winter and summer, along the Red River," being "frequently killed in the immediate vicinity of the settlements at Pembina." * Mr. Henry M. Rice also states that in the spring of 1847 a party of Red River hunters, numbering twelve hundred carts, went in a body south to Devil's Lake, in Minnesota (now Dakota); † while Mr. J. E. Fletcher states that twenty thousand buffaloes were at this time annually killed in the country of the Sioux and Chippewa Indians, south of the United States and British boundary, § mostly within the present Territory of Dakota. The Hon. H. H. Sibley has given an interesting account of a buffalo-hunt in Eastern Dakota (then a part of Minnesota Territory) in Schoolcraft's great work on the Indian Tribes of the United States, ‡ and incorporates therewith a detailed account, furnished him by the Rev. Mr. Belcourt, ‖ of the chase of the buffalo on the Pembina Plains. It contains not only much valuable information respecting the peculiar modes of hunting pursued by the Red River hunters, but also important statistics respecting the rate of their destruction at the date of writing (1853).

Mr. A. W. Tinkham, in the "Itinerary" of his route from St. Paul to Fort Union, in June and July, 1853, speaks of using the *bois de vache* for fuel on Maple River, and reports killing his first buffalo on the Shayenne, one of the chief tributaries of the Red River. At this time, he says, large herds roamed over the prairies of the Shayenne River, and extended as far south as the South Fork of the Shayenne. He also met with recent indications of the buffalo on the White Earth River. ¶

Governor Stevens, in speaking of the abundance of the buffalo on the Shayenne River, near Lake Zisne, the same year, says: "About five miles

* Report of an Exploration of the Territory of Minnesota. (Congressional Reports, 31st Congr., 1st Session, Senate Doc. No. 42, p. 27.)

† Congress. Rep., 31st Congr., 1st Sess., House Ex. Doc., Vol. VIII, No. 51, p. 8.

‡ Ibid., p. 41.

§ Schoolcraft's History, Condition, and Prospects of the Indian Tribes of the United States, Vol. IV, pp. 101 – 110.

‖ The account given by Mr. Sibley as that furnished by Mr. Belcourt seems to be merely a translation of Mr. Belcourt's account of buffalo-hunting by the Red River half-breeds originally contained in a letter addressed by Mr. Belcourt to Major S. Woods, and dated "St. Paul, November 25, 1845." This document was published by Major Woods in his Report of his Expedition to the Pembina Settlement in 1849 (Congressional Documents of the 31st Congress, 1st Session, House Doc. No. 51, pp. 44 – 52).

¶ Pacific R. R. Explorations and Surveys, Vol. I. Governor Stevens's Report, pp. 252 – 258.

from camp, we ascended to the top of a high hill, and for a great distance ahead every square mile seemed to have a herd of buffalo upon it. Their number was variously estimated by the members of the party, some as high as half a million. I do not think it is any exaggeration to set it down at 200,000. I had heard of the myriads of these animals inhabiting these plains, but I could not realize the truth of these accounts till to-day, when they surpass everything I could have imagined from the accounts which I had received." *

According to Assistant Surgeon Asa Wall, buffaloes were still common about Fort Abercrombie, on the Red River, as late as 1858.†

Mr. W. H. Illingworth, the well-known photographer of St. Paul, informs me that in 1866, when he made a journey from St. Cloud westward to the Yellowstone, he met with immense herds for two days in passing the Coteau des Prairies, west of the James River. They seem to have wholly disappeared east of the Missouri soon after this date, surviving in Southern Dakota, however, between the James and Missouri Rivers, for some years after their extermination over the plains of the Red River. As already stated, they were exterminated east of the Red River as early as about the year 1850,‡ and, being at that time rapidly pressed westward by the Red River hunters, were wholly exterminated during the few years next following throughout the whole basin of the Red River, and even throughout the whole of the northern half of Dakota. In Southern Dakota, between the James and the Missouri, they lingered for some years later, but wholly disappeared east of the Missouri prior to the year 1870.

Region between the Upper Missouri and 49th Parallel.—The former existence of the buffalo over the whole of the region drained by the Upper Missouri is well substantiated by the evidences they themselves have left, and which exist in the form of well-defined trails and osseous remains. When Lewis and Clarke ascended the Missouri in 1804, they met with them at frequent points along almost its whole course, from the mouth of the Big Sioux to the Forks,§ and subsequent explorers found them on its remotest sources. As late as 1856 this whole region was occupied, at least temporarily, by roving bands. Lambert, in his general report respecting the topography of this

* Pacific R. R. Rep. of Expl. and Surveys, Vol. XI, pt. 1, p. 59.

† Med. Statistics U. S. Army, 1855–1860, p. 34.

‡ See above, p. 144.

§ Expedition, etc., Vol. I, pp. 67, 75, 77, et seq.

region, speaks of the extensive plains between the meridian of Fort Union and the Rocky Mountains as being the "pasture-grounds of unfailing millions of the uncouth and ponderous buffalo." * Lieutenant Saxon, in his report of a journey down the Missouri, from Fort Benton to Fort Union, made in 1853, says that during the last few days of their journey, as they approached Fort Union, they saw innumerable herds of buffalo-cows, in many places extending in every direction as far as the eye could reach. † Lieutenant Groger, the same year (October, 1853), also found large bands on the Missouri from the Musselshell to the Milk River,‡ and small bands were also seen by Tinkham west of the Great Falls, on the Sun River,§ where herds were also observed in January, 1854, by Lieutenant Groger. ‖ In December, 1853, they occurred in great numbers on Big Hole Prairie, on the head of the Jefferson Fork.¶ They were also reported as occurring on the Milk River, near Camp Atchison, and also on other of the neighboring northern tributaries of the Missouri.

Dr. Cooper states that in 1860 "the buffalo herd of the Upper Missouri was spread from the Rocky Mountains, near latitude 49°, southeast," and says that he "found them along the Missouri, from its upper Great Bend, west to about fifty miles above Milk River, but nowhere in great numbers. Remains of their skeletons, left about five years since, were abundant west of Fort Benton, and," he adds, "I saw one or more old skulls daily in the valley of the Little Blackfoot and Hell Gate Rivers [west of the mountains], quite down to the junction with the Bitter Root." **

Lieutenant M. E. Hogan, 22d United States Infantry, who for some years previous had been in the United States military service in the Department of Dakota, informed me in 1873 that the buffaloes had recently crossed the Marias and Teton Rivers, in Northwestern Montana, from the northward, and were abundant throughout the region about Fort Shaw, and that there were "millions of buffaloes" on Milk River.

Respecting the present range of the buffalo between the Missouri River and the 49th parallel, and the evidences of their recent occupation of this

* Pacific R. R. Rep. of Expl. and Surveys, Vol. I, Governor Stevens's Rep., p. 167.

† Ibid., p. 264.

‡ Ibid., p. 494.

§ Ibid., p. 369.

‖ Ibid., p. 500.

¶ Ibid., p. 167.

** American Naturalist, Vol. I, p. 538.

whole belt of country, I am indebted to Dr. Elliott Coues for the subjoined important communication. Two seasons spent in this region as naturalist of the United States Northern Boundary Survey have given him opportunities for collecting much important information respecting this region. The communication, dated "Washington, March 2, 1875," is as follows:—

"The time when the buffalo ranged in this latitude [parallel of 49°], eastward of the Red River of the North, passed so long since that the traces of their former presence have become effaced. The present generation of hunters in Manitoba and adjacent portions of the United States trail to the westward, by several well-known routes, in pursuit of robes and meat. In travelling from the river I saw no sign whatever until in the vicinity of Turtle Mountain, where an occasional weather-worn skull or limb-bone may be observed. Thence westward to the Mouse River, the bony remains multiply with each day's journey, until they become common objects; still, no horn, hoof, or patch of hide. In the space intervening between this river and the point where the Coteau de Missouri crosses the parallel of 49°, quite recent remains, as skulls still showing horns, nose-gristle, or hair, and portions of skeletons still ligamentously attached, are very frequent. At La Rivière de Lac, a day's march west of the Mouse River, there was a grand battue a few years since, as evidenced by the numbers of bones, the innumerable deserted badger-holes, and the circles of stones denoting where Indian lodges stood. Within the Coteau the most recent remains are the rule; and a hundred miles from such edge (nearly north of the mouth of the Yellowstone) living animals were seen in the summer of 1873.

"Thus comparing the two great basins of the Red River and of the Missouri, respectively, it will be seen that the animal left the whole United States portion of the former before it was driven from parts of the Missouri basin equally far east, or even further eastward. This is borne out by observations made on my journey from the Mouse River due south to Fort Stevenson, on the Missouri. There were few skulls (about as many as between Mouse River and Turtle Mountain) until I struck the Coteau, within which they at once multiplied.

"In the western portion of the Red River basin numberless buffalo-*trails* still score the ground, with a general north-south trend.

"In the summer of 1871 I approached the parallel of 49° in a southwesterly course from the mouth of the Yellowstone. The whole country offered a fair amount of skeletal remains, in many cases ligamentously cohering, and was furrowed with trails. But there were no living animals in the region eastward of Frenchman's River, which is one of the first of many north-south tributaries of Milk River. A day's march west of this river brought us to the edge of the 'Yellowstone Herd,' as the northerly division of the buffalo is termed, where the first buffalo were seen and killed. Small straggling droves, or single animals, were observed every day thence to the vicinity of the Sweet Grass Hills (or Three Buttes, as they are called on the map), where they become very abundant. In this vicinity many thousands, if not some hundreds of thousands, passed the season. During the latter part of August we travelled for several days in continual sight of droves on every side on the road between the Sweet Grass Hills and Fort Benton; one day the plain was uniformly dotted, as far as the eye could reach, in at least a quadrant of a circle.

"In the comparatively short distance between the Sweet Grass Hills and the Rocky Mountains we encountered no buffalo, but this was a mere fortuitous circumstance for the particular days; the 'chips' were everywhere. They were traced, however, by their remains into the very heart of the Rocky Mountains, at an altitude of at least 5,000 feet; and I was informed that the various glades were a winter resort of some of the animals that pass that season in this latitude. But I could obtain no indication that the buffalo ever [here] crossed the mountains. Hunters and guides familiar with the region for years agree that this barrier is not surmounted, and had never been passed, either within their memory or according to tradition; indeed, the Kootanie Pass has been always known as the point where Indians from the westward have come annually to hunt on the opposite side.

"It is sufficiently attested that buffaloes pass the winter in this region, or at least have very recently done so. In exploring the Sweet Grass Hills I followed up one gorge where for a mile or so skulls and skeletons lay almost touching each other in the cul-de-sac. Here was evident indication that a drove, in attempting to cross from the hog-back on one side to the other, had sunk in the snow which filled the ravine, and lost many of their number. The buffaloes are more expert and venturesome climbers than their unwieldy forms would indicate. Upon the summits of the Sweet Grass Hills, inaccessible on horseback, and where a man can only go about by scrambling, their dung and bones are found, with those of the mountain sheep. The hillsides here, and the equally steep banks in places along the heads of the Milk River and its tributaries, too declivous in their natural state to afford footing to a horse or mule, are cut by innumerable hoofs into a series of narrow terraces, each a buffalo trail.

"In the whole region just north of the Milk River, absolutely treeless excepting along a part of the stream, and on the Sweet Grass Hills, buffalo chips are everywhere at hand for fuel.

"In descending the Missouri River from Fort Benton, buffalo were seen almost daily during that part of the voyage which embraced the rapid portion of the river flowing between the bluffs of the Bad Lands. Small droves were seen surmounting peaks which, it would seem, only a mountain sheep could scale; and in one instance, indeed, the attempt was a failure, and the animal rolled down hill in a cloud of dust. No more were seen below the mouth of the Musselshell, where the Missouri widens and enters a flatter country. The limit on the Missouri corresponds in longitude, in a general way, with that above noted on the parallel of 49°."

It thus appears that twenty years ago buffaloes were accustomed to frequent the whole region between the Missouri River and the 49th parallel, from the western boundary of Dakota, or the 104th meridian, westward to the Rocky Mountains, occurring even throughout the foot-hills of the latter as well as over the head-waters of the Bitter Root, or St. Mary's River, one of the sources of Clarke's Fork of the Columbia, but that they are now restricted to the region between Frenchman's Creek, near the 107th meridian, and the Rocky Mountains, over much of which area their occurrence is merely irregular and more or less fortuitous, their main range being between the 110th and the 112th meridians.

Region between the Upper Missouri and Platte Rivers.—It is so well known that the buffalo formerly ranged throughout this region that there is little need of presenting further evidence of the fact than will be given incidentally in tracing the boundaries of their present range, and in sketching the history of their extirpation over the greater part of this extensive territory. Beginning at the eastward, we find that Bradbury in 1810, in crossing from the Platte River northward to the Mandan Villages, met with a few buffaloes in what is now Eastern Nebraska, on the Elk Horn River, and that they were then plentiful on the Canon Ball and Heart Rivers, in what is now Southwestern Dakota.* They lingered in Southwestern Dakota till within a very short time. The last buffalo killed near Fort Rice was taken in 1869,

* Bradbury (John), Travels in the Interior of North America in the years 1809, 1810, and 1811, pp. 53, 134.

when three were killed from a herd of ten old bulls that had wandered considerably to the eastward of the main herds. According to Dr. W. J. Hoffman, to whom I am indebted for other interesting facts relating to the subject of the present paper, the buffaloes disappeared from the region between the Cheyenne and Grand River Agencies at about the same time (1869), although occasional stragglers frequented the plains toward the Black Hills till somewhat later. He states that fresh hides were brought into the Grand River Agency in 1872, that were obtained about one hundred miles to the westward of that place.* Dr. Hayden also informs me that a few were found until a few years since south of the Black Hills, on the sources of the Niobrara and Cheyenne Rivers, from which localities they have, however, been since exterminated.

As already stated, they were abundant about Fort Union at the mouth of the Yellowstone, in 1853, and for some distance below this point west of the Missouri, where they remained for some years later. Dr. Hayden informs me that they were abundant there as late as 1859, and that even as late as 1866 they occupied much of the country between Fort Union and Fort Pierre. In 1861 Dr. Hayden published the following general statement in relation to the range of the buffalo at that time on the Upper Missouri. "They occur," he says, "in large bands in the valley of the Yellowstone River, and in the Blackfoot country, but their numbers are annually decreasing at a rapid rate. Descending the Yellowstone in the summer of 1854, from the Crow country, we were not out of sight of large herds for a distance of 400 miles. . . . . In 1850 they were seen as low down on the Missouri River as the Vermilion, and in 1854 a few were killed near Fort Pierre. But at the present time (1861) they seldom pass below the 47th parallel on the Missouri. Every year, as we ascend the river, we can observe that they are retiring nearer and nearer to the mountainous portions." †

General W. F. Raynolds, in passing from Fort Pierre westward in July, 1859, says that the whole country, for one hundred and forty miles, was a dry, desolate tract, a few antelopes forming the only living things met with; "but buffaloes," he says, "have evidently been here, and may return at more favorable seasons of the year. Six bulls were seen to-day in the distance, as we drove into camp, being our first sight of the famous 'lords of the prairie.' We are now approaching the Black Hills, however, and will

* In a letter dated April 16, 1875.

† Transact. Amer. Phil. Soc., Vol. XII, 2d Series, p. 150.

soon have them around us in abundance."* This locality was on the head-waters of the Cheyenne. Again, in speaking of the valley of the Yellowstone, he says: "This valley has long been the home of countless herds of buffalo. . . . . When my party first reached the bluff overlooking the Yellowstone the sight was one which in a few years will have passed away forever. I estimated that about fifteen miles in length of the wide valley was in view. The entire tract of forty or fifty square miles was covered with buffalo as thickly as in former days in the West (when cattle were driven to an Eastern market) a pasture-field would be which was intended only to furnish subsistence to a large drove for a single night. I will not venture an estimate of their probable numbers."†

In 1873 I made a journey from Fort Rice, on the Missouri, to the Yellowstone and Musselshell Rivers, accompanying the "Yellowstone Expedition" of that year (General D. S. Stanley commanding) as naturalist of the expedition. From my report on the collections made I quote the following: "Recent signs of the buffalo were first met with in the valley of the Yellowstone, near the mouth of the Rosebud,— tracks of single old bulls that had passed down to the river for water within a period of a few weeks. Above this point considerable numbers seemed to have frequented the river valley during the early part of the season (1873), and tracks but a few days old were frequent for the last ten miles before reaching Pompey's Pillar. The first buffalo *seen* was observed about twelve miles west of Pompey's Pillar. Eight miles further west, on the divide between the Yellowstone and the Musselshell, we found large herds had grazed but a day or two before our arrival, and fresh tracks of cows and calves, as well as of bulls, were abundant. From this point to the Musselshell we were frequently in sight of large bands, and quite a number of individuals were killed. They moved off rapidly, however, as we approached, and at no time were more than a few hundred in sight at once. We found later that the valley of the Musselshell and its adjoining prairies had been the recent feeding-ground of large herds, immense numbers having evidently spent the early part of the season there. They seemed not, however, to have visited the valley in large numbers before for many years, as all the trails and other signs had evidently been made within the few weeks immediately preceding our arrival. Traces of ancient trails remained, but they were few and insignificant

* Exploration of the Yellowstone, p. 27.

† Ibid., p. 11.

as compared with those of the present year. The herds seemed to have occupied the whole valley as far as we followed it (from the 109th meridian to the Big Bend), as well as the plains on either side. Considerable bands had also ranged over the divide between the Musselshell and the Yellowstone, particularly along the two Porcupine Creeks. General Custer met with small herds still further to the eastward, and the main expedition came in sight of a few near the mouth of Custer's Creek, where several were killed by the scouts. On our return we found that during our absence small bands had visited the valley of the Yellowstone itself, and had ranged as far down as Powder River, while quite large herds had recently passed up Custer's Creek.

"Occasional skeletons and buffalo chips in a good state of preservation occur eastward nearly to the Missouri, but the only very recent signs observed this year east of the Yellowstone were the tracks of a few old straggling bulls a few miles east of the river."* I was also informed by credible authorities that they then wintered in great numbers on the head-waters of the Big Horn, Tongue, and Powder Rivers, passing northward in spring to the Yellowstone and Musselshell. Mr. Reynolds, a hunter and scout of great experience, and an unquestionable authority, informed me that the buffalo range of the Upper Missouri embraced the regions of the Powder, Tongue, Big Horn, and Upper Yellowstone Rivers, and thence northward over the Musselshell, Teton, and Marias Rivers, to the Milk River.

The recent rapid extermination of the buffalo over Southwestern Dakota and the adjoining portions of Wyoming has been undoubtedly effected mainly by the Sioux Indians, who have of late ranged over this region. This at least is the view taken by Colonel Dodge, and apparently with good reason. He refers to the subject as follows: "The great composite tribe of Sioux, driven by encroaching civilization from their homes in Iowa, Wisconsin, and Minnesota, had crossed the Missouri and thrust themselves between the Pawnees on the east and the Crows on the north and west. A long-continued war between the tribes taught at least mutual respect, and an immense area, embracing the Black Hills and the vast plains watered by the Niobrara and White Rivers, became a debatable ground, into which none but war parties ever penetrated. Hunted more or less by the surrounding tribes, immense numbers of buffalo took refuge in this debatable land, where they were comparatively unmolested, remaining there summer and winter

* Proc. Boston Soc. Nat. Hist., Vol. XVII, pp. 39, 40, 1874.

tered survivors of the former large herds, and which of course will not long remain. He also says that a few were met with in the valley of the Gros Ventres as late as 1860, and in the valley of the upper part of the Snake River Valley in 1870, — the two latter localities of course being on the western slope of the Rocky Mountains.

It thus appears that the present range of the buffalo between the Platte and the Missouri is confined to the comparatively small area drained by the principal southern tributaries of the Yellowstone, namely, the Powder, the Tongue, and the Big Horn Rivers, from which they range northward over the middle portions of the Yellowstone and the Musselshell Rivers to the Missouri.

Former Boundaries of the Range of the Buffalo within the British Possessions, and its present Distribution within that Area.

The range of the buffalo, as previously remarked, formerly extended continuously from the plains of the United States northward to Great Slave Lake, in latitude 62° to 64° north, being apparently almost as numerous over the plains of the Red River, the Assinniboine, Qu'appelle, both branches of the Saskatchewan, and the Peace River, as over the plains of the Missouri. Franklin, in 1820, met with a few at Slave Point, on the north side of Great Slave Lake,* and Dr. Richardson states that in 1829 they had recently, according to the testimony of the natives, wandered to the vicinity of Great Marten Lake, in latitude 63° or 64°.† In respect to the distribution of the buffalo in the "Fur Countries," Dr. Richardson speaks as follows: "As far as I have been able to ascertain, the limestone and sandstone formations, lying between the great Rocky Mountain ridge and the lower eastern chain of primitive rocks, are the only districts in the fur countries that are frequented by the bison. In these comparatively level tracts there is much prairie-land, on which they find good grass in the summer; and also many marshes overgrown with bulrushes and carices, which supply them with winter food. Salt springs and lakes also abound on the confines of the limestone, and

* "A few frequent Slave Point, on the north side of the lake, but this is the most northern situation in which they were observed by Captain Franklin's party." — Sabine, *Zoological Appendix* to *Franklin's Journey*, p. 668.

† Fauna Boreali-Americana, Vol. I, p. 279. See also Zoological Appendix to Parry's Second Voyage, p. 332.

there are several well known salt-licks, where bison are sure to be found at all seasons of the year. They do not frequent any of the districts formed of primitive rocks, and the limits of their range to the eastward within the Hudson Bay Company's territories may be correctly marked on the map by a line commencing in longitude 97° on the Red River which flows into the south-end of Lake Winipeg, crossing the Saskatchewan to the westward of the Basquian hill, and running thence by the Athapescow to the east end of Great Slave Lake. Their migrations to the westward were formerly limited by the Rocky Mountain range, and they are still unknown in New Caledonia and on the shores of the Pacific to the north of the Columbia River; but of late years they have found out a passage across the mountains near the sources of the Saskatchewan, and their numbers to the westward are said to be annually increasing." * The range of the buffalo in British America was hence co-extensive with the prairies, meeting the range of the musk-ox on the north, and the prairies and plains of the United States on the south. It was not, however, exclusively confined to the plains, and apparently less so at the northward than toward the south. Besides positively forsaking the more exposed portions of the northern plains and seeking refuge in the woods during the severer periods of cold in winter, they are said to frequent, at all seasons, the timber adjoining the prairie districts. In a later work Dr. Richardson refers to the range of this animal as follows: "The bison, though inhabiting the prairies in vast bands, frequents also the wooded country, and once, I believe, almost all parts of it down to the coasts of the Atlantic; but it had not until lately crossed the Rocky Mountain range, nor is it now known on the Pacific Slope, except in a very few places. Its most northern limit is the Horn Mountain [in latitude 62°]." † To the northward of the Saskatchewan, the prairie country is confined to limited areas, and there buffaloes range extensively through the open woods.‡ The habitat of the bison north of the United States, at the beginning of the present century, hence embraced a triangular area, extending through about seventeen degrees of longitude (from 96° to 113°) on the northern boundary of the United States, decreasing in breadth northward to a narrow point

* Fauna Boreali-Americana, Vol. I, pp. 279, 280.

† Arctic Searching Expedition: A Journal of a Boat-Voyage through Rupert's Land and the Arctic Sea, American ed., p. 99, 1852.

‡ Hind believes that the so-called "prairie" buffalo, as distinguished by the hunters from the "wood" buffalo, formerly "ranged through open woods, almost as much as he now does through the prairies."—*Assinniboine and Saskatchewan Expedition*, Vol. II, p. 106.

at Great Slave Lake. At present, however, they are confined within much narrower limits than formerly, and are quite absent over large areas that once were among their favorite resorts.*

The following abstracts and quotations embrace the more important references to the range and extermination of the buffalo in British North America, and are arranged nearly in a chronological order. In 1790 Mackenzie found buffaloes in considerable numbers on Peace River, along which they extended westward to the base of the Rocky Mountains.† At this time they abounded also on the plains between the Assinniboine, Red, and Missouri Rivers, as well as on both branches of the Saskatchewan and their tributaries.‡

Ross Coxe, in June, 1812, also found the buffalo in small numbers on the head-waters of the Assinniboine River and its tributaries,§ but from all this

* According to the observations of Mr. W. H. Dall, and others, a near ally of the buffalo (the *Bison antiquus* Leidy = *B. crassicornis* Richardson) formerly existed considerably to the northwestward of the former range of the living species, extending throughout probably nearly the whole of Alaska. The evidences of this consist in the occurrence of their fossil remains at different localities in the valley of the Yukon and elsewhere. In answer to inquiries of mine, Mr. Dall wrote me, under date of San Francisco, Cal., January 23, 1871, as follows, respecting the distribution of these remains: "Your letter is at hand, and in reply I can only say that the bones of the bison are found on the Upper Yukon, from the ramparts eastward and northward, and also at Kotzebue Sound. They are found, like all the remains of tertiary mammals in that region, on or very near the surface, and are especially abundant on the Kotlo River, which falls into the Yukon above Fort Yukon [latitude 66°, longitude 141°,—just west of the United States and British boundary]. The remains I have seen, with those of the elephant (in similar situations), are black and fossilized. The bones of the musk-ox and mountain goat, on the contrary, are white, and look very recent. The latter animal is still rarely found living on the mountains near the Upper Yukon. The bison remains which I have seen have been principally horn-cores and the remains of the cranium and lower jaws. The indications are that the *Elephas primigenius* and the fossil bison were contemporaries, but that the musk-ox was a later comer. However, this idea rests merely on the appearance of the bones, as the bones of all (as well as the remains of fossil horses) are found together in a bed of blue clay, near the surface, at Kotzebue Sound, and (barring the horses) all over the Upper Yukon Valley, in similar positions, irregularly scattered on the ground. I found the cranium of an elephant in the grass at the mouth of the Yukon, skulls of musk oxen and bisons on the surface in little valleys in the Ramparts, and on the alluvial plain near Fort Yukon."

In addition to the above, I have since been informed by Mr. Dall that he obtained a complete skull, except the lower jaw, on the Sitzikunten River, just below the Ramparts of the Yukon, in about latitude 65° and longitude 151°, and other fragments about fifty miles lower down the Yukon. The skull was unfortunately lost during the subsequent journey down the river. [The above should have been inserted in connection with the history of *Bison antiquus*, but was accidentally omitted.]

† Mackenzie (Sir Alexander), Travels to the Polar Sea and to the Pacific Ocean in the years 1789–91, Vol. II, pp. 147, 155, 156, 377.

‡ Ibid., pp. lxi, lxii, lxv, lxix.

§ Adventures on the Columbia River, p. 259.

region they have now nearly or quite disappeared. Hind reports finding bones and horns of buffaloes on the Assinniboine River, between Fort Garry and Prairie Portage, in 1857, but makes no mention of the occurrence of the animals themselves there at that date, but says they were still found on the sage plains further north. The Red River hunters at this time, he says, went part to the plains of the Saskatchewan, and part to the Yellowstone and Coteau de Missouri for their buffaloes.* Alexander Ross, writing at about the same date, also says, "Formerly all this part of the country [Red River Plains] was overrun by wild buffalo, even as late as 1810"; but adds, "Of late years the field of chase has been far distant from the Pembina Plains." †

Simpson reports that buffaloes were abundant on the plains south of the Saskatchewan in the winter of 1836, and that the country about Carlton House was completely intersected with their deeply-worn trails, and strewed with their skeletons; from this region they had been temporarily driven by the autumnal fires. He also met with a few buffaloes on the Clear Water River, a little above its junction with the Athabasca. In January, 1840, they were also extremely abundant about Carlton House. ‡

Respecting the range and the migrations of the buffalo within the British Possessions about the year 1858, Hind observes as follows: "Red River hunters recognize two grand divisions of buffalo, those of the Grand Coteau and Red River, and those of the Saskatchewan. . . . . The north-western buffalo ranges are as follow. The bands belonging to the Red River Range winter on the Little Souris, and south-easterly towards and beyond Devil's Lake, and thence on to Red River and the Shayenne. Here, too, they are found in the spring. Their course then lies west towards the Grand Coteau de Missouri until the month of June, when they turn north, and revisit the Little Souris from the west, winding round the flank of Turtle Mountain to Devil's Lake, and by the Main River (Red River), to the Shayenne again. In the memory of many Red River hunters, the buffalo were accustomed to visit the prairies of the Assinniboine as far north as Lake Manitobah, where in fact their skulls and bones are now to be seen; their skulls are also seen on the east side of the Red River of the North, in Minnesota, but the living

* Hind (H. Y.), Canadian, Red River, Assinniboine, and Saskatchewan Exploring Expeditions, Vol. II, p. 272.

† The Red River Settlement: its Rise, Progress, and Present State, p. 15.

‡ Simpson (Thomas), Narrative of the Discovery of the North Coast of America, London, 1843, pp. 40, 45, 46, 60, 402, 404.

animal is very rarely to be met with. A few years ago they were accustomed to pass on the east side of Turtle Mountain, through the Blue Hills of the Souris, but of late years their wanderings in this direction have ceased; experience teaching them that their enemies, the half-breeds, have approached too near their haunts in that direction.

"The country about the west side of Turtle Mountain, in June, 1858, was scored with their tracks at one of the crossing places on the Little Souris, as if deep parallel ruts had been artificially cut down the hill-sides. These ruts, often one foot deep and sixteen inches broad, would converge from the prairie, for many miles to a favorite crossing or drinking place; and they are often seen in regions in which the buffalo is no longer a visitor.

"The great western herds winter between the south and north branches of the Saskatchewan, south of the Touchwood Hills, and beyond the north Saskatchewan in the valley of the Athabaska; they cross the South Branch in June and July, visit the prairies on the south side of the Touchwood Hill range, and cross the Qu'appelle valley anywhere between the Elbow of the South Branch and a few miles west of Fort Ellice, on the Assinniboine. They then strike for the Grand Coteau de Missouri, and their eastern flank often approaches the Red River herds coming north from the Grand Coteau. They then proceed across the Missouri up the Yellow Stone, and return to the Saskatchewan and Athabaska as winter approaches, by the flanks of the Rocky Mountains. We saw many small herds, belonging to the western bands, cross the Qu'appelle valley and proceed in single file towards the Grand Coteau de Missouri in July 1858. The eastern bands, which we had expected to find on the Little Souris, were on the main river (Red River is so termed by the half-breeds hunting in this quarter). They had proceeded early thither, far to the south of their usual track, in consequence of the devastating fires which swept the plains from the Rocky Mountains to Red River in the autumn of 1857. We met bulls all moving south, when approaching Fort Ellice; they had come from their winter quarters near the Touchwood Hill range. As a general rule the Saskatchewan bands of buffalo go north during the autumn and south during the summer. The Little Souris and main river bands go north-west in summer and south-east in autumn."* Hind also states that the buffaloes still frequented the eastern flank of the Rocky Mountains.†

* Hind (J. H.), Narrative of the Canadian Red River Expedition of 1857, and of the Assinniboine and Saskatchewan Exploring Expeditions of 1858, Vol. II, pp. 107-109. See also Vol. I, pp. 295, 306, 338, 342, 356.

† Ibid., Vol. II, p. 106.

The Earl of Southesk, in his recently published narrative of his sporting adventures in British North America in 1859,* makes but few references to the buffalo, and adds nothing of much importance to our knowledge of its distribution. He speaks, however, of their occurrence on the plains west of Fort Ellice, and of meeting with large herds between the North and South branches of the Saskatchewan. He also met with their recent remains near Old Bow Fort, on the South Saskatchewan, at the base of the Rocky Mountains. "The plains," he says, "are all strewn with skulls and other vestiges of the buffalo, which came up this river last year in great numbers. They were once common in the mountains. At the Kootanie Plain I observed some of their wallowing-places, and even so high as a secluded little lake near where the horses were taken up to the ice bank, I saw traces of them. They are now rapidly disappearing everywhere." A few were also seen near the Touchwood Hills, west of Fort Pelly, in November, which was about the most easterly point at which they were seen.†

Captain W. F. Butler, writing in 1872, thus speaks of the region of the Touchwood Hills: "This region bears the name of the Touchwood Hills. Around it, far into endless space, stretch immense plains of bare and scanty vegetation, plains scored with the tracks of countless buffalo, which, until a few years ago, were wont to roam in vast herds between the Assinniboine and the Saskatchewan. Upon whatever side the eye turns when crossing these great expanses, the same wrecks of the monarch of the prairie lie thickly strewn over the surface. Hundreds of thousands of skeletons dot the short, scant grass; and when fire has laid barer still the level surface the bleached ribs and skulls of long-killed bison whiten far and near the dark burnt prairie."‡

Captain Butler crossed the plains from Fort Ellice in a northwest direction to Fort Carlton (Carlton House), and journeyed thence up the North Saskatchewan River to the base of the Rocky Mountains; but he seems not to have met with any living buffalo throughout his journey. He again refers to the vast diminution the buffalo has undergone, and mentions the wholesale slaughter formerly practised by the Cree Indians on the plains of the Saskatchewan, and describes a hunt he himself participated in on the plains of Nebraska. Referring to the rapidity with which the buffalo is vanishing

* Saskatchewan and the Rocky Mountains, 1875.

† Ibid., pp. 52, 254, 306.

‡ The Great Lone Land, p. 217, 1873.

from the "great central prairie land," he says: "Far in the northern forests of the Athabasca a few buffaloes may for a time bid defiance to man, but they, too, must disappear, and nothing be left of this giant beast save the bones that for many an age will whiten the prairies over which the great herds roamed at will in times before the white man came."*

Mr. Huyshe, writing in 1871 of the region about Fort Garry, says: "Buffalo are no longer found nearer than three hundred miles west of Fort Garry, and are gradually being driven further and further west by the advancing stream of civilization." †

In a valuable communication respecting the present and former range of the buffalo in the British Possessions, kindly sent me by Mr. J. W. Taylor, U. S. Consul at Winnipeg, Mr. Taylor, under date of "United States Consulate, Winnipeg, B. N. A., April 26, 1873," writes as follows: "In preparing this reply to your note requesting information respecting the comparative numbers and present range of the buffalo, I have consulted Mr. Andrew McDermott, an old and intelligent resident of Selkirk Settlement, now known as the province of Manitoba. This gentleman, when a very young man, was in the service of the Hudson Bay Company,—from 1812 to 1821,—and has since been a successful trader. His position in the country is attested by his recent appointment as the Manitoba Director of the Canada Pacific Railway Company.

"My informant, in 1818, was in the midst of a large herd, only two miles west of Fort Garry, where I am writing. His party stood for an hour in the midst of the black moving mass, with difficulty preventing themselves, by the constant discharge of fire-arms, from being trampled to death. Now, in 1873, the nearest point where the animal is found is at the Woody Hills, upon the International frontier, three hundred miles southwestwardly, while you must go five hundred miles west to meet large bands. Formerly a variety called the wood buffalo was very numerous in the forests surrounding Lakes Winnipeg and Manitoba, the last survivor having been killed only two years ago, on Sturgeon Creek, ten miles west of Fort Garry. The wood buffalo is smaller than its congener of the plains, with finer and darker wool, and a superior quality of flesh. It more resembles the 'bison' of naturalists.

"The Saskatchewan plains, near the Rocky Mountains, have always been a great resort of the buffalo, and although the traditions of their immense

* The Great Lone Land, pp. 315, 320.

† Huyshe (G. L.), The Red River Expedition, p. 230, 1871.

multitudes fifty years ago have hardly been sustained of late, yet I am inclined to the opinion that the extension of settlements in Dakota and Montana, the navigation of the Missouri by steamers, and the construction of the Northern Pacific Railroad are concentrating the herds which had previously retreated northward from the great overland route now traversed by the Union Pacific Railroad, upon the tributaries of the Saskatchewan. Quite recently, a party of hunters in the district adjoining the country of the Blackfoot Indians, in longitude 110°, latitude 51°, was seven days in passing through a herd. The Saskatchewan district sent 17,930 buffalo-robes through Minnesota to market during the year ending September 30, 1872, while an equal number was either consumed in the country or despatched to Europe by vessels from York Factory, on Hudson's Bay."

Respecting the present range of the buffalo in that portion of the British Possessions immediately north of the United States line, I have been favored, through Principal J. W. Dawson of McGill College, Montreal, with the following important communication from Professor George M. Dawson, Geologist of the British and United States Boundary Survey, dated McGill College, Montreal, June 3, 1875: "Understanding from Principal Dawson that you wish to collect information as to the range of the buffalo in British North America, I have marked on the enclosed portion of a map the range of the animal on the forty-ninth parallel, of which alone I can speak from

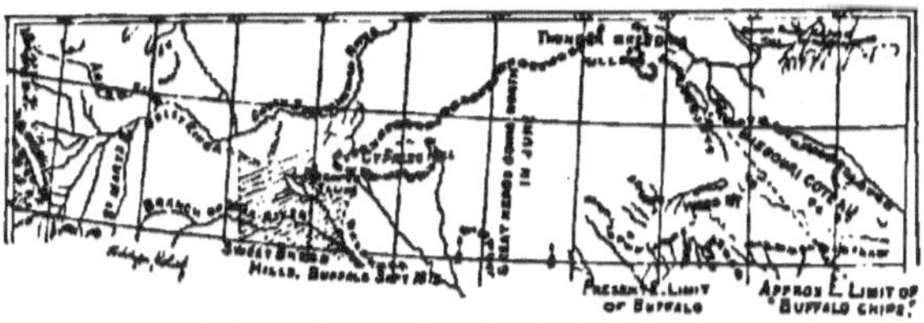

A reduced copy of the map above referred to by Professor Dawson.

The oblique dotted line to the right indicates approximately the eastern limit of "buffalo chips" in 1784; the arrows near the centre, the paths of migration in June, 1874; the shaded area to the left, the range in September, 1874.

personal knowledge. During the last sixteen years it would appear that the buffaloes have been driven back over two hundred miles on the forty-ninth parallel, and now do not extend in any force beyond White Mud River, or Frenchman's Creek (longitude 107° 30'). They reached this point when we arrived there late in June of last summer, and were going north in great herds, followed by the Sioux Indians. This migration seems to have ceased before about the 20th of July, when they were confined to the limits stated on the map,* and remained so till we left the country, in September. The Sweet Grass Hills form their centre in the vicinity of the Line. The pasture is good, and the region is besides a sort of neutral ground among the Indian tribes. We saw abundant traces of the passage of great herds in spring on the upper branches of Milk River, and they come in to the foot of the Rocky Mountains. I do not think they ever cross the mountains in the vicinity of the forty-ninth parallel, though I have seen their bones as far up the South Kootanie Pass as the last grassy meadow."

On the map referred to in the above-given letter, and reproduced in the adjoining wood-cut, it will be seen that a line drawn along Frenchman's Creek or White Mud River is given as the eastern limit of the present range of the buffalo, while the region a little to the west of this line is marked as the district where "great herds" were seen "going north in June." The line drawn parallel to the Little Souris River, and about forty miles to the westward of it, following the Coteau de Missouri, is given as the "approximate eastern limit of 'buffalo chips.'"

In addition to the information contained in Professor Dawson's letter, I find the following in his recent "Report on the Geology and Resources of the Region in the Vicinity of the Forty-ninth Parallel," etc.: "From what I could learn," says Professor Dawson, "I believe that, at the present rate of extermination, twelve to fourteen years will see the destruction of what now remains of the great northern band of buffalo, and the termination of the trade in robes and pemican, in so far as regards the country north of the Missouri River." †

Present Range of the Northern Herd. — From the foregoing it appears that what may be termed the great *Northern Herd* of buffaloes ranges from the principal southern tributaries of the Yellowstone northward over a large part of Montana, far into British North America, extending northward, doubtless, to the wooded region of the Athabasca and Peace Rivers. To the westward, north of the United States, buffaloes still range to the base of the Rocky Mountains, though doubtless somewhat irregularly, and usually

* A belt about seventy-five miles wide, situated on both sides of the 111th meridian, but lying mainly between the 111th and 112th meridians, and stretching northward towards the South Saskatchewan.

† Report on the Geology and Resources of the Region in the Vicinity of the Forty-ninth Parallel, etc., 1875, p. 296.

only in small numbers; while their eastern limit does not appear to extend beyond the longitude of Carlton House, or to the eastward of the 106th meridian. They have thus, within the last thirty years, become exterminated over more than half of the more fertile portion of the region north of the United States formerly occupied by them, including the whole of the vast prairie region drained by the Assinniboine and Qu'appelle Rivers, and are now confined principally to the arid plains between the two forks of the Saskatchewan, where, as Professor Dawson believes, they cannot survive for many years longer. Their numbers and the extent of their range north of the North Saskatchewan I have at present no means of determining, but it seems probable that their range has here also become greatly restricted since the time of Richardson and Franklin's visits to this region.

General Remarks respecting the rapid Diminution of the Buffalo, and its evident Destiny of speedy Total Extermination.

It thus appears that the buffalo has become so reduced in numbers, and so circumscribed in its range, that, instead of roaming over nearly half of the continent, as formerly, it is restricted to two small widely separated areas, the southern of which embraces portions of Texas, Colorado, and Kansas, scarcely exceeding in area the smaller of these States, while the northern embraces only the larger portion of the Territory of Montana and an adjoining area to the northward of nearly equal extent. Even as late as the beginning of the present century the buffalo occupied the whole of the region between the Mississippi and the Rocky Mountains, and extended from the Rio Grande on the south to Great Slave Lake on the north, and also over a considerable area west of the Rocky Mountains, or through thirty-five degrees of latitude and about twenty degrees of longitude. This immense habitat of almost a third of the continent has been reduced in three fourths of a century to a region not larger in the aggregate than the present Territories of Dakota and Montana. Over a large part of the former vast region they inhabited they were as numerous as they now are in Western Kansas or Northern Texas, and ranged at different seasons over the whole. Particular portions of this area have ever formed their favorite places of resort, where they were sure to be found at almost any season of the year. There is, for instance, abundant historic evidence that over the plains of Kansas, especially near the forks of the Platte, along the Republican, the Pawnee, the Canadian, and other tributaries of the Arkansas, they were as numerous when these parts were first visited by the early explorers as they have ever been since, and that subsequent travellers have always found them in immense numbers at all these points, the plains there literally swarming with them.

In this connection two questions naturally arise, especially in the minds of those not fully conversant with the subject: Have the buffalo really decreased to the extent these statements imply? or have they simply been driven in by the "encroachments of civilization" and concentrated upon a smaller area? Not a few otherwise intelligent persons, on visiting Western Kansas or Northern Texas and seeing the herds which there recently literally blackened the plains, at once adopt the latter hypothesis, and proclaim that this vast amount of talk about the decrease of the buffalo is all "nonsense"; that they are just as numerous as ever, and are not at all decreasing; that the extermination of the wolves and the Indians more than compensates for the slaughter made by the professional hunters and by the numerous sporting parties from the East.* The hunters often adopt the same theory, from the most evident reason of self-interest, fearing that some restrictions, which will act unfavorably upon their business, may be placed upon the wholesale and indiscriminate slaughter now carried on; yet the more candid are willing to admit that, at the present rate of destruction, the buffalo can last but a few years longer. That such is the truth is evident on a moment's reflection, when one has a full knowledge of the facts. Less than fifty years ago the buffaloes swarmed in as great — or certainly in very nearly as great — numbers as at the present time, *not only* over the regions they now frequent, but *at the same time* over the Laramie Plains, over much of the Green River Plateau, over the head-waters of the Colorado and Columbia Rivers, over the plains of the Yellowstone, and especially over the vast plains of the Red River of the North and the Grand Coteau de Missouri; throughout all of which region they have been gradually exterminated, leaving nothing to mark their former presence but their rapidly crumbling skeletal remains and their well-worn trails. Over much of this region

* In General Meigs's MS. notes on the buffalo, already quoted, he says: "It is a question whether the buffalo west of the Mississippi have diminished or increased in numbers to this time," and quotes General Sheridan's opinion in confirmation of this view. He says: "General Sheridan, the year after the Grand Duke of Russia hunted with him on the Kansas Pacific, told me that he thought there were probably *more buffalo that year than there had ever been before.* He had travelled through seventy miles of buffalo. He thought the killing by strychnine of wolves for the hides had saved many buffalo-calves, and the hostilities with Indians had prevented them from hunting as freely as usual for some years."

they have been not merely *driven out* and pressed on to some more secure retreat, but actually *exterminated*, the vast majority *being killed on the spot*, as we have seen was the case east of the Mississippi during the last quarter of the eighteenth century.

This shows with the utmost certainty what is to be the destiny of this former "monarch of the prairies," unless rigidly protected by legal restrictions, defining not only the seasons at which the animals may be killed, but also protecting the young and the bearing females. At the present time, as well as heretofore, those animals are most sought after on which the perpetuation of the race depends, — the young animals of both sexes and the cows. The older bulls are alike generally useless both to the Indian and the white hunter. The skins of cows are alone used by the Indians in furnishing themselves with robes; the young and middle-aged cows are regarded as especially desirable by the white hunters, since they afford the best meat for the market, although along with them are killed yearlings, and two- and three-year-olds of both sexes; but bulls older than five or six years are not generally desired, though many have of late years been killed merely for their hides. The hunting season being chiefly in the fall and winter, the cows are then with young, and thus two animals are killed in securing one.

Recent Destruction of the Buffalo in Kansas. — Some idea of the havoc recently made with the buffalo in Kansas can be formed from the following well-attested statements. At the time of the completion of the Atchison, Topeka, and Santa Fé Railroad to Dodge City, which occurred September 23, 1872, the principal trade of the town consisted in the "outfitting of hunters, and exchange for their game." The number of hides shipped during a period of three months, beginning with this date (Sept. 23), is reported to have been 43,029, and the shipment of meat for the same time 1,436,290 pounds.* The forty-three thousand hides of course represent forty-three thousand dead buffaloes, and the one million and a half pounds of meat — the saddles only being saved — represent at least six or seven thousand more, making a total of at least fifty thousand killed in three months. The same authority states that the returns for the January following exceeded those of the preceding months by over *one hundred and fifty per cent*, thus making the number of buffaloes killed merely "around Fort Dodge and the neighborhood," for this period of four months, exceed one hundred thousand!

* *Forest and Stream*, February, 1873.

This, too, is aside from those killed in "wanton cruelty, miscalled sport, and for food for the frontier residents."

Another report of about the same date, referring to a locality about one hundred miles southeast of Fort Dodge, says: "Thousands upon thousands of buffalo hides are being brought here [Wichita, Kansas] by hunters. In places whole acres of ground are covered with their hides, spread out, with their fleshy side up, to dry. It is estimated that there are, south of the Arkansas and west of Wichita, from one to two thousand men shooting buffalo for their hides alone." * Another account † states that during the season of 1872–73 not less than *two hundred thousand* buffaloes were killed in Kansas merely for their hides. ‡ It is also stated that in 1874, on "the south fork of the Republican, upon one spot, were to be counted six thousand five hundred carcasses of buffaloes, from which the hides only had been stripped. The meat was not touched, but left to rot on the plains. At a short distance hundreds more of carcasses were discovered, and, in fact, the whole plains were dotted with the putrefying remains of buffaloes. It was estimated that there were at least two thousand hunters encamped along the plains hunting the buffalo. One party of sixteen stated that they had killed twenty-eight hundred during the past summer, the hides only being utilized." The same account says that the extent of the slaughter of the buffalo for their hides was so great that the market for them became glutted to such an extent that whereas a few years before they were worth three dollars apiece at the railroad stations, skins of bulls would now bring only a dollar, and those of cows and calves sixty and forty cents respectively. § While on the plains in 1871, I had an opportunity of witnessing some of the evidences of the wholesale slaughter of buffaloes for their hides, as practised at that time along the line of the Kansas Pacific Railway in Northwestern Kansas, where sometimes several scores and even hundreds of decaying carcasses, from which nothing but the hides had been taken, could be seen from a single point of view. During the season of 1871 meat and hides representing over twenty thousand individuals were shipped over the Kansas Pacific Railway.

Mr. W. N. Byers, editor of the "Rocky Mountain News," in referring to this wholesale slaughter (in the letter previously quoted), characterizes it as

* *Wichita* (Kansas) *Eagle*.

† *Forest and Stream*, Oct. 15, 1873.

‡ General M. C. Meigs in his MS. notes says that one hundred and eighty thousand hides are reported to have passed over the Atchison, Topeka, and Santa Fé road alone in a single season.

§ Baird's Annual Record of Science and Industry for 1871, p. 304.

"simply inhuman and outrageous." He adds: "The slaughter-ground is mainly in Kansas, reaching only into the edge of Colorado. Practised hunters follow the herds day after day, and shoot them down by scores. Sixty, seventy, eighty or more a day is no unusual number. A good shooter will keep five or six 'skinners' at work. I heard a young man say within a week past that during the winter of 1873–74 he killed over three thousand buffaloes, — in one day eighty-five, in another sixty-four," etc.

Another writer thus refers to the same subject: "The butchery still [summer of 1875] goes on. Comparatively few buffalo are now killed, for there are comparatively few to kill. I was, in October of 1874, on a short trip to the buffalo region south of Sidney Barracks. A few buffalo were encountered, but there seemed to be more hunters than buffaloes. The country south of the South Platte is without water for many miles, and the buffaloes must satisfy their thirst at the river. The south bank was lined with hunters. Every approach of the buffaloes to water was met by rifle bullets, and one or more bit the dust. Care was taken not to permit the others to drink, for then they would not return. Tortured with thirst, the poor brutes approach again and again, always to be met by bullets, always to lose some of their number. But for the favoring protection of night the race would before now have been exterminated. In places favorable to such action, as the south bank of the Platte, a herd of buffalo has, by shooting at it by day and by lighting fires and firing guns at night, been kept from water for four days, or until it has been entirely destroyed. In many places the valley was offensive from the stench of putrefying carcasses. At the present time the southern buffalo can hardly be said to have a range. The term expresses a voluntary act, while the unfortunate animals have no volition left. They are driven from one water-hole to meet death at another. No sooner do they stop to feed than the sharp crack of a rifle warns them to change position. Every drink of water, every mouthful of grass, is at the expense of life, and the miserable animals, continually harassed, are driven into localities far from their natural haunts, — anywhere to avoid the unceasing pursuit. A few, probably some thousands, still linger about their beloved pastures in the Republican country. A few still hide in the deep cañons of the Cimarron country, but the mass of southern buffalo now living are to be found far away from the dreaded hunter, on a belt of country extending southwest across the upper tributaries of the Canadian, across the northern end of the Staked Plain to the Pecos River. The difficulty of getting the hides to market from these remote and Indian-infested regions is some guaranty that the buffalo will not be extinct for a few years."*

These facts are sufficient to show that the present decrease of the buffalo is extremely rapid, and indicate most clearly that the period of his extinction will soon be reached, unless some strong arm is interposed in his behalf. As yet no adequate game-laws for the protection of the buffalo, either by the different States and Territories included within its range, or by the general government, have been enacted. In a country so sparsely populated as is that ranged over by the buffalo, it might be difficult to enforce a proper law, yet the parties who prosecute the business of buffalo-hunting professionally are so well known that it would not be difficult to intercept them and bring them to justice, if found unlawfully destroying the buffalo. It is evident that restrictions should be made, not only in respect to season, but the young and the bearing females should be protected at all seasons. The government might even set apart certain districts within which the buffalo should be constantly exempt from persecution.†

Historical and Statistical Remarks respecting the Destruction and Reckless Waste of the Buffalo.

In addition to the statistics already given relating to the recent destruction of the buffalo in Kansas, it seems fitting in this connection to here append such additional statistical data as can be conveniently gathered concerning its destruction at large, together with a few remarks in respect to the causes and motives that have led to such a waste of life, and the agencies that have effected it.

The excitement of the chase, as is well known, seems almost universally to beget a spirit of wanton destructiveness of animal life. Wherever civil-

* Colonel Richard I. Dodge — See *Chicago Inter-Ocean* of August 5, 1875.

† Respecting this matter the following suggestions were made in Professor Baird's "Annual Record of Science and Industry" for 1874, p. 304: "As these animals range almost entirely within the Territories of the United States, it is within the province of Congress to enact laws prohibiting their destruction, but the difficulties lie in the matter of enforcing them. Possibly some provision for seizing and confiscating the green hides, along certain lines of railway or during certain seasons of the year, as a part of the penalty to be attached to the violation of the law on the subject, might accomplish the result; but, at any rate, the subject is one that demands the prompt attention of legislators, in view of the relationship of these animals to the welfare of the Indians, and the reaction which their destruction will produce upon the scattered white settlements in the vicinity of the range of both buffaloes and Indians."

ized man has met with the larger mammalia in abundance, as has often happened in the experience of explorers and pioneer settlers of newly discovered countries, the temptation to slaughter for the mere sake of killing seems rarely to be resisted. In the case of the carnivorous species an exterminating persecution is often pardonable, and to some extent necessary. The fur-bearing species, even when hunted to excess, are seldom destroyed wantonly, though often imprudently, the trapper blindly considering only his immediate profits. In the case of the harmless herbivorous species, the ungulates especially, self-interest, it would seem, would prompt an economical treatment of the game in newly settled districts. But the history of America shows that no such principle has here been regarded, where other animals than the buffalo — as the elk, moose, deer, prong-horn, and mountain sheep — have been slaughtered with the utmost recklessness. When stress of weather, for instance, or other circumstances, have brought these animals within the hunter's power, scores and even hundreds have often been killed by single parties already so well supplied with the products of the chase that they had no need for and could make no use of the animals thus destroyed. The buffaloes, from their great numbers and the little tact required in their capture, have probably been the victims of indiscriminate, improvident, and wanton slaughter to a greater extent than any other North American animal. As already stated, thousands are still killed annually merely for so-called "sport," no use whatever being made of them; thousands of others of which only the tongue or other slight morsel is saved; hundreds of thousands of others for their hides, which yield the hunter but little more than enough to pay him for the trouble of taking and selling them; while many more, though escaping from their would-be captors, die of their wounds and yield no return whatever to their murderers.* Of the hundreds of thousands that for the last few years have been annually killed, probably less than a fourth have been to any great extent utilized. While this wanton and careless waste has ever characterized the contact of the white race with the sluggish and inoffensive bison of our plains and prairies, the Indians have likewise been improvident in their slaughter of this animal, often killing hundreds or even thousands more during their grand

* Professional buffalo-hunters of the Kansas plains repeatedly assured me that they believe that an average of not more than one in three of the buffaloes killed by them were secured and made use of. From extended observations, however, I felt convinced that this was quite too high an estimate of the proportion unrecovered of those killed. Yet the waste is actually enormous, even in the contingencies of hunting for legitimate purposes, namely, for frontier consumption and shipment to Eastern markets.

annual hunts than they could possibly use, or from which they saved merely the tongues. The wolves were formerly also a great check upon the increase of the buffalo, but the hunters by means of poison have reduced their number much more rapidly than even that of the buffalo, so that the influence of the wolves in hastening the extirpation of the buffalo is now but slight. The Indians, too, have vanished before the westward advance of the white man more rapidly even than the buffalo, so that the destruction of the buffalo by the Indians is now relatively far less than formerly. Hence the opinion, as stated in the preceding pages, has been advanced, and to some extent publicly advocated, that the present rate of the decrease of the buffalo is actually less than formerly, notwithstanding the vast numbers annually killed by white hunters, in consequence of the greatly reduced numbers of the wolves and the Indians. A slight glance at the history of the decline of the buffalo, however, is sufficient to at once indicate the fallacy of such an opinion; and none are better aware of this than the most active participators in their destruction,— the professional buffalo-hunters themselves,— many of whom are candid enough to admit that, through the almost utter extermination of the buffalo, their present occupation will soon pass away, unless the general or local governments enforce the most peremptory restrictions upon their slaughter.

The Indians, prior to the discovery of the continent by Europeans, appear not to have seriously affected the number of buffaloes, their natural increase equalling the number destroyed both by the Indians and the wolves. When the Jesuit missionaries penetrated the range of the buffalo east of the Mississippi, in the seventeenth century, they found this animal the main subsistence of the Indian tribes, as it doubtless had been for centuries, its flesh serving them for food, its skins for shields, clothing, and tents, and its hair, wool, horns, hoofs, and bones for various articles of ornament and use. No sooner, however, had Europeans made settlements within its range, than the buffaloes began to disappear, and were either wholly destroyed or driven from their favorite haunts in the short space of a very few years. The destruction increased with the increase of the white population till they were totally exterminated east of the Mississippi (at least, south of the present State of Minnesota), as already shown, prior to the beginning of the nineteenth century. Even as late as fifty years ago they occupied a considerable area west of the Rocky Mountains, all the extensive parks and valleys within these mountains, and all the vast plains and prairies between them and the Mississippi River. The fur-hunters and trappers appear to have begun at this date to contribute appreciably toward their rapid diminution, but not until the establishment of the "overland trails," and the constant passing of large emigrant parties across the plains, did their numbers here become very greatly diminished. Steadily pressed back on their eastern boundary by advancing settlements, they were at the same time rapidly thinned along the line of the great emigrant routes. These thoroughfares becoming from year to year more numerously travelled, especially the more northern route by way of the South Pass, the buffaloes were driven to the right and left of the line of travel, till finally by this intersection their range was divided into two essentially distinct regions. The construction of the Union Pacific Railroad completely severed the northern from the southern herds, while the Kansas Pacific and the Atchison, Topeka, and Santa Fé Roads opened up new highways to their most populous holds. In the mean time adventurers and miners either gradually exterminated them in the parks and valleys of the mountains, or drove them eastward into the plains, while they were at the same time preyed upon by the great buffalo-hunting parties from the Red River Settlements and the United States, until they have dwindled to a few hard-pressed bands lingering chiefly in the least-frequented parts of their formerly almost undisturbed haunts.

A century ago the rapid extermination of the buffalo had begun to attract the attention of travellers, Romans, as early as 1776, alluding to the wanton destruction of "this excellent beast, *for the sake of perhaps his tongue only*." * As early as 1820 Major Long thought it highly desirable that some law should be enforced for the preservation of the bison from wanton destruction by the white hunters, who, he said, were accustomed to attack large herds, and from *mere wantonness* slaughter as many as they were able and leave the carcasses to be devoured by the wolves and birds of prey.†

Gregg, in 1835, also alludes to the wanton slaughter of these animals by travellers and hunters, and the still greater havoc made among them by the Indians, who often kill them merely for their skins and tongues. Their total annihilation he regarded as only a question of time, although he believed that if they were only killed for food, their natural increase would perhaps replenish the loss.‡ Almost every intelligent traveller who has crossed the

* Natural History of Florida, p. 174.

† Long's Expedition, Vol. I, p. 482.

‡ Commerce of the Prairies, Vol. II, p. 213.

plains or spent much time in the buffalo country has also called attention to this exterminating slaughter, and predicted their complete annihilation at no very distant date. Some writers believed twenty or thirty years ago that they would hardly survive to the present time unless protected by the government.

Dr. Leidy, in 1852, says: "The day is not far distant when it [the buffalo] will become quite extinct, unless protected by a munificent republic, as has been done by the Emperor of Russia in the case of the aurochs, or European bison." * Professor Baird, writing at about the same time, says: "Still, vast as these herds are, their numbers are much less than in earlier times, and they are diminishing with fearful rapidity. Every year sees more or less change in this respect, as well as alterations of their great line of travel. . . . . If it were possible to enforce game-laws, or any other laws on the prairies, it would be well to attach the most stringent penalties against the barbarous practice of killing buffalo merely for the sport, or perhaps for the tongues alone. Thousands are killed every year in this way. After all, however, it is perhaps the Indian himself who commits the mischief most wantonly." †

General W. F. Raynolds, in his report of his Exploration of the Yellowstone in 1859 and 1860, thus refers to this matter: ‡ "And here I would remark, that the wholesale destruction of the buffalo is a matter that should receive the attention of the proper authorities. It is due to the fact that the skin of the *female* is alone valuable for robes. The skin of the male over three years old is never used for that purpose, the hair on the hind quarters being not longer than that on a horse, while on the fore quarters it has a length of from four to six inches. The skin is also too thick and heavy to be used for anything but lodge coverings, while the flesh is coarse and unpalatable, and is never used for food when any other can be had. The result is that the females are always singled out by the hunter, and consequently the males in a herd always exceed the females, in the proportion of ten to one. Another, but far less important cause of their extinction is the immense number of wolves in the country, which destroy the young. The only remedy that would have the slightest effect in the case would be a prohibition of the trade of buffalo-robes, and a premium upon wolf-skins. I fear

* Mem. Extinct Species of American Ox, p. 4 (Smith. Contrib., Vol. V, Art. III).

† Pat. Off. Rep., Agricult., 1851 – 52, Part II, p. 123.

‡ Exploration of the Yellowstone, p. 11, published in 1868.

it is too late for even this remedy, and notwithstanding the immense herds that are yet to be found, I think it is more than probable that another generation will witness almost the entire extinction of this noble animal."

During the fifteen years that have passed since this was written, the wolves have in a great measure been exterminated over much of the buffalo range, but something far more fatal to the buffalo than anything then known — the railroad — has penetrated its range, and while the females and the young are still slaughtered with the same recklessness as before, the old bulls have of late been hunted with almost equal eagerness.

Statistics relating to the Destruction of the Buffalo, based principally on the Trade in Robes. — Frémont, in 1845, published some statistics furnished him by Mr. Sanford, a partner of the American Fur Company, respecting the number of robes annually obtained from the Indians by the different fur companies. The average return for the preceding eight or ten years is given as ninety thousand annually. "In the Northwest," says Mr. Sanford, "the Hudson's Bay Company purchase from the Indians but a very small number — their market being Canada, to which the cost of transportation nearly equals the produce of the furs; and it is only within a very recent period that they have received buffalo robes in trade; and out of the great number of buffalo annually killed throughout the extensive regions inhabited by the Camanches and other kindred tribes [Texas, the Indian Territory, and Kansas] no robes whatever are furnished for trade. During only four months of the year (from November until March) the skins are good for dressing; those obtained in the remaining eight months being valueless to traders; and the hides of bulls are never taken off or dressed as robes at any season. Probably not more than one third of the skins are taken from the animals killed, even when they are in good season, the labor of preparing and dressing the robes being very great; and it is seldom that a lodge trades more than twenty skins in a year. It is during the summer months, and in the early part of autumn, that the greatest number of buffalo are killed, and yet at this time a skin is never taken for the purpose of trade." *

Besides the number of robes traded by the Indians, as many or a greater number were at this time annually used by the Indians themselves. This would make, at a moderate estimate, the annual number of about two hundred thousand robes, which represent, according to the competent authority above cited, only *one third* of the buffaloes killed during about *one third of the*

* Frémont's First and Second Expeditions, p. 145.

year, and during that part of the year, too, when the smallest number are destroyed. Taking the above data as a basis for an estimate, the whole number killed annually by the Indians must have equalled eighteen hundred thousand (1,800,000). Allowing a slight addition for the relatively greater number killed during the warmer parts of the year, we have, in round numbers, the startling total of about two millions as the average annual number destroyed by only those tribes of Indians who were accustomed to collect robes for the market. These embraced only a small portion of the tribes living within or on the borders of the great buffalo range; so that probably two millions a year is much less than half the number killed at this time by the Indians alone. Besides this, travellers and white hunters killed annually hundreds of thousands more. When we consider that this enormous destruction continued for several decades, we need no longer be surprised at the rapid numerical decrease of the buffalo that has marked the last forty or fifty years of his history.

In 1852 Professor Baird wrote: "Mr. Picotte, an experienced partner of the American Fur Company, estimated the number of buffalo-robes sent to St. Louis in 1850 at one hundred thousand. Supposing each of the sixty thousand Indians on the Missouri to use ten robes for his wearing apparel every year, besides those for new lodges and other purposes, by the calculation of Mr. Picotte, we shall have an aggregate of four hundred thousand [*sic*] robes [seven hundred thousand?]. We may suppose one hundred thousand as the number killed wantonly or destroyed by fire or other casualties, and we will have the grand total of half a million [eight hundred thousand?] of buffalo destroyed every year. This, too, does not include the numbers slaughtered on Red River and other gathering points."* In this estimate the important fact is overlooked that the robes are all taken during three months of the year, at a season too when the smallest number are killed, and that only about one third of those killed during these three months are utilized for robes. If this number should be multiplied by nine, as it evidently must be from the above-quoted statements of Mr. Sanford, and which from general considerations also seems probable, we should have the immense total of from five to seven millions as the number killed yearly by the Indians who furnished the one hundred thousand robes for the St. Louis market! Ten robes, however, seems to be a large number to be used annually by each person. If we reduce the number to three, we shall still have an

* Pat. Off. Rep., Agricult., 1851-52, Part II, p. 125.

annual aggregate of nearly three and a half millions as the number destroyed by the Upper Missouri tribes alone. South of this region there were at this time upwards of forty thousand Indians belonging to other tribes living within the range of the buffalo, besides the numerous populous tribes inhabiting the buffalo range north of the United States. The number that must have been killed each year by all these tribes together is a startling sum to contemplate.

In 1854 the Hon. H. H. Sibley, in his paper on the buffalo contained in Schoolcraft's "History, Condition, and Prospects of the Indian Tribes of the United States," gives a later estimate of their annual destruction in the Missouri region. He says: "From data which, although not mathematically correct, are sufficiently so to enable us to arrive at conclusions approximating the truth, it has been estimated that for each buffalo-robe transported from the Indian country, at least five animals* are destroyed. If it be borne in mind that very few robes are manufactured of the hides of buffalo except such as, in hunter's parlance, are killed when they are in season, that is during the months of November, December, and January, and that even of these a large proportion are not used for that purpose, and also that the skins of the cows are principally converted into robes, those of the males being too thick and heavy to be easily reduced by the ordinary process of scraping; together with the fact that many thousands are annually destroyed through sheer wantonness, by civilized as well as savage men, it will be found that the foregoing estimate is a moderate one. From the Missouri region the number of robes received varies from forty thousand to one hundred thousand, so that from a quarter to half a million of buffaloes are destroyed in the period of each twelvemonth." †

From the preceding remarks it is evident that Mr. Sibley's estimate is far below the truth. Since as many robes are doubtless used by the Indians themselves as they sell, this number must include not more than half of the robes taken during only three or four months of the year. Hence instead of one fourth to half a million representing the number annually killed at this date in the Missouri region, probably a million to a million and a half would be a much nearer estimate.

In June, 1873, I met at Fort Abraham Lincoln, Dakota Territory, Mr. F.

* Evidently quite too low an estimate.

† Schoolcraft's History, Condition, and Prospects of the Indian Tribes of the United States, Vol. IV, p. 94.

F. Gerard, the well-known Cree interpreter, whose twenty-five years' experience in the Upper Missouri country, nearly every part of which he had visited, together with his having been formerly an agent of the American Fur Company, had given him much valuable information respecting not only the fur trade but the former range and the recent great decrease in numbers of many of the larger mammals of that region. From him I learned that in 1857 the trade in buffalo-robes at the principal posts on the Upper Missouri was about as follows: At Fort Benton, the number received amounted to 3,600 bales, or 36,000 robes; at Fort Union, 2,700 to 3,000 bales, or about 30,000 robes. At Forts Clarke and Berthoud, 500 bales at each post, or about 10,000 robes; at Fort Pierre, 1,900 bales, or 19,000 robes; giving a total for one year of about 75,000 robes, which he informed me was about the annual average at that period. Allowing that the Indians retained only as many more for their own use, and estimating as before that one robe represents the destruction of three buffaloes, gives four hundred and fifty thousand as the number killed by a portion only of the Upper Missouri Indians in one third of a year, or over a million and a third annually. To this number, as already noticed, must be added the number killed by the Indians to the northward and southward of this region, as well as the great numbers destroyed by the Red River half-breeds and by white men.

Respecting the number killed by the Red River hunters, I have met with no satisfactory statistics, but that it must have been immense is evident from the number of persons engaged in their hunting expeditions. Mr. Ross, in his history of the Red River Settlement, states that the number of carts assembled for the first trip in 1820 was five hundred and forty. Subsequently the number regularly increased to one thousand two hundred and ten in 1840. In his description of the hunt of this year, he states that the number of hunters engaged was six hundred and twenty for two months, who were accompanied by six hundred and fifty women, and three hundred and sixty boys and girls, the party numbering altogether sixteen hundred and thirty souls. The party was armed with seven hundred and forty guns, and had with them eleven hundred and fifty-eight horses and five hundred and eighty-six draught oxen, with other equipments in proportion. During the first day of the hunt no less than thirteen hundred and seventy-five buffalo tongues were brought into camp, and during the first two races not less than twenty-five hundred animals were killed. Of these he estimates that less than one third were properly utilized, as he considers that seven hundred and fifty animals, making all due allowance for waste, would have been ample for the amount of pemmican and dried meat saved from them. The rest, he says, was wasted; "and this," he adds, "is only a fair example of the manner in which the plain business is carried on under the present system. Scarcely one third in number of the animals killed are turned to account."*

Dr. Hayden, in 1861, says that as near as he could determine, about one hundred thousand robes were then annually made by the Indians of the Upper Missouri country.† Dr. Hayden also states that at this period the bulls outnumbered the cows ten to one; which personal experience led me to think was a fair estimate of the proportion of the sexes in 1871 on the plains of Kansas.

Through the kindness of E. T. Bowen, Esq., General Superintendent of the Kansas Pacific Railway, I have obtained a statement of the "estimated shipments of buffalo products over the Kansas Pacific Railway during the year 1871." This estimate, carefully prepared by the Auditor of the Company, is as follows: Dry hides, three hundred and forty-one thousand, one hundred and fifty-one (341,151) pounds, estimated at twenty-five pounds per hide, and thus representing thirteen thousand six hundred and forty-six (13,646) buffaloes; eleven hundred and sixty-one thousand four hundred and nineteen (1,161,419) pounds of meat, estimated at two hundred pounds per saddle, and thus representing five thousand eight hundred and seven (5,807) buffaloes. No return is here made of the large amount of salted and cured meat also sent to Eastern markets. The somewhat less than six thousand "saddles" represented by the above statement must, it appears to me, be far below the actual number, as one hunter informed me that he had himself alone killed over three thousand buffaloes a year for several years, and I met other persons who claimed to have each killed an equal number. These statistics would alone indicate a slaughter of at least twenty thousand buffaloes along the line of the Kansas Pacific Railway during the year 1871, to which must be added other thousands killed by travellers and amateur hunters, and by the officers and soldiers stationed at the different military posts in the same region.

I have been unable to obtain statistics of the shipment of buffalo products over this road since 1871, as such information, writes the present Superintendent of the road, is not in available shape, and to obtain it would

* Ross (Alexander), The Red River Settlement; its Rise, Progress, and Present State, pp. 242-265.

† Trans. Am. Phil. Soc., New Series, Vol. XII, p. 151.

involve considerable expense. There has, however, been a great falling off in the annual amounts shipped since that date, in consequence of the great decrease of the buffalo throughout the region through which this road passes.

Respecting the quantity of the products of the buffalo shipped over the Atchison, Topeka, and Santa Fé Railroad during the years 1872, 1873, and 1874, I have been favored with the following statement by the General Superintendent, Mr. C. F. Morse:—

Statement of Buffalo Products shipped over the Atchison, Topeka, and Santa Fé Railroad during a period of three years, from 1872 to 1875.

Hides, in 1872,	165,721
" in 1873,	251,443
" in 1874,	42,289
Robes, in 1872,	No account.
" in 1873,	" "
" in 1874,	18,489
Meat, in 1872,	No account.
" in 1873,	1,617,600 lbs.
" in 1874,	632,800 "
Bones, in 1872,	1,135,300 lbs.
" in 1873,	2,743,100 "
" in 1874,	6,914,900 "

From the above statement it appears that the number of hides shipped over this road during a period of three years was nearly half a million, while the robes, of which the number shipped in a single year only is given, would make the number exceed this sum. In addition to this number we have to add, for the number of buffaloes utilized or sold as meat, only the small number of from three to eight thousand a year more!

In answer to inquiries respecting the shipment of buffalo products over the Union Pacific Railroad, I have been kindly informed by Mr. E. P. Vining, General Freight Agent, that no large amount of buffalo products has been received by this road, and that consequently no statistics of the business have been kept, as is the case with all the important branches of their business. These statistics respecting the shipments over the railroads relate only to the Kansas range of the buffalo, and hence refer merely to a limited district, and to the slaughter by white hunters alone.

In respect to the recent destruction of the buffalo north of the United States, Mr. J. W. Taylor, United States Consul at Winnipeg, B. N. A., whose valuable communication on the buffalo has been previously quoted, informs me that about eighteen thousand robes were sent to the Minnesota market from the Saskatchewan district alone during the year ending September 30, 1872, while as many more were either consumed in the country or sent to Europe by the way of York Factory, or about forty thousand in all. By far the larger part of the buffaloes killed in the Saskatchewan district, however, are converted into pemmican and dried meat, and, being killed in summer, do not enter at all into the above statement made by Mr. Taylor. From these data it is evident that the destruction of the buffalo in the Saskatchewan region in 1872 must have amounted to considerably more than a million, and these mainly cows.

In forming a general estimate of the annual destruction of the buffalo in recent years, it is necessary to add to the large sums already given the large number killed by the different Indian tribes still residing in or near the ranges of the two herds, as well as the thousands killed for frontier consumption, and the many thousands more of which no use is made. Even approximate data for the last-named elements of the problem of course do not exist, but the total killed between 1870 and 1875 cannot have been less than about two and a half millions annually. The effect of this destruction upon the already terribly thinned herds has been most marked, and if continued at a proportional rate will unquestionably in a few years exterminate the race.

2. — Products of the Buffalo.

The flesh of the buffalo is, of course, its most important product, either to the white man or the Indian.' It has not only always formed a large part of the food of the Indian tribes living within its range, but has also proved hardly less important to the whites during their first exploration of the country it inhabited. The various military and other surveys of the great central plateau of the continent, as well as the numerous private expeditions to the same region, could have been accomplished only at greatly increased expense and privation had not the buffalo supplied to the persons engaged in these enterprises a never-failing and ready means of subsistence.

The buffaloes, in common with deer and elks, have also often been invaluable to the pioneer settler, insuring him food during the first few years at least of his frontier life. As already noticed, Boone and his party subsisted almost wholly during their first winter in Kentucky on the flesh of this animal, and throughout the prairie portions of the country, from Illinois westward to the Rocky Mountains, the buffalo has subserved a most important purpose in the westward progress of civilization. The vast influx of settlers that follows the opening of new railroads across the Plains, such as that which still sets into the valley of the Arkansas along the line of the Atchison, Topeka, and Santa Fé Railroad, thus find a sure subsistence until they can open up and improve their farms; and, as one writer has remarked, "by the time the last buffalo has disappeared from Kansas, the frontier will be subdued to civilization and be self-supporting."

From lack of speedy and cheap means of transportation the consumption of buffalo meat was, until recently, necessarily limited to the people living near or within its actual range, and to parties traversing the country it inhabited. Upon the opening of the Kansas railways, however, many car-loads, as already shown by the above-given statistics, were shipped during winter to the Eastern cities. While Chicago, St. Louis, Cincinnati, and the other larger cities of the Mississippi Valley formed the principal markets for its sale, it was also sent in large quantities to Boston, New York, Philadelphia, Baltimore, and the other chief cities of the East.* When arriving in good condition, as was usually the case, it rivals beef and venison in cheapness, if not in quality, besides having the special feature of novelty.

The meat of the buffalo is often spoken of as being dry and tough, and far inferior in quality to beef. This is in a measure true, the flesh of middle-aged and elderly bulls being of this character, that of old bulls being eaten only when none other can be obtained. The flesh of a young fat cow, or of a yearling or two-year-old bull, however, is not surpassed by the finest beef, from which it cannot usually be distinguished. During some two months spent on the Kansas plains in 1871–72, I ate it daily, and would never ask

* As already noticed, upward of one million pounds were shipped, as saddles, over the Kansas Pacific Railway during the winter of 1871–72, besides hundreds of barrels of tongues and cured "hams" during the same period. Since that time the shipments over this road have greatly diminished, but the reduction was for a year or two more than balanced by the additional shipments over the Atchison, Topeka, and Santa Fé road, which in 1873 were over one and a half million (1,617,600) pounds. In 1874, however, the shipment was less than half this amount, there having been already a marked decline in the amount of buffalo products transported over this road also.

for, as indeed I have never tasted, finer beef than the buffalo meat, which was almost exclusively used. Often at the hotel in Hays City, as well as at other public tables in the buffalo country, have I heard the beef praised by Eastern travellers, who frequently expressed their surprise at the excellent quality of this article set before them. Often, too, in the same connection, our Eastern traveller would ask about buffalo meat, whether it was fit to eat, whether it was much used for food, and whether he would be likely to get a chance to taste it in his journey across the plains. When told that he had just partaken of it, that it was buffalo beef which he had been praising, and that it was the staple meat of the table throughout the buffalo country, at the hotels and restaurants as well as in the hunter's camp, his surprise amounted almost to incredulity, which only the strongest assurances would remove. The age and condition of the animal, as already stated, has much to do with the quality of the meat, and a more miserable semblance of food could hardly be set before one than a steak cut from one of the old "lords of the prairie."

The tongue of even an old bull is always regarded as a delicate morsel, and is often saved when no other part of the animal is touched. The hump is generally considered to be next in delicacy and tenderness. A few hunters killed buffaloes during the autumn months for the purpose of curing the meat. The best pieces only, from young and tender animals, were selected, and when properly cured were fully equal to the best dried and smoked beef found in the Eastern markets. A single hunter at Hays City shipped annually for some years several hundred barrels thus prepared, which the consumers probably bought for ordinary beef.*

Further northward, on the plains of the Saskatchewan, Assinniboine, Red River, and Upper Missouri, large quantities of the meat were formerly made into pemmican. In this form it proves invaluable to the Northern *voyageurs* and trappers, of whose commissariat it formed the chief resource. Hind states that the Hudson's Bay Company formerly obtained from the Plain Crees, the Assinniboines, and the Ojibways, pemmican and dried meat to

* Dr. Richardson's testimony respecting the quality of bison meat is as follows: "The flesh of the bison, in good condition, is very juicy and well flavored, much resembling that of well-fed beef. The tongue is deemed a delicacy, and may be cured so as to surpass in flavor the tongue of an English cow. The hump of flesh covering the long spinous processes of the first dorsal vertebræ is much esteemed. It . . . . has a fine grain, and when salted and cut transversely, it is almost as rich and tender as the tongue." — *Fauna Boreali-Americana*, Vol. I, p. 282.

supply the brigades of boats in their expeditions to York Factory, on Hudson's Bay, and throughout the interior.*

Pemmican, though made sometimes from the meat of other animals, as deer, elk, moose, mountain sheep, and reindeer, is prepared principally from the buffalo. It is put up in bags of from ninety to one hundred and ten pounds' weight (according to different authorities), and consists of nearly equal parts, by weight, of pounded dried meat and tallow. The method of its preparation has been repeatedly described by different Northern travellers,† whose accounts differ somewhat in respect to the details, as they do in respect to its flavor and desirability as an article of food. The Earl of Southesk ‡ speaks of it as scarcely endurable, and Captain Butler says that when prepared in the best form it "can be eaten, provided the appetite be sharp and there is nothing else to be had, — this last consideration is, however, of importance." § It proves, however, to be exceedingly nutritious, and is the favorite food of the Indians and the half-breed *voyageurs*, and was formerly so extensively used in the Red River Settlement that the supply was never adequate to the demand.‖ According to Mr. Sibley's account, as furnished him by the Rev. Mr. Belcourt,¶ a Catholic priest residing among the Red River half-breeds, the dried meat and the pemmican are prepared by these people as follows: —

"The meat, when taken to the camp, is cut by the women into long strips, about a quarter of an inch thick, which are hung upon the lattice-work prepared for that purpose, to dry. This lattice-work is formed by small pieces of wood placed horizontally, transversely, and equi-distant from each other, not unlike an immense gridiron, and is supported by wooden uprights (trépieds). In a few days the meat is thoroughly desiccated, when it is bent into proper lengths, and tied in bundles of sixty or seventy pounds' weight. This is called dried meat (viande séche). Other portions, which are destined

* Narrative of the Canadian Exploring Expedition, Vol. I, p. 311.

† See Ross, The Red River Settlement, pp. 262–264; Sibley, in Schoolcraft's History, Condition, and Prospects of the Indian Tribes, Part IV, p. 107; Hind, Canadian Exploring Expedition, Vol. I, p. 312; Butler, The Great Lone Land, p. 153, etc.

‡ Saskatchewan and the Rocky Mountains, p. 302.

§ The Great Lone Land, p. 134.

‖ Ross, Red River Settlement, p. 165.

¶ Mr. Belcourt's account appears to have been previously communicated to Major S. Woods, by whom it was published in the original French as early as 1840, in his report of his Expedition to the Pembina Settlements. See Congress. Rep., 31st Congress, 1st Session, House Ex. Doc., Vol. VIII, No. 54, pp. 44–52.

to be made into *pimikchigan*, or pemican, are exposed to an ardent heat, and thus become brittle, and easily reducible to small particles by the use of a flail; the buffalo-hide answering the purpose of a threshing-floor. The fat, or tallow, being cut up and melted in large kettles of sheet-iron, is poured upon this pounded meat, and the whole mass is worked together with shovels, until it is well amalgamated, when it is pressed, still warm, into bags made of buffalo-skin, which are strongly sewed up, and the mixture gradually cools and becomes almost as hard as a rock. If the fat used in the process is taken from the parts containing the udder, the meat is called *fine pemican*. In some cases dried fruits, such as the prairie-pear and cherry, are intermixed, which make what is called *seed pemican*. The lovers of good eating judge the first described to be very palatable; the second, better; the third, excellent. A taureau of pemican weighs from one hundred to one hundred and ten pounds. Some idea may be formed of the immense destruction of buffalo by these people when it is stated that a whole cow yields one half a bag of pemican, and three fourths of a bundle of dried meat; so that the most economical calculate that from eight to ten cows are required for the load of a single vehicle." * The same account says that "the men break the bones; which are boiled in water to extract the marrow to be used for frying and for other culinary purposes. The oil is then poured into the bladder of the animal, which contains, when filled, about twelve pounds; being the yield of the marrow-bones of two buffaloes." † Ross states that "a bull in good condition will yield forty-five pounds of clean rendered tallow," and that cows when in good order yield on an average about thirty-five pounds. ‡

Prior to the time of railroad communication with the Plains, however, the most important commercial product of the buffalo was its robes. For many years, as is evident from the statistics already given, not less than one hundred thousand robes were annually purchased of the Indians, a considerable portion of which found their way to European markets. In recent years there has been a marked decline in the production of robes, owing in part to the rapid extirpation of the buffalo, but more especially to the great depopulation, through wars and contagious diseases, of the Indian tribes of the Plains, by whom most of the robes have hitherto been prepared. A few are still gathered in the United States by the Indian traders, and of late

* Schoolcraft's History, Condition, and Prospects of the Indian Tribes, Part IV, p. 107.

† Ibid., p. 107.

‡ Red River Settlement, p. 262.

white hunters have turned their attention to their preservation. Thus in the above-given returns of the shipment of buffalo products over the Atchison, Topeka, and Santa Fé Railroad occurs the item of eighteen thousand four hundred and eighty-nine robes in the statement for the year 1874.

To the Indians of the Plains the buffalo has not only ever been an unfailing source of food, — whose flesh, Catlin states,* they prefer to that of the antelope, deer, or elk, — but has also furnished them, to a great extent, with shelter and clothing; the heavier, coarser skins of the bulls being used as lodge-coverings, and those of the cows for beds and clothing.

According to the Jesuit missionaries, the women of the Illinois Indians used to employ the hair of the buffalo in making bands, belts, and sacks; and these and other tribes used also to make shields of the hides, and spoons, ladles, etc., from the horns and bones. Gomara, in speaking of the Indians of the Plains, says, "and of their hides they make many things, as houses, shooes, apparell, and ropes: of their bones they make bodkins: of their sinewes and haire, thread: of their dung, fire: and of their calves-skinnes, budgets, wherein they drawe and keepe water. To bee short, they make so many things of them as they have need of, or as many as suffice them in the use of this life." †

During the last few years many skins of buffaloes have been taken by the white hunters for the purpose of preparing leather from them. At the lowest estimate more than a million buffaloes have been sacrificed for this purpose in Kansas alone during the last five years. I say *sacrificed* in this connection advisedly, because the amount realized by the hunters from the sale of these hides scarcely brings them a return equal to the wages of an ordinary laborer in other pursuits. The "buffalo-skinners," as they are sometimes derisively termed, practise their ignoble calling mainly during the warmer months, when the weather will not permit of the shipment of meat to the Eastern markets, and seem to follow the business more from a love of the wild, semi-barbarous, out-door life of the plains-hunter than for any anticipated profit.

Generally in hunting buffaloes for their hides only the old bulls are killed, which are of little account in a pecuniary point of view for any other purpose, but some hunters are so reckless of even their own interest as to take any animal that comes in their way. Aside from the diminution in the

* North American Indians, Vol. I, p. 24.

† Translation in Hakluyt's Voyages, Vol. III, p. 456.

number of buffaloes resulting from this reckless and almost unremunerative slaughter, the herds are harassed and kept wandering from place to place the whole year, which of course greatly interferes with their multiplication. It should be said, however, that this destruction of the buffalo in summer for its hide has not generally met with the approval of the better class of hunters, among whom there has been at times a strong feeling against it, it being chiefly carried on by those who were too unthrifty to seek employment in other pursuits during the time when buffalo-hunting for the Eastern market was not in season. Sometimes the more intelligent and influential portion of the hunters would warn the transgressors to desist from their unseasonable slaughter or immediately leave the country, on pain of summary treatment,—an admonition which was generally so effective as not to require a repetition.

The hide of the buffalo makes but an inferior, porous kind of leather, useful, however, for certain purposes, such as covers for carriage-tops, belt-leather, etc. The average net price realized by the hunter is generally less than a dollar per hide, usually from fifty to seventy-five cents, while it occasionally happens that in shipping a car-load of hides to the Eastern market the hunter is left in debt to the broker, whose deduction for freight and charges for commission exceed the price allowed for the skins.

The coarse wool of the buffalo early attracted attention as an article of commercial value. The early Jesuit explorers stated that the Indians were accustomed to weave it into ornamental or useful fabrics, and usually enumerated it as one of the products of the buffalo that would render the animal valuable under domestication. Charlevoix says that the wives of the Illinois Indians were accustomed to spin the buffalo-wool and make it as fine as that of English sheep.* Marquette says, referring to the same tribes, "they presented us with belts, garters, and other articles made of the hair of bears and buffaloes"; and adds that "their chiefs are distinguished from the soldiers by red scarfs made of the hair of buffaloes, curiously wrought." † Father Marest also enumerates among the employments of the Illinois Indians the making of "bands, belts, and sacks" from the hair of the buf-

* Charlevoix says, in describing the Illinois Indians: "Their Wives are sufficiently dexterous: They spin the Buffalo's Wool, and make it as fine as that of *English* Sheep. Sometimes one would even take it for Silk. They make Stuffs of it, which they dye black, yellow, and a dark red. They make Gowns of it, which they sew with the Thread made of the Sinews of Roe-Bucks." — *Letters*, etc., English ed., p. 293.

† Hist. Coll. Louisiana, Vol. II, p. 288.

falo.* Brackenridge, in a work published in 1814, says: "The wool of the buffaloe has a peculiar fineness, even surpassing that of the merino. I have seen gloves made of it, little inferior to silk. But for the difficulty of separating the hair, it might become a very important article of commerce. Should any means be discovered of effecting this, or should it be found that at certain seasons there is less of this mixture, the buffalo wool must become of prime importance in manufactures." This author adds in a footnote as follows: "It is curious to observe, that in the instruction to Iberville by the King of France, two things were considered of the first importance, the *pearl fishery* and the *buffaloe wool*. Charlevoix observes, that he is not surprised that the first should not have been attended to, but he thinks it strange that the second should be neglected even to his time."†

The early explorers of the country east of the Mississippi evidently very generally looked upon the buffalo as an animal that would prove of very great economic value. M. de la Galissonière, in a "Memoir on the French Colonies in North America," written in 1750, speaks especially of the prospective value of the buffalo to the French settlers of the Illinois country. After describing the vast prairies "waiting only for the plough," he refers to their being "covered with an innumerable multitude of buffaloes,—a species," he says, "which will probably not run out for many centuries hence, both because the country is not sufficiently peopled to make their consumption perceptible and because, the hides not being adapted to the same uses as those of the European race, it will never happen that the animals will be killed solely for the sake of their skins, as is the practice among the Spaniards of the River de la Plata.

"If the Illinois buffaloes do not supply the tanneries with much," M. Galissonière continues, "eventually, advantages at least equivalent may reasonably be expected, on which we cannot prevent ourselves dwelling for a moment.

"1st These animals are covered with a species of wool, sufficiently fine to be employed in various manufactures, as experience has demonstrated.

"2d It can scarcely be doubted that, by catching them young and gelding them, they would be adapted to ploughing; perhaps, even, they would possess the same advantage that horses have over domestic oxen, that is, superior swiftness; they appear to be as strong, but perhaps are indebted for

* Kip's Early Jesuit Missions, p. 199.

† Views of Louisiana, p. 57.

this to wild breeding; in other respects, they do not seem difficult to tame; a 4 or 5 year old Bull and Cow have been seen that were extremely gentle.

"3d Were the Illinois country sufficiently well settled to admit of the people inclosing a great number of these animals in parks, some of them might be salted, a business susceptible of being extended very considerably, without Illinois possessing a large population for that purpose. This trade would perhaps enable us to dispense with Irish beef for Martinico, and even to compete with the English, and at a lower rate, for the supply of the Spanish Colonies." *

It appears that in 1821 a joint-stock company was formed in the British Red River Colony, under the high-sounding title of the "Buffalo Wool Company," whose express objects were "to provide a substitute for wool, which substitute was to be the wool of the wild buffalo, which was to be collected in the Plains, and manufactured both for the use of the colonists and for export, and to establish a tannery for manufacturing the buffalo-hides for domestic purposes." A capital of two thousand pounds sterling was raised, and orders sent to England for machinery, implements, dyes, and skilled workmen. Two immigrations of operatives arrived, including "curriers, skinners, sorters, wool-dressers, teasers, and bark manufacturers, of all grades, ages, and sexes." For a time money was plenty, wages high, and the prospects golden. But events proved the scheme to be grounded on miscalculation, which, with the extravagant expenditure indulged in by the company, soon brought grief, not only to all the participants, but in a measure affected the fortunes of the whole colony. It was found that "the wool and the hides were not to be got, as stated, for the picking up; the hides soon costing the company 6*s.* each, and the wool 1*s.* 6*d.* per pound." But, according to Ross (from whom these statements are compiled), "the bottle and the glass" were too freely circulated; spirits were imported by the hogshead, and scenes of disorder and intemperance followed; both officials and operatives were "wallowing in intemperance"; the hides were allowed to rot, the wool to spoil, and the tannery proved a complete failure. The company, besides expending their capital, found themselves irretrievably in debt to their bankers, and bankruptcy followed. "A few samples of cloth," continues Mr. Ross, "had, indeed, been made and sent home; but that which cost two pounds ten shillings per yard in Red River would only fetch four

* Documents relative to the Colonial History of the State of New York; procured in Holland, England, and France, by John Romeyn Brodhead, Esq., etc., Vol. X, pp. 230, 231.

shillings and sixpence in England!" But, though the enterprise itself disastrously failed, mainly through mismanagement and gross indiscretion, its indirect results were nevertheless beneficial to the colony.*

Dr. Richardson also states that the wool of the buffalo "has been manufactured in England into a remarkably fine and beautiful cloth, and in the colony of Osnaboyna, on the Red River, a warm and durable coarse cloth is formed of it."†

Although the soft woolly hair of the buffalo is evidently well adapted for the manufacture of cloth, I have heard of no other attempts towards its utilization. Of late, however, a traffic has sprung up along the line of the Kansas railroads in the bones, which are gathered for the purpose of shipment east for the manufacture of a fertilizing material. Mr. C. F. Morse, the General Superintendent of the Atchison, Topeka, and Santa Fé Railroad, writes, under date of June 2, 1875, that the "bone business is still quite heavy, and will probably last for one or two years longer." From his accompanying statements of buffalo products shipped over that road during the last three years, it appears that the shipment of bones in 1872 amounted to eleven hundred and thirty-five thousand three hundred pounds; for 1873, twenty-seven hundred and forty-three thousand one hundred and ten pounds; for 1874, sixty-nine hundred and fourteen thousand nine hundred pounds, or treble the amount of the previous year, and six times that of 1872.

Among the products of the buffalo, mention of "buffalo chips," or *bois de vache*, as the French *voyageurs* term it, should not be omitted. This material, as most persons doubtless well know, is simply the dried excrement of the buffalo, which the traveller on the treeless plains finds a very serviceable substitute for wood. As Dr. Elliott Coues has recently remarked, in an interesting and very humorously written article on this subject, "As an agent in the progress of civilization, the spirit of which is expressed in the remark that westward the course of empire takes its way, the buffalo-chip rises to the plane of the steam-engine and the electric telegraph, and acquires all the dignity which is supposed to enshroud questions of national importance or matters of political economy. I am not sure, indeed, that it is not entitled to still higher rank, for it is certain, at any rate, that we move in some parts of the West without either steam or electricity (mules replacing both), where it would be as impossible to live without buffalo chips as to exist

* Ross (Alexander), The Red River Settlement, pp. 69-72.

† Fauna Boreali-Americana, Vol. I, p. 282.

without flour, coffee, and tobacco."* In the narratives of military reconnaissances and other government explorations of the Plains, as well as of those of private explorers and travellers, the first meeting with buffalo chips is chronicled as something intimately affecting the welfare of the party, as it not only generally gives promise of soon meeting with herds of the animals themselves, but insures fuel for the camp-fire and for culinary purposes in regions where other sources of fuel are either precarious or entirely wanting. In the history of travel across the great interior plains, from those of Texas to those of the Saskatchewan, no other element, not even water, figures more prominently. Its absence in the treeless districts necessitates the transportation of wood as an indispensable part of the camp stores, while its presence not only renders this needless, but insures all those ordinary comforts of camp life that the conveniences of a camp-fire always bring. Hence its importance as a civilizing agent cannot well be overrated. The misery experienced when, during rainy seasons, it is temporarily too wet to burn, — the deprivation of the "cup that cheers but not inebriates," and of all means of cooking, — gives one a most vividly realizing sense of what his condition might be, for days and weeks, were it not for this invaluable resource.

How long the chip will endure the vicissitudes of the weather under the dry atmosphere of the Plains it is impossible to say, but its decomposition is slow, as it will remain in serviceable condition for years. After an exposure of six months it burns quite readily, but is not at its best as an article of fuel till it has had the suns and frosts of a year. It burns in much the same manner as peat, and though making but little flame yields a very intense heat. Strips of buffalo fat thrown on at intervals during the evening add a bright blaze, furnishing the explorer with ample light by which to write up his notes of the day's work, and enlivening the camp with all the cheer afforded by the piñon and pitch-pine camp-fires of the mountains or other wooded districts. Especially grateful does this "buffalo-chip" fire thus become in the long cold evenings of the hunter's winter camp on the Plains.

Another use to which buffalo chips are sometimes put is that of marking trails, and even surveyor's lines and points, it temporarily serving the office of stones and stakes in places where timber and stones are not to be obtained, as is the case over so large a part of the Great Plains.

* "Chips from the Buffalo's Workshop" — *Forest and Stream*, April 1, 1875.

3.—The Chase.

An account of the means and methods by which the buffalo has become so nearly exterminated forms an interesting chapter in its history, since they have varied at different times and at different localities, in accordance with the customs of the different Indian tribes, and with the wants and implements of the white man.

When the Jesuit missionaries first visited the Illinois prairies, it seems to have been a general custom with the Indians of the Mississippi Valley to hunt the buffalo by the aid of fire, accounts of which have been left us by Hennepin, Du Pratz, Charlevoix, and others. Hennepin says: "When the Savages discover a great Number of those Beasts together, they likewise assemble their whole Tribe to encompass the Bulls, and then set on fire the dry Herbs about them, except in some places, which they leave free; and therein lay themselves in Ambuscade. The Bulls, seeing the Flame round them, run away through those Passages where they see no Fire; and there fall into the Hands of the Savages, who by these Means will kill sometimes above sixscore in a day."*

Charlevoix's account of the Indian method of hunting the buffalo is as follows: "In the Southern and Western Parts of *New France*, on both Sides the *Mississippi*, the most famous Hunt is that of the Buffaloe, which is performed in this Manner: The Hunters range themselves on four Lines, which form a great Square, and begin by setting Fire to the Grass and Herbs, which are dry and very high: Then as the Fire gets forwards, they advance, closing their Lines: The Buffaloes, which are extremely afraid of Fire, keep flying from it, and at last find themselves so crouded together that they are generally every one killed. They say that a Party seldom returns from hunting without killing Fifteen Hundred or Two Thousand. But lest the different Companies should hinder each other, they all agree before they set out about the Place where they intend to hunt," etc.†

Mr. J. G. Shea also alludes to the general custom among the Indians of the Upper Mississippi of hunting buffaloes by fire, of which the buffaloes have a great dread. Finding it approaching them, "they retire towards the centre of the prairie, where, being pressed together in great numbers, the Indians

* A New Discovery of a Vast Country in America, p. 90, London, 1698.

† Letters, Goadby's English Ed., p. 68.

rush in with their arrows and musketry, and slaughter immense numbers in a few hours."*

Mr. Catlin, in his "North American Indians," has described with considerable detail the methods of hunting the buffalo among the Sioux Indians, and has given a series of six plates illustrative of the chase.† According to this author, the chief hunting amusement of the Indians of the vicinity of the Teton River, a small tributary of the Missouri, which joins the latter at old Fort Pierre, in Southern Dakota, consists in the chase of the buffalo. Being bold and desperate horsemen, they almost invariably pursue the buffalo on horseback, despatching him with the bow and lance with apparent ease. The horses, being well trained to the chase, as well as very fleet, soon bring their riders alongside their game. The Indian, as well as his horse, is divested of everything that might prove an encumbrance in running, the Indian even throwing off his shield and quiver as well as his clothing; taking in his left hand five or six arrows drawn from his quiver, he holds them ready for instant use, while he plies a heavy whip with his right. Riding near the rear of the herd he selects his animal, which he separates from the mass by dashing his horse between it and the herd, and, riding past it to the right, discharges his deadly arrow at the animal's heart, which penetrates "to the feather." Some, our author says, also pursue the animal with the lance. In this manner the Sioux were accustomed to destroy immense numbers of the buffalo, pursuing them in large hunting-parties, and killing hundreds and even thousands in a single hunt. Mr. Catlin refers to one of these grand hunts that occurred just before his arrival at the Fur Company's post at the mouth of the Teton, in May, 1833. A large herd of buffaloes appearing in sight on the opposite side of the river, a band of five hundred or six hundred Sioux horsemen forded the river about midday, and, recrossing the river at sundown, brought with them to the post *fourteen hundred fresh buffalo tongues*, which they readily exchanged for a few gallons of whiskey, "which was soon demolished," as our narrator states, "indulging them in a little and harmless carouse." Not a skin, nor a pound of meat, except the tongues, was saved from these slaughtered hundreds.

In winter, when from the depth of the snow these huge creatures are unable to move rapidly, they fall an easy prey to the Indian, who overtakes them readily upon his snow-shoes, and despatches them with his bow and

* Discovery and Exploration of the Mississippi Valley, p. 18, footnote.

† North American Indians, Vol. II, plates cvii–cxiii.

arrow, or drives his lance to their hearts. This being the season for gathering the robes, it is also a period of great slaughter. The skins being stripped off, the carcasses are generally left to the wolves, the Indians laying in during the fall a supply of dried meat for the winter. Catlin has also given an illustration of Indians disguised in wolf-skins creeping upon a herd that is unsuspectingly grazing on the level prairie, where they are shot down before they are aware of their danger by their disguised enemies.*

Lewis and Clarke describe a very novel method of destroying the buffaloes formerly practised by the Minnetarees of the Upper Missouri. This mode of hunting was to select one of the most active and fleet young men, who, disguised with a buffalo-skin fastened about his body, with the horns and ears so secured as to deceive the buffalo, placed himself at a convenient distance between the herd of buffalo and some of the river precipices, which sometimes extend for miles. His companions in the mean time get in the rear and along the flanks of the herd, and, showing themselves at a given signal, advance upon the herd. The herd thus alarmed runs from the hunters toward the disguised Indian, whom they follow at full speed toward the river. The Indian who thus acts as a decoy, when the precipice is reached, suddenly secures himself in some crevice of the cliff which he had previously selected, leaving the herd on the brink. It is then impossible for the foremost of the herd to retreat or to turn aside, being pressed on by those behind, who see no danger except from the pursuing Indians. They are thus tumbled headlong over the cliff, strewing the shore with their dead bodies. The Indians then select as much meat as they wish, the rest being abandoned to the wolves. A little above the mouth of the Judith River, on the Missouri, Lewis and Clarke passed a precipice, about one hundred and twenty feet in height, at the base of which lay scattered the fragments of at least one hundred carcasses of buffaloes, although many had already been carried away by the water.†

Lewis and Clarke also describe the Indian method of hunting the buffalo on the ice, as witnessed by them March 29, 1805, at their wintering-post on the Missouri River, about thirty miles above the present site of Fort Abraham Lincoln, Dakota Territory. Every spring, say these authors, as the river is breaking up, the plains are set on fire by the Indians. The buffaloes are thus tempted to cross the river in search of the fresh green grass that springs

* North American Indians, Vol. II, pp. 249 - 251.

† Lewis and Clarke's Expedition, Vol. I, p. 235.

up immediately after the burning. In crossing they often find themselves insulated on large pieces of floating ice. The Indians seize these opportunities for their attack, passing nimbly across the trembling ice, where the footsteps of the huge animals are unsteady and insecure. The buffalo being thus unable to offer resistance, the hunter gives him his death-wound and paddles his ice-raft to the shore and secures his prey.*

The Indians of the Northern Plains were long in the habit of hunting the buffalo by impounding them, or by driving them into an artificial enclosure constructed for the purpose, within which the buffaloes were at their mercy. Various descriptions of this method have been given by different travellers, but one of the most recent is that by Hind, in his "Narrative of the Assinniboine and Saskatchewan Expedition," † where he describes the method as practised in 1859 by the Plain Cree Indians of the Qu'appelle and Saskatchewan Plains. The pound is described as circular, enclosing an area of about one hundred and twenty feet in diameter, formed of the trunks of trees set in the ground and bound together by withes, and braced by external supports. Converging rows of bushes extend from the pound a distance of several miles into the prairie, where their extremities are about one and a half to two miles apart. These bushes are termed "dead men," and serve to guide the buffaloes into the pound. When all is ready for action, skilled hunters, mounted on fleet ponies, partly surround a herd and start them in the direction of the pound, being aided by confederates stationed in hollows, who, when the buffaloes take a wrong direction, rise and wave their robes to change their course. If when the "dead men" are reached the buffaloes are disposed to pass through them, Indians stationed behind appear, and by the shaking of robes urge on the herd toward the pound. Thus the band is pressed on between the narrowing lines of "dead men" to the entrance of the pound. This is closed by a heavy tree-trunk placed about a foot from the ground, inside of which is a ditch sufficiently deep to prevent the enclosed buffaloes from jumping out. No sooner has the fatal leap been made than the imprisoned animals rush wildly around the enclosure in search of some point of escape. With the utmost silence, women and children hold their robes before every orifice, until the whole herd is brought in. When all are enclosed the slaughter begins; the hunters, climbing to the top of the fence, spear or shoot, with bows and arrows or firearms, the bewildered buf-

* Lewis and Clarke's Expedition, Vol. I, p. 175.

† Canadian Exploring Expeditions, etc., Vol. I, pp. 355 – 359.

faloes now so wholly within their power. Soon rendered frantic with rage and fear, the stronger toss, crush, or impale the weaker. In this dreadful scene of confusion and slaughter, says Hind, "the shouts and screams of the excited Indians rise above the roaring of the bulls, the bellowing of the cows, and the piteous moaning of the calves. The dying struggles of so many huge and powerful animals crowded together create a revolting and terrible scene, dreadful from the excess of its cruelty and waste of life, but with occasional displays of wonderful brute strength and rage; while man, in his savage, untutored, and heathen state, shows, both in deed and expression, how little he is superior to the noble beasts he so wantonly and cruelly destroys."

"The conflict over," says Hind, "animals of every age, from old bulls to young calves of three months old, were huddled together, in all the forced attitudes of violent death. Some lay on their backs, with eyes starting from their heads, and tongues thrust out through clotted gore, and others were impaled on the horns of the old and strong bulls. Others again, which had been tossed, were lying with broken backs, two or three deep. One little calf hung suspended on the horns of a bull, which had impaled it in the wild race round and round the pound." Of the two hundred to two hundred and fifty animals usually killed at each impounding, only the best and fattest are utilized, the flesh of these being removed and dried in the sun.

Sometimes the attempts at impounding are unsuccessful, an instance of which is mentioned by Mr. Hind. After the pound was nearly full, an old bull espied a narrow crevice which had not been closed by the robes of those on the outside, whose duty it was to conceal every orifice; making a dash at this, he forced himself through, breaking the fence, when the whole herd ran helter-skelter through the gap, a few only being speared or shot through with arrows in their attempt to escape.

Simpson says that in January, 1840, the buffaloes were so numerous about Carlton House as to render it necessary to remove the haystacks into the Fort to prevent their being devoured by the buffaloes. In the vicinity of the Fort were three camps of Assinniboines, each of whom had its buffalo pound, into which they drove forty or fifty animals daily; "and I afterwards learned," says Simpson, "that in other places these pounds were actually formed of piled-up carcasses." *

Audubon states that the Gros Ventres, Blackfeet, and Assinniboines often also took the buffalo in large pens in a similar manner. Two converging

* Simpson (Thomas), Narrative of the Discoveries on the North Coast of America, etc., pp. 402, 404.

fences, built of sticks, logs, and brushwood, form in a similar way a funnel-shaped entrance to the enclosure or "park," as it is usually called, which may be either square or round according to the nature of the ground. The narrow end or entrance is always on the verge of a sudden break in the prairie, ten or fifteen feet deep, and is made as strong as possible. When the pen is ready a young man, very swift of foot, starts at daylight towards the herd that is to be taken, provided with a bison's hide and head, with which he is to disguise himself for the purpose of acting as a decoy. On nearing the herd he bleats like a calf, and makes his way slowly towards the mouth of the converging fences leading to the pen. Repeating the cry at intervals, the buffaloes follow the decoy, while mounted Indians, riding to and fro along the flanks and rear of the herd, urge them on towards the funnel. A crowd of men, women, and children then come and assist in frightening them, the disguised Indian still occasionally bleating. As soon as the buffaloes have fairly entered the road to the pen, the decoy runs to the edge of the precipice, quickly descends, and makes his escape by climbing over the fence forming the pen. The herd follows on until the leader is forced to leap down into the pen, and is followed by the whole herd, which being thus ensnared is easily destroyed, even the women and children participating in the slaughter.*

This method, if not still practised in the Yellowstone country, was in use there at no distant date, since while with the Yellowstone Expedition of 1873 I several times met with the remains of these pounds and their converging fences in the region above the mouth of the Big Horn River. They are here, I was told, used in entrapping the elk and deer as well as the buffalo; and, according to Charlevoix, the Indians of Canada formerly hunted the moose, the caribou, and the deer in a somewhat similar manner.

On the plains, where no timber is available for the construction of pounds, the Indians pursue a different but an almost equally destructive method. The hunting party, numbering usually hundreds of horsemen, select such a portion of a large herd as they desire to destroy, and, surrounding them, thus cut them off from the rest of the herd, and prevent their escape in every direction by enclosing them with a cordon of armed horsemen. The slaughter is begun simultaneously on all sides; and whichever way the herd moves they encounter their invincible and deadly enemies. The slaughter usually continues until the whole "surround" is killed, often numbering hun-

* Audubon and Bachman's Quadrupeds of North America, Vol. II, p. 49.

dreds of animals. In their casual hunts the Indians simply follow the herds on horseback, shooting from the saddle when in full pursuit, using either bows and arrows or the modern fire-arms with great dexterity.

Descriptions of the systematic expeditions of the Red River half-breed hunters have been given with greater or less fulness by McLean, Ross, Hind,* and others. The distinctive features of these grand hunting expeditions are their magnitude, the number of persons engaged in them, and the almost military character of their organization. As previously stated, these expeditions generally numbered from five hundred to upwards of twelve hundred carts, accompanied by from two hundred and fifty to six hundred hunters, nearly twice this number of women and children, besides a draught animal (either a horse or an ox) and a dog to each cart, and riding animals in addition for the hunters. Setting out from Fort Garry, the expeditions for many years hunted over the Pembina plains, extending their trips southward and westward over the prairies and plains of the Red River, the Shayenne, and the Coteau de Missouri. The Red River half-breed hunters have undoubtedly done more to exterminate the buffalo than any other single cause, and have long since wholly extirpated them throughout not only this vast region, but also over the extensive prairies of the Assinniboine, the Qu'appelle, and the lower Saskatchewan. Their method of hunting was for several hundred horsemen armed with fire-arms to make a grand simultaneous rush into the very midst of the immense herds. An attack that Mr. Ross witnessed he thus describes: "Our array in the field must have been a grand and imposing one to those who had never seen the like before. No less than four hundred huntsmen, all mounted, and anxiously waiting for the word 'Start!' took up their position in a line at one end of the camp, while Captain Wilkie, with his spy-glass at his eye, surveyed the buffalo, examined the ground, and issued his orders. At eight o'clock the whole cavalcade broke ground and made for the buffalo; first at a slow trot, then at a gallop, and lastly at full speed. Their advance was over a dead level, the plain having no hollow or shelter of any kind to conceal their approach. . . . . When the horsemen started the cattle might have been a mile and a half ahead; but they had approached to within four or five hundred yards before the bulls curved their tails or pawed the ground. In a moment more

* McLean (John), Notes of Twenty-five Years' Service in the Hudson's Bay Territory, Vol. II, pp. 297–302; Ross (Alexander), The Red River Settlement, pp. 255–264; Hind (H. Y.), Canad. Expl. Expedition, Vol. II, pp. 110, 111.

the herd took flight, and horse and rider are presently seen bursting in among them; shots are heard, and all is smoke, dust, and hurry. The fattest are first singled out for slaughter, and in less time than we have occupied with the description a thousand carcasses strew the plain. Those who have seen a squadron of horse dart into battle may imagine the scene, which we have no skill to depict. The earth seemed to tremble when the horses started; but when the animals fled it was like the shock of an earthquake. The air was darkened; the rapid firing, at first distinct, soon became more and more faint, and at last died away in the distance. Two hours, and all was over; but several hours elapsed before the result was known, or the hunters reassembled; . . . . in the evening no less than thirteen hundred and seventy-five tongues were brought into camp." *

The dexterity in loading and firing on horseback while at full speed exhibited by these half-breeds, as well as their tact in recognizing their game on the field of slaughter after the killing is over, is represented as surprising. Formerly, when hunting with the old flint-lock musket, says Mr. Taylor,† they would drop a charge of powder into the palm of the hand, thence into the muzzle of the gun, following it with a bullet from a stock carried in the mouth, firing as often as this operation could be repeated. The use of modern breech-loading arms, however, long since rendered this process needless. They seldom leave a mark to designate their own animals, though some do so, leaving first a cap, then a sash, and so on, until, as often happens, these means of designation fail, five or six to a dozen buffaloes being generally killed in a single run by a good hunter. Riding in clouds of dust and smoke, in company with hundreds of other horsemen, crossing and re-crossing each other's tracks, among dead and wounded as well as among the terrified and fleeing animals, it certainly evinces, on the part of the hunter, no small degree of discriminating power, after an hour of such wild, bewildering confusion, to tell not only the number of animals he has killed, but also the exact spot where each lies. Yet this, we are told, is constantly done.

According to Simpson, the Red River hunter, in winter, when the snow was too deep to pursue them on horseback, approached the buffaloes by crawling to them on the snow, disguised sometimes by a close dun-colored cap, furnished with upright ears, to give him the appearance of a wolf, which, through constant association, the buffaloes regard without dread. Towards

* Red River Settlement, pp. 255 557.

† MS. Notes, as previously cited.

spring, when the deep snow is covered with a hard crust, which, while it supports the hunter, proves a great impediment to the buffaloes, they are easily run down by the hunters, and despatched with daggers while floundering in the deep drifts, even women and boys assisting in killing the then almost helpless animals.*

The two modes of hunting the buffalo chiefly practised at present are the pursuit on horseback and the "still hunt." The first named is the one usually chosen when sport and excitement are the things mainly desired, the still hunt being practised when a supply of meat or of hides is the object. The latter method affords but little excitement, and entails, with proper precautions, little or no risk of life or limb on the part of the hunter. Parties hunting for pleasure prefer the chase on horseback, shooting from the saddle with heavy revolvers at close range when at full gallop. Success depends almost wholly, provided the hunter is a good rider, upon the speed and bottom of his horse, and is really about as noble sport as attacking a herd of domestic cattle would be. The chase on horseback of a drove of Texan cattle would be far more dangerous, and attended probably with as much excitement, except that in the case of the buffalo the hunter has the consciousness of pursuing a nominally wild animal, and hence legitimate game. That the chase on horseback affords the wildest excitement is an undeniable fact. The swift pursuit of the flying mass of buffaloes, the mingling with the terrified herd, the singling out of the victim, the rapid shots at the huge moving bulk of hair and flesh, at so close range that the game is almost within reach of the hand, the tottering fall or the headlong tumble of the doomed animal, the risk of pursuit by a wounded bull maddened with pain, the general din and confusion, with the double risk of collision with the blindly fleeing monsters, or of being thrown by treacherous marmot or badger holes, or anon the long pursuit of an animal which, though pierced with a dozen balls, still rushes on, can, of course, yield only excitement of the intensest kind, both for the rider and his steed. This method is the favorite one with hunting parties from the East or from abroad, as well as of the officers and soldiers of the United States Cavalry, when the latter are stationed within or near the range of the buffalo, or are passing through its range, at the expense, usually, of several of the best horses in the command. The destruction of the buffalo during these hunts is not generally very great, though amounting annually, in the aggregate, to many thousands; but the demoralization of the

* Narrative of the Discoveries on the North Coast of America, etc., p. 404.

herd produced by the fright and the chase has a most deleterious influence on their stability and increase.

The still hunt is far more fatal, and is the method adopted by the professional hunter, who throughout the year makes it his chief business to hunt the buffalo for its commercial products. The buffalo being naturally unsuspicious and sluggish, even to stupidity, is readily approached within easy range, even in a level country, where the slight herbage of the plains is the only shelter. Buffalo-hunting hence requires much less tact and skill than the hunting of most other large game, especially deer and pronghorns. The chief precaution necessary is to keep to the leeward of the herd, in order not to give them the "scent," as this alarms them even when no enemy is in sight, being sufficient to "stampede" a herd at a long distance. The buffaloes can ordinarily be approached to within a thousand yards in a perfectly level and open country, and with a slight growth of herbage for shelter it is easy to creep up to within a hundred yards, and by aid of ravines to within twenty or thirty paces. I have seen hunters approach within thirty yards of a herd when their only cover was grass and weeds a foot or so in height. The old bulls are always less wary than the cows and younger bulls; they also, to a great extent, keep in the rear and on the outskirts of the herd. As generally only the younger animals are desired, and especially the young cows, the hunters often have to creep past the old bulls in order to get within range of the cows. Where slight inequalities of the ground have favored the hunters, I have seen them pass within a few paces of the quietly reclining, ruminating old bulls, in trying to get within range of the more desirable game beyond without the patriarchs of the herd being alarmed by the hunter's approach. The half-wild Texan steers are often far more wary than the unsuspecting herds of buffaloes.

The professional hunter, when desiring to load his teams with meat, will rarely make his first shot at a greater distance than fifty to seventy-five yards. If the shot result fatally, the herd rarely moves more than fifty yards before stopping to look for the cause of the mishap to their fallen companion, and turning half round to get a good view rearward, they thus present themselves in the best possible position to the hunter at still short range. Here others fall before the hunter's shots; the herd, again slightly startled, moves on a few paces, and again stops to gaze. The hunter, still keeping prostrate, approaches, if necessary, under cover of those already killed, and continues the work of destruction. The shots are thus often repeated till fifteen, twenty, or even thirty buffaloes are killed before the herd becomes thoroughly alarmed and, in hunter's parlance, "stampedes." By keeping prostrate the hunter is able to creep up to the herd again as it recedes, till he has killed enough to furnish loads for his teams; and even sometimes he has to rise and drive away the stupid creatures to prevent the living from playfully goring the dead! When the hunter is thus successful, it is termed "getting a stand on the herd." A "stand" is most surely made in nearly level ground. In shooting from ravines, the herd usually runs away after three to five or six of their number have fallen. During the rutting season, if a cow falls at the first shot, the hunter is pretty sure of a "stand," and of getting a dozen or more shots, if he keeps prostrate and uses due caution. As soon as he rises the buffaloes seem at once to recognize the cause of their trouble, and generally immediately stampede; but so long as he remains prone they seem to have no perception of the character of their enemy, and often do not notice him at all. A "stand" can usually be obtained, by due care, at any time from May to December, but during the rest of the year the buffaloes are more wary, and often very lean, and the hunters say that the poorer they get, the wilder they become.

The Kansas hunter for several years was generally able to reach the herds by an easy drive from either of the railroads that now intersect the State. Generally equipped with one to three four-mule teams, he was able for a part of the season at least, to make daily trips from the herds to the points of shipment, although not unfrequently two days were required to enable him to load his teams and make the round trip. The chief of a party is usually mounted on a pony, and, riding in advance, often has enough animals killed to furnish loads for his teams by the time the latter reach the scene of action. The dead buffaloes are then speedily "butchered," * a few minutes sufficing for each. The "saddle," or the two hind quarters, and the tongue are usually the only parts saved, but in the case of calves and very fat yearlings the whole carcass is taken. The usual weight of a saddle is about two hundred pounds, which is sold at an average price of about three cents per pound delivered at the cars, the buyer being generally on the spot to inspect it and superintend its packing for shipment.

The regular or "professional" hunter formerly followed the buffalo herds the whole year, moving eastward or westward along the lines of railroad as the

* The hunters appear to generally restrict this term to the dressing of the slain animals; "butchering," in their parlance, does not include the killing.

buffaloes at different seasons changed their range. When the weather was too warm to allow of the shipment of the meat to Eastern cities, they killed the creatures for their hides, each hunter in this way destroying hundreds in the course of a few months, though getting hardly enough for them to pay his expenses. A few of the more enterprising preserved a portion of the meat by salting and smoking it. As no skins can be taken from those from which the quarters are taken, an animal is thus sacrificed for each hide taken and for each saddle saved.

The life of a buffalo-hunter is one of hardship and exposure, and yet one of remarkable fascination to those who have ever engaged in such pursuits. In winter, owing to sudden changes of temperature, the hunter is often in great danger, since he is liable to be overtaken by storms and extreme cold when far out on the prairie, many miles from any means of protection. The early part of the winter of 1871 – 72 was one of remarkable severity in the West, even as far south as the plains of Northern Kansas, where in December, 1871, several hunters perished from the cold, and many others were maimed from having been frost-bitten, some of whom narrowly escaped with their lives. Within the winter range of the northern herds of the Kansas buffaloes, a lone tree here and there, at the head of some ravine, usually forms the hunter's sole dependence for firewood. His own improvidence, however, often deprives him of many comforts, as well as a considerable degree of security, which a little trouble and care would secure to him.

The life of a hunter seems always to tend more or less to barbarism, but especially is this the case with the buffalo-hunter. The "buffalo rangers" of the Red River Settlements are described by Ross, Hind, and others, as speedily becoming unfitted for agricultural or other civilized pursuits. Improvident and unthrifty in their habits, they riot in plenty during a part of the year, and again verge upon starvation before the arrival of their annual hunting season. The buffalo-hunter of the Plains contrasts unfavorably in many respects with his Rocky Mountain brother. With the less degree of skill required in the chase of the stupid, unwieldy bison, as compared with the tact and caution required in the successful pursuit of the watchful prong-horn, the timid deer, the elk, or the bighorn, there is a corresponding lack of thrift and energy on the part of the hunter. In place of the buckskin suit of the Rocky Mountain hunter, the buffalo-hunter goes clad in a coarse dress of canvas, stiffened with blood and grease. His hair often goes uncut and uncombed for months together, and his hands are frequently unwashed for many days. The culinary apparatus of a whole party consists of a single large coffee-pot, a "Dutch oven," and a skillet, and the table-set of a tin cup to each man, the latter vessel often consisting merely of a battered fruit-can. Each man's hunting-knife not only does duty in butchering the buffalo, but is the sole implement used in despatching his food, supplying the places of spoon and fork as well as knife. The bill of fare consists of strong coffee, often without milk or sugar, "yeast-powder bread," and buffalo meat fried in buffalo tallow. When the meal is cooked the party encircle the skillet, dip their bread in the fat, and eat their meat with their fingers. When bread fails, as often happens, "buffalo straight," or buffalo meat alone, affords them nourishing sustenance. Occasionally, however, the fare is varied with the addition of potatoes and canned fruits. They sleep generally in the open air, in winter as well as in summer, subjected to every inclemency of the weather. As may well be imagined, a buffalo-hunter, at the end of the season, is by no means prepossessing in his appearance, being, in addition to his filthy aspect, a paradise for hordes of nameless parasites. They are yet a rollicking set, and occasionally include men of intelligence, who formerly possessed an ordinary degree of refinement. Generally none are more conscious of their unfitness for civilized society than themselves, and after a few years of such free border-life they can hardly be induced to abandon it and resume the restraints of civilization.

Although successful in the pursuit of the buffalo, their success arises from the unsuspicious nature of their victims rather than from skill in the use or selection of their arms. The improved breech-loading United States musket is their favorite weapon, and most of them will use no other. A few employ Sharp's and Winchester rifles; arms of small calibre, however, they generally despise. Yet with these heavy arms, used, as they are, at short range, only about one shot in three proves fatal, many of the poor beasts getting but a broken leg in place of a fatal shot.* This is owing in part to carelessness or lack of skill in shooting, and in part to the inaccuracy of the arms. However good the gun may be originally, it soon deteriorates and is eventually ruined by rough usage. A few of the hunters have good guns, take good care of them, and use them effectively, killing their game as readily at three hundred and four hundred yards as do the others at one fourth that distance. A rifle

* When returning from a buffalo-hunt on the Kansas plains in January, 1872, my party fell in with a small band of these unfortunates, about thirty in number, nearly all of whom were in some way maimed, the greater part having broken legs.

having a calibre of $\frac{44}{100}$ inches is as effective a weapon against the buffalo as need be used, if accurate and skilfully employed, the fatality of the shot depending not so much upon the size of the ball used as upon the part of the animal hit. I have seen, for instance, an old buffalo bull shot entirely through the body at a distance of two hundred and thirty yards by a ball from a six-pound rifle, having a calibre of only $\frac{45}{100}$ inches, the wound killing the animal almost instantly.

4.—Domestication of the Buffalo.

Now that the buffalo is apparently so nearly exterminated, it is greatly to be regretted, not only that its ultimate extinction has been so rapidly hastened by improvident and wanton slaughter, but that no persistent attempts have as yet been made to utilize this valuable animal by domestication. Never, perhaps, was the time more favorable for such experiments than now, since there are not only intelligent settlers living within or near the boundaries of its range, where the experiments might be tried without any of the risks that would attend a change of climate, but easy access to its haunts from the Eastern States is afforded by railroads, by means of which, at comparatively little cost and trouble, numbers might be taken to any portion of the older States of the Union.

The early explorers of the Mississippi Valley believed that the buffalo, besides being valuable for its flesh and hide, might be made to take the place of the domestic ox in agricultural pursuits, and at the same time yield a fleece of wool equal in value, in respect to quality, to that of the sheep. That the buffalo calf may be easily reared and thoroughly tamed needs not at this late day to be proved. The known instances of their domestication are too many to admit even of enumeration, but they have usually been kept merely as objects of curiosity, and little or no care has been given to their reproduction in confinement, and few attempts have been made to train them to labor.

As early as 1750, Kalm states that young buffaloes had frequently been taken to Quebec, and kept among the tame cattle, but he adds that the climate there seemed too severe for them to bear, and that they commonly died in three or four years. The same writer also states that the calves of "the wild cows and oxen . . . . which are to be met with in Carolina and other provinces to the south of Pennsylvania," had been obtained by "several people of distinction," who "brought them up among the tame cattle." "When grown up," he adds, "they were perfectly tame, but at the same time very unruly, so that there was no enclosure strong enough to resist them if they had a mind to break through it; for as they possess a great strength in their neck, it was easy for them to overthrow the pales with their horns, and to get into the cornfields; and as soon as they had made a road, all the tame cattle followed them; they likewise copulated with the latter, and by that means generated, as it were, a new breed." *

Bernard Romans also says (writing a century ago), "The bounteous hand of nature has here given us an animal which, *by experience*, we know may easily be domesticated, whose fine wooll might yield good profit, and whose flesh is equal at least to our beef, and yields as much tallow; i mean the buffaloe." †

Gallatin also says that they were not only domesticated in Virginia, but that they were bred with domestic cattle, and that the mixed breed was fertile. "As doubts have lately been raised upon that point," he says, writing forty years ago, "I must say that the mixed breed was quite common fifty [now ninety] years ago, in some of the northwestern counties of Virginia; and that the cows, the issue of that mixture, propagated like all others. No attempt that I know of was ever made by the inhabitants to tame a buffalo of full growth. But calves were occasionally caught by the dogs and brought alive into the settlements. A bull thus raised was for a number of years owned in my immediate vicinity by a farmer living on the Monongahela, adjoining Mason and Dixon's line. He was permitted to roam at large, and was no more dangerous to man than any bull of the common species. But to them he was formidable, and would not suffer any to approach within two or three miles of his own range. Most of the cows I knew were descended from him. For want of a fresh supply of the wild animal they have now merged into the common kind. They were no favorites, as they yielded less milk. The superior size and strength of the buffalo might have improved the breed of oxen for draft, but this was not attended to, horses being almost exclusively employed in that quarter for agricultural

* Kalm (Peter). Travels in North America (Forster's translation), Vol. I p. 162.

† Nat. Hist. of East and West Florida, p. 174.

pursuits."* He adds that the buffalo is very intractable, and is not known to have been domesticated by the Indians.†

Sibley observes, in speaking of the buffalo of the Red River of the North, that "in spring the calves are easily weaned, and when trained to labor become quite useful. One farmer, who had broken a bull to the plough, performed the whole work of the field with his aid alone."‡

Mr. Robert Wickliffe, in a letter addressed to Messrs. Audubon and Bachman, dated Lexington, Kentucky, November 6, 1843, has quite fully recorded the results of his own efforts at domesticating the buffalo. He says: "The herd of buffalo I now possess have descended from one or two cows that I purchased from a man who brought them from the country called the Upper Missouri; I have had them for about thirty years, but from giving them away and the occasional killing of them by mischievous persons, as well as other causes, my whole stock does not exceed ten or twelve. I have sometimes confined them in separate parks from other cattle, but generally they herd and feed with my stock of farm cattle. . . . . On getting possession of the tame buffaloes I endeavored to cross them as much as I could with my common cows, to which experiment I found the tame bull unwilling to accede, and he was always shy of the buffalo cow, but the buffalo bull was willing to breed with the common cow.

"From the domestic cow I have crossed half-breeds, one of which was a heifer; this I put with a domestic bull, and it produced a bull calf. This I castrated and it made a very fine steer, and when killed produced very fine beef. I bred from the same heifer several calves, and then, that the experiment might be perfect, I put one of them to the buffalo bull, and she brought me a bull calf, which I raised to be a very fine large animal, perhaps the only one in the world of his blood, namely, a three-quarter, half-quarter, and a half-quarter of the common blood. After making these experiments, I have left them to propagate their breed themselves, so that I have only had a few half-breeds, and they always proved the same, even by a buffalo bull. The full-blood is not as large as the improved stock, but as large as the ordinary stock of the country. The crossed or half-blood are larger than either

* Gallatin (Albert), A Synopsis of the Indian Tribes of North America; Trans. Amer. Antiquarian Soc., Vol. II, p. 139, footnote.

† Dr. Woodhouse states that he had seen "a few of these animals tamed in the Creek nation, running with the common cattle." — SITGREAVES'S *Report of an Exped. down the Zuñi and Colorado Rivers*, p. 57.

‡ Sibley (H. H.), in Schoolcraft's History, Condition, and Prospects of the Indian Tribes of the United States, Vol. IV, p. 110.

the half-blood or common cow. The hump, brisket, ribs, and tongue of the full and half-blooded are preferable to those of the common beef, but the round and other parts are much inferior. The udder or bag of the buffalo is smaller than that of the common cow, but I have allowed the calves of both to run with their dams upon the same pasture, and those of the buffalo were always the fattest; and old hunters have told me that when a young buffalo calf is taken, it requires the milk of two cows to raise it. Of this I have no doubt, having received the same information from hunters of the greatest veracity. The bag or udder of the half-breed is larger than that of full-blooded animals, and they would, I have no doubt, make good milkers.

"The wool of the wild buffalo grows on their descendants when domesticated, but I think they have less of wool than their progenitors. The domesticated buffalo still retains the grunt of the wild animal, and is incapable of making any other noise, and they will observe the habit of having select places within their feeding-grounds to wallow in.

"The buffalo has a much deeper shoulder than the tame ox, but is lighter behind. He walks more actively than the latter, and I think has more strength than a common ox of the same weight. I have broken them to the yoke, and found them capable of making excellent oxen; and for drawing wagons, carts, or other heavily laden vehicles on long journeys, they would, I think, be greatly preferable to the common ox. I have as yet had no opportunity of testing the longevity of the buffalo, as all mine that have died did so from accident, or were killed because they became aged. I have some cows that are nearly twenty years old, that are healthy and vigorous, and one of them has now a sucking calf.

"The young buffalo calf is of a sandy red or rufous color, and commences changing dark brown at about six months old, which last color it always retains. The mixed breeds are of various colors; I have had them striped with black, on a gray ground, like the zebra, some of them brindled red, some pure red with white faces, and others red without any markings of white. The mixed bloods have not only produced in my stock from the tame and the buffalo bull, but I have seen the half-bloods reproducing, viz., those that were the product of the common cow and wild buffalo bull. I was informed that, at the first settlement of the country, cows that were considered best for milking were from the half-blood, down to the quarter, and even eighth, of the buffalo blood. But my experiments have not satisfied me that the half-buffalo bull will produce again. That the half-breed heifer will be productive from either race, as I have before stated, I have tested beyond the possibility of a doubt.

"The domesticated buffalo retains the same haughty bearing that distinguishes him in his natural state. He will, however, feed or fatten on whatever suits the tame cow, and requires about the same amount of food. I have never milked either the full-blood or mixed breed, but have no doubt they might be made good milkers, although their bags or udders are less than those of the common cow; yet, from the strength of the calf, the dam must yield as much or even more milk than the common cow." *

From the foregoing the following facts are sufficiently attested: (1) That the buffalo is readily susceptible of domestication; (2) that it interbreeds freely with the domestic cow; (3) that the half-breeds are fertile; and (4) that they readily amalgamate with the domestic cattle. The advantages that arise from the mixed race are less clearly apparent, as their adaptability to labor seems as yet to have not been properly tested, although the experiments of Mr. Wickliffe offer encouragement in this direction. A larger race than either of the original stocks seems, however, to result from the crossing of the buffalo with the cow, and a probable improvement in milking qualities.

The domestication of the buffalo has heretofore been undertaken only in regions where farm-labor was done chiefly by the use of horses or mules. Galissonière, as already noticed (see *antè*, p. 198), writing a century and a quarter ago, believed the buffalo would "be adapted to ploughing," and that

* Audubon and Bachman's Quadrupeds of North America, Vol. II, pp. 52–54. Mr. Wickliffe's account of his observations and experiments has been repeatedly quoted by different writers on the subject of the domestication of the buffalo (see Baird, Patent-Office Report, Agriculture, Part II, 1851–52, pp. 120–128; Hind, Canadian Exploring Expedition, Vol. II, p. 113), and embraces nearly all of importance as yet published relating to the subject.

In this connection may be noticed the astonishing dogmatism with which Schoolcraft, four years after the publication of Mr. Wickliffe's account of his experiments in domesticating the buffalo, and three years after its republication by Professor Baird, asserts that while "the calf of the bison has often been captured on the frontiers, and brought up with domestic cattle," and been "measurably tamed," that "*it produces no cross*," and "*is utterly barren in this state*." He alludes also to the statement of Gomara that it is susceptible of domestication, his statement being revived, Schoolcraft adds, and "in a manner galvanized by a justly eminent writer [Humboldt], after the *uniform observation* of the French and English colonists of America, *disaffirming* [!], for more than two centuries, the practicability of its domestication"; and further states that "*all* visitors and travellers who have spoken on the subject coincide in the opinion that the bison is *incapable of domestication*, and that it is not without imminent peril to themselves that the fierce and untamable herds of it are hunted." — *History, Condition, and Prospects of the Indian Tribes of the United States*, Part V (1856), p. 49.

"they would possess the same advantage that horses have over domestic oxen, that is, superior swiftness," but the question has as yet received little attention. Being more active than the domestic ox, it seems highly probable that they might make a superior farm animal, especially since, as Professor Shaler suggests to me, they would be far better able to endure the intense heat of summer than ordinary cattle, besides being swifter and stronger.

From what is already known of the behavior of the buffalo under domestication, it seems altogether tractable and docile. A letter written by Mr. P. B. Thompson, Sr., to Professor Shaler, respecting the domestication of the buffalo in Kentucky, bears further on this point. Mr. Thompson says (under date of "Harrodsburg, Ky., October 30, 1875"): "In reply to your inquiry relative to the buffaloes formerly owned by Colonel George C. Thompson of Shawnee Springs, Mercer County, permit me to say that my remembrance of them runs back at least fifty years. My first recollection is that there was a bull and three cows. They were kept in a park of about sixty acres of blue-grass. In the same park were about fifty deer, and from seven to twelve elk. The animals in the park were fed but little, and given the same food as other cattle. The elk and deer were but slightly domesticated, but the buffaloes became as gentle as any other cattle that were not constantly handled. I have been often within a few feet of them, and have no doubt that they could have been used as beasts of labor, or that the females would have submitted to milking. There were but few young, they being poor breeders, which was probably the effect of neglect. They were very long-lived; one of them must have been thirty years old, the others over twenty. The bull died many years ago, the last cow about a year since.

"During the whole time I do not think they ever broke a fence, or went beyond the limits of the park unless driven. Other cattle were put in the park, and it was used at times for a calf lot. They were not vicious to either cattle, horses, hogs, or sheep. "The two last left were cows, who survived the bull at least fifteen years. They were calved in the park, and, as I have said before, were docile and harmless."

No attempt appears as yet to have been made to perpetuate an unmixed domestic race of the buffalo. Probably after a few generations they would lose much of their natural untractableness, and when castrated would doubtless form superior working cattle, from their greater size and strength and great natural agility. While on the Plains in

1871 I made extensive inquiries as to the possibility of the buffalo being domesticated and trained to work, and while the general opinion seemed to be that such a thing was wholly feasible, I could not learn that it had been properly attempted. I heard of instances where buffaloes had been broken to the yoke, and, though strong and serviceable, they were at times rather unmanageable. When on a journey they are liable, it is said, when thirsty, "to break for water," rushing precipitately down the steep banks of the nearest stream to slake their thirst, dragging after them the wagon to which they may be attached, with, of course, rather unpleasant results.

The fate of extermination so surely awaits, sooner or later, the buffalo in its wild state that its domestication becomes a matter of great interest, and is well worthy of the attention of intelligent stock-growers, some of whom should be willing to take a little trouble to perpetuate the pure race in a domestic state. The attempt can be hardly regarded otherwise than as an enterprise that would eventually yield a satisfactory and probably a profitable result, with the possibility of adding another valuable domestic animal to those we already possess. It seems probable, also, that a mixed race might be reared to good advantage.

APPENDIX.

I.

Occurrence of the Buffalo in Union County, Pennsylvania. — On pages 87 and 108 reference is made to the traditional evidence afforded by such names as "Buffalo Valley" and "Buffalo Creek," of the former existence of the buffalo near Lewisburg, in Union County, Pennsylvania. Through the kindness of my friend, Professor C. H. Hamlin, I am now able to show that such names owe their origin to the former presence of buffaloes at this locality. Professor Hamlin, on writing to Professor J. R. Loomis, of the University at Lewisburg, received from him the following in reply to his inquiries. In a letter dated Lewisburg, Pa., March 14, 1876, Professor Loomis writes as follows: "I have made such inquiries as I could. One man whose grandfather he well remembers, as well as much of his conversation, and who lived here one hundred years ago, never heard of the bison being native of this valley. I went to see the oldest native-born citizen of our town, who is now eighty-six years old. He says there were no buffaloes in his early days, but it was a current notion in his boyhood days that there had formerly been. . . . . Since writing the above I have received the enclosed note from Mr. Wolfe, the first gentleman referred to on the other page. The information, ... coming so directly, ... is probably the best that can now be gathered up."

In the note from Mr. J. Wolfe to Professor Loomis, Mr. Wolfe states as follows: "Since seeing you this morning I have had a conversation with Dr. Beck, and he informs me that buffaloes, at an early day, were very abundant in this valley, and that the valley received its name from that circumstance. The Doctor received his information from Colonel John Kelly, who was a prominent and early settler in the valley. Kelly told the Doctor that he shot the last one that was seen in the valley. Kelly received his information of the abundance of buffaloes from an old Indian named Logan, friendly to the whites, and who remained among the whites after the Indians were driven away."

Under date of March 30, 1876, Professor Loomis wrote again to Professor Hamlin respecting the same matter, from which I quote the following: "I sought an interview with Dr. Beck. . . . . The Colonel Kelly referred to was a soldier and officer in the Revolutionary War, and was a leading man in some fight in New Jersey during the war. A small monument is in our cemetery to his memory, from which I take the following inscription: 'Col. John Kelly died Feb. 18th, 1832, aged 88 years & 7 days.' He owned a farm about five miles from Lewisburg, in Kelly township, which was named from him. About 1790 or 1800 (such is the indefiniteness) Colonel Kelly was out with his gun on the McClister farm (which joined that of Colonel Kelly), and just at evening saw and shot a buffalo. His dog was young, and at so late an hour he did not allow it to pursue. The next morning he went to hunt his game, but did not find it. Nearly a week later word was brought him that it had been found, dead, some mile or two away. He found the information correct, but the animal had been considerably torn and eaten by wolves. He regarded the animal as a stray one, and had never heard of any in the valley at a later day. Dr. Beck had the account from Colonel Kelly about three months before his death. . . . . The Colonel also told him that the valley was wooded originally with large but scattered trees, so that the grass grew abundantly and furnished good pasturage for the buffalo, and that the animal had been from this circumstance very abundant in the valley. The Colonel repeated the statement of a friendly Indian, Logan (probably *not* the native chief of that name), who said that the buffalo had been very abundant. He, Dr. Beck, had the same statement from Michael Grove, also one of the first settlers in the valley. . . . . I was more particular than I should ordinarily have been, because this is about the last stage when reliable tradition can be had."

This, of course, affords satisfactory proof of the former existence of the buffalo in the region about Lewisburg, which forms the most easterly point to which the buffalo has been positively traced.*

* In respect to the supposed remains of *Bison americanus* from the Carlisle bone-caves, Professor Baird, in a recent letter to me (dated May 13, 1876), expressed some doubt as to their being referable to that species. A re-examination of them he thinks would be necessary in order to determine "whether they are of the bison, and if so of which species." During my recent visit to Washington, quite careful search was made for the specimens, but unfortunately without finding them, though they are doubtless still stored somewhere in the Museum of the Smithsonian Institution, and will some day be found.

Buffaloes on the Shenandoah River, Virginia. — On pages 85 to 87 evidence is cited in proof of the former occurrence of the buffalo on the sources of the James. My attention has since been called by Mr. Geo. Graham to the following passage in Watson's "Annals of Philadelphia":* "The latest mention of buffaloes nearest to our region of country is mentioned in 1730, when a gentleman from the Shanadore, Va., saw there a buffalo killed of 1,400 pounds, and several others came in a drove at the same time." This was probably a wandering herd from the region of the Upper James River, where, as already shown, they at that time existed.

A "Buffalo Creek" in Southern Georgia. — As will be presently noticed, the buffalo extended, about 1720 to 1750, considerably to the southward, in the States of Mississippi and Louisiana, of its range at the time De Soto and La Salle traversed these States. Catesby also found the buffalo on the Upper Savannah River, about "Fort Moore," in 1754, while Bartram refers to the existence, in 1774, of a locality known as "Great Buffalo Lick" on the divide between the Savannah and Altamaha Rivers, — a region well known to have been traversed by De Soto and others, one hundred to two hundred and thirty years earlier, and who did not either meet with or hear anything of the existence of buffaloes anywhere in that section of the country. In the extreme southeastern part of Georgia (Camden County), however, there is found a small creek emptying into the Santilla River, at its great bend to the eastward, which still bears the name of "Buffalo Creek." If this is to be taken as sufficient proof of the former presence there of buffaloes, it may imply that the region was casually visited by a roving band of buffaloes from the region northward some time probably between the years 1700 and 1770. During the sixteenth and seventeenth centuries this region was traversed by several different explorers, who, as is evident from their writings, did not meet with or hear of buffaloes here. It is, however, quite possible that subsequently buffaloes may have occasionally wandered to Southeastern Georgia, and even to portions of Florida. In all other cases the name "Buffalo Creek" proves to have had its origin in the former presence of buffaloes in the vicinity of the streams so named.

While it is certain that many of the allusions to the existence of the buffalo in Florida do not refer to the present area of Florida, it is possible that some of the later ones already discussed (see pages 97 – 101) may refer to a brief occupation of portions of that State by this animal during the

* Page 674 of the edition of 1830; Vol. II, p. 431, of the later edition.

early part of the eighteenth century. That it was not there earlier seems to me fully evident, and that if it was ever found there it must have existed there at a comparatively recent date and for only a very short period. As already stated (see page 101), I have met with no writer who claims to have himself seen buffaloes within the present limits of Florida, though if it ever occurred there an unquestionable record of the fact will yet doubtless be found.

The Buffalo in Mississippi.—On pages 102 and 115 I state that I had been unable to find any evidence of the former existence of the buffalo south of the Tennessee River, and the statement of Du Pratz that the Indians of Lower Louisiana leave that country in winter to hunt the buffalo is cited in proof of its supposed absence from that region. Du Pratz's statement in full on this point is as follows: "This buffalo is the chief food of the natives, and of the *French* also for a long time past..... They hunt this animal in winter; for which purpose they leave *Lower Louisiana* and the river *Missisipi*, as he cannot penetrate thither on account of the thickness of the woods; and besides loves to feed on long grass, which is only to be found in the meadows of the high lands."* This notice appears in the chapter devoted to an account of the quadrupeds of Louisiana, and being misled by the import of the term *Lower Louisiana*, which at that time was generally applied to all the Lower Mississippi country, or that portion south of the 35th parallel, and by the fact of the almost unquestionable absence of the buffalo from the country south of the Tennessee at the time De Soto crossed this region in 1539 and 1540, I inadvertently omitted to examine with due care the earlier portions of Du Pratz's work. My attention, however, has since been kindly directed (by my friend, Mr. L. Carr) to other reference by Du Pratz to the buffalo as a former inhabitant of a considerable portion of the present State of Mississippi. In his detailed account of the "Lands of Louisiana" Du Pratz says: "From the sources of the river of the *Pasku Ogoulas*, quite to those of the river of *Quesoncté*, which falls into the Lake *St. Louis*, the lands are light and sterile, but something gravelly, on account of the neighborhood of the mountains, that lye to the North. This country is intermixt with extensive hills, fine meadows, numbers of thickets, and sometimes woods,

* The History of Louisiana, etc., English Ed., Vol. II, p. 49. The original reads as follows: "Ce Bœuf est la viande principale des Naturels, & a fait long-tems aussi celle des François. . . . . On va à la chasse de cet Animal dans l'hyver, & on s'écarte de la Basse Louisiane & du Fleuve S. Louis, parce qu'il ne peut y pénétrer, à cause de l'épaisseur des Bois, & que d'ailleurs il aime la grande herbe qui ne se trouve que dans les Prairies des *terres hautes*." — *Histoire de la Louisiane*, etc., Tom. II, p 67.

thick set with cane, particularly on the banks of rivers and brooks; and is extremely proper for agriculture. The mountains which I said these countries have to the North, form nearly the figure of a chaplet, with one end pretty near the *Missisipi*, the other on the banks of the *Mobile*. The inner part of this chaplet or chain is filled with hills; which are pretty fertile in grass, simples, fruits of the country, horse-chestnuts, and wild-chestnuts, as large and at least as good as those of *Lyons*. To the North of this chain of mountains lies the country of the *Chicasaws*, very fine and free of mountains: it has only very extensive and gentle eminences, or rising grounds, fertile groves and meadows. . . . . All the countries I have just mentioned are stored with game of every kind. The buffalo is found on the rising grounds; the partridge in thick open woods, such as the groves in meadows; the elks delight in large forests, as also the pheasant; the deer, which is a roving animal, is every where to be met with, because in whatever place it may happen to be, it always has something to browse on." *

Later he says in speaking of the country further north: "But to the east [of the Mississippi River], the lands are a good deal higher [than on the present Louisiana side], seeing from *Manchac* [near the present site of Baton Rouge] to the river Wabache [Ohio] they are between an hundred and two hundred feet higher than the *Missisipi* in its greatest floods. . . . . All these high lands are, besides, surmounted, in a good many places, by little eminences, or small hills, and rising grounds running off lengthwise, with gentle slopes. . . . . All these high lands are generally meadows and forests of tall trees, with grass up to the knees. . . . . Almost all these lands are such as I have described; that is, the meadows are on those high grounds, whose slope is very gentle; we also find there tall forests, and thickets in the low bottoms. In the meadows we observe here and there groves of very tall and straight oaks, to the number of fourscore or an hundred at most. There are others of about forty or fifty, which seem to have been planted by men's hands in these meadows, for a retreat to the buffaloes, deer, and other animals, and a screen against storms, and the sting of the flies. . . . . Those rising meadows and tall forests abound with buffaloes, elk, and deer, with turkeys, partridges and all kinds of game; consequently wolves, catamounts, and other carnivorous animals are found there." †

* The History of Louisiana, Vol. II, pp. 251 – 253.

† The History of Louisiana, Vol. II, pp. 262 – 267. The last quotation reads in the original as follows: "Ces Côteaux en Prairies & ces futayes sont abondantes en Bœufs, Cerfs & Chevreuils, en Dindes, en Perdrix & en toute sorte de gibier," etc. — *Histoire de la Louisiane*, Tom. I, p. 267.

On one of his accompanying maps this region is marked as "Terres Hautes," while the low country, or "drowned lands," of the present Lower Louisiana is marked "Terres Plates." Hence, when in his later description of the buffalo he speaks of the Indians leaving "Lower Louisiana" to hunt the buffalo, he simply means that they leave the low flat country immediately bordering the coast and the river, especially the low country south and west of Baton Rouge, to hunt in the higher lands of the present State of Mississippi, where, if we take Du Pratz as trustworthy authority, the buffalo must, at that time (about 1720 and later), have been abundant. Yet when this very region was crossed by De Soto, two hundred years earlier, the buffalo was evidently not to be found there. It hence appears to have spread in the mean time from the region more to the northward. West of the Mississippi, also, the buffalo, in Du Pratz's time, extended southward over regions where it was not met with by De Soto or by La Salle, which affords further evidence that the buffalo extended its range considerably to the southward and eastward in the valley of the Lower Mississippi between 1540 and 1720, or even between 1685 and the latter date, as seems to have been also the case in South Carolina and Georgia.

It hence appears evident that at one time the buffalo occupied probably most of the region between the Tennessee and Mississippi Rivers. On Du Pratz's map, however, the course of the Tennessee is very incorrectly laid down, as it is also on the earlier map of De l'Isle, and on maps published much later even than Du Pratz's, its southern bend on Du Pratz's map not reaching the 36th parallel, while it actually crosses the 33d. He seems not to have himself passed above the Chickasaw Bluffs, and his knowledge of the country beyond on the east side of the river was evidently very vague.

The presence of "Bœufs" in the country drained by the Mobile River is also mentioned by *un Officier de Marine*, in a letter published with Chevalier de Tonti's "Relation" * (the authorship of which work, however, Tonti disowns).

The presence of a creek in Southwestern Mississippi still bearing the name of "Buffalo Creek" may be considered as further evidence of the former existence of the buffalo in this region.

It is to be regretted that Adair, who spent many years (1735 to 1767) as a trader and government official among the tribes south of the Tennessee River, has left so little on record respecting the range of the buffalo at that

* Relation de la Louisiane, 1720, Vol. I, p. 11.

period. In his "General Observations on the North American Indians" he refers to their use of buffalo flesh as food, and its skins, horns, wool, and sinews in the manufacture of clothing and utensils, but without specifying by what tribes or at what localities.* Among the tribes mentioned are those that lived north of the Tennessee River, and hence where the buffalo was at that time abundant. In an account of one of his journeys he mentions the killing of buffaloes somewhere, apparently, in the mountains of Northern Georgia,† in 1749, and this is the only allusion in his work that bears directly upon the range of the buffalo. He states also, however, that "the buffaloes are now become scarce, as the thoughtless and wasteful Indians used to kill great numbers of them, only for the tongues and marrow-bones, leaving the rest of the carcase to the wild beasts."‡ Elk, deer, bears, and turkeys, however, are frequently mentioned as affording a supply of food to the southern tribes of Indians, but in these statements he never alludes to the buffalo.

Former Abundance of the Buffalo along the Ohio River, with Notes respecting the Date of its Extirpation in the State of Ohio. — On pages 106, 107, and 111 evidence has already been given respecting the former occurrence of the buffalo in Ohio. In answer to recent inquiries of mine, Mr. George Graham of Cincinnati, well known as a reliable authority on matters relating to the early history of the West, has kindly given me reference to notices of the buffalo as an inhabitant of Ohio in Craig's *Olden Time*, and also unpublished traditional facts bearing upon the date of its extirpation from that State.

The "Journal of George Croghan,"§ published in *Olden Time*,‖ states that buffaloes, bears, turkeys, and other game abounded about the mouth of the "Conhawa," in 1765, as well as at the mouth of "Bottle River," and also on the prairies bordering the "Ouabache."¶ They were also found and killed by Washington, according to the "Journal of a Tour to the Ohio River in 1770," at the mouth of the Kanhawa and also near the "Great Bend" of the

* See Adair (James), History of North American Indians, pp. 375 – 450.

† Ibid., p. 335.

‡ Ibid., p. 415.

§ Not Colonel Croghan of Kentucky.

‖ The Olden Time: a Monthly Publication devoted to the Preservation of Documents and other Authentic Information in relation to the Early Explorations, and the Settlement and Improvement of the Country around the Head of the Ohio. Edited by Neville B. Craig, Esq. Two volumes, small 4to. Pittsburg, 1846 – 1848.

¶ *Olden Time*, Vol. I, pp. 405, 410, 411.

Ohio, in 1770.* According to the "Journal of General [Richard] Butler," buffaloes were killed by his party at the mouth of Big Sandy Creek, in October, 1785, and also on Buffalo Lick Creek and Licking Creek the same year,† at which time the buffaloes were there still quite abundant.

"In 1791," says Mr. Graham in one of his letters to me (dated "Cincinnati, April 11, 1876"), "General Massie laid out the town of Manchester in the Virginia Military District of Ohio, about thirty-five miles from Cincinnati. This was the first settlement in the Virginia Military District. The woods in the neighborhood supplied game, — deer, elks, buffaloes, bears, and turkeys, — while the river furnished a variety of excellent fish. In 1794 and 1795 McArthur‡ was settling a plan for his winter operations, when he fell in with George Hardick, an experienced hunter and trapper, who was never at ease but when he was ranging through the solitary woods. Agreeing to go into partnership for a winter hunt, they made a light canoe, procured ammunition and beaver-traps, and set off from Manchester, travelling down the Ohio River to the mouth of the Kentucky River, thence up the Kentucky far above the settlements. Game of every description was found in abundance; deer and buffalo were killed for their hides and tallow. Beaver and otter were the principal game pursued, and were caught in great numbers. They went up the river as far as they could find water to float their canoe, and spent the winter in the spurs of the Cumberland Mountains, more than a hundred miles from the habitations of civilized men," returning in spring by the same route to Manchester.

"The last reliable account of killing buffalo," says Mr. Graham, in the same letter, "is taken from the Lacross manuscripts, and partly from tradition from the lips of the children and grandchildren of those who were present. Of the French who settled at Gallipolis, Ohio, in 1790, but one person ever killed a buffalo. This man's name was Duteil. He was out hunting in the summer of 1795, about two miles west from Gallipolis, and saw a herd of buffaloes. He fired without aiming at any particular one, and luckily killed a large one. He was so elated with this feat that without stopping to examine the animal he ran as fast as he could to the town, and, having announced his luck, came back, followed by the entire body of colonists, men, women, and children. They quickly formed a procession, with

* *Olden Time*, pp. 426, 427.

† Ibid., Vol. II, pp. 447, 450, 453, 456, 458, 497.

‡ "'McDonald's Sketches,' published in Cincinnati, in 1838, by E. Morgan, gives the life of General McArthur."

musicians playing violins, flutes, and hautboys in front, the fortunate hunter proudly marching with his gun on his shoulder, and the animal swinging from poles thrust through between its tied feet, followed by the crowd, singing and rejoicing at the prospect of good and hearty fare. The animal was quickly skinned and dressed on its arrival at the town, and for several days there was feasting, as the first and last buffalo of Gallipolis was served up in such a variety of ways and means as none but the French could devise; Charles Francis Duteil remaining until his death the renowned marksman who killed the first and last buffalo of all the emigrants from France who settled the town of Gallipolis."

Mr. Graham adds that he has "no information that can be relied upon of buffalo being killed in Ohio after the year 1795 or 1796." In a later letter he says, "From all that I know of the early settlement and history of the West, I am under the impression that the buffalo disappeared from Ohio, Illinois, Indiana, and Kentucky about the year 1800."

The Bison seen by Cortes in the City of Mexico.—According to De Solis, Cortes found specimens of the bison in Mexico, among the wonderfully varied possessions of Montezuma. In describing the animals in Montezuma's menagerie, De Solis says: "In the second Square of the same House were the Wild Beasts, which were either presents to Montezuma, or taken by his Hunters, in strong Cages of Timber, rang'd in good Order and under Cover: Lions, Tygers, Bears, and all others of the savage Kind which *New-Spain* produc'd; among which, the greatest Rarity was the *Mexican* Bull; a wonderful Composition of divers Animals: It has crooked Shoulders, with a Bunch on its Back like a Camel; its Flanks dry, its Tail large, and its Neck cover'd with Hair like a Lion: It is cloven footed, its Head armed like that of a Bull, which it resembles in Fierceness, with no less Strength and Agility."* These captive individuals appear to have been the first specimens of the American Bison seen by Europeans.

Specimens of the Bison taken alive to Spain prior to 1558.—According to Thevet, living specimens of the bison were taken to Spain prior to 1558, of one of which Thevet claims to have seen the skin.†

* De Solis's (Antonio de) History of the Conquest of Mexico by the Spaniards. Townsend's English translation (London, 1724). Book III, Chap. XIV, p. 76.

† "Lon en amena une fois deux tous vifs en Espagne, de l'un desquels j'ay veu la peau & non autre chose, & n'y peurent vivre long temps." — *Les Singularitez de la France antarctique*, etc., p. 144.

II.

ON THE AGE OF THE BISON IN THE OHIO VALLEY.

BY N. S. SHALER.

In the foregoing Memoir of Mr. Allen, allusion is made to certain researches carried on by me at Big Bone Lick in Kentucky, which have some reference to the question of the age of the Buffalo in the Ohio Valley. These investigations, begun in 1868 and continued in 1869, have only been sufficient to point the way to further studies which it is in the plan of the Kentucky Geological Survey to prosecute, but which it may not be in its power to undertake for some time to come. I therefore give a short sketch of the evidence collected at Big Bone Lick with a view to showing the limits of the observations that have been made there.

The springs at Big Bone Lick, as at all the other licks of Kentucky, are sources of saline waters derived from the older Palæozoic rocks. These saline materials, as has been suggested by Dr. Sterry Hunt, have their origin in the imprisoned waters of the ancient seas, or in the salts derived therefrom, which have been locked in the depths of the strata below the reach of the leaching action of the surface water. Whenever the rocks lie above the line of the drainage, these salts have been leached away. As we go below the surface they increase in quantity until we reach the level, where these waters remain saturated with the materials which existed in the old sea-waters. The displacement of these old imprisoned waters is brought about by the sinking down of water on the highlands through the vertical interstices of the soil and rock, and the consequent tendency of the water below the surface to restore the hydrostatic balance. This action is particularly likely to occur when the rocks above the drainage are limestones or shales; while a bed of rock at some distance below the drainage is of sandstone and permeable to water. This is the case at Big Bone Lick, where at about two hundred feet below the surface we have the calciferous sandstone with a structure open enough to admit the free passage of water in a horizontal direction. That some such process is at work is shown by the fact that the water will rise ten feet or more above the surface of the soil if enclosed in a pipe.

The fact that the reservoir of these waters is below the general surface causes them to appear in the bottom of the valleys, and the considerable abstraction of matter from the underlying beds, probably amounting to some hundred cubic feet per annum in the case of Big Bone Lick, causes a depression at the point of escape, and generally brings about the formation of a swamp in a depressed and constantly lowering basin, through which the spring water creeps away, or is evaporated. This swamp forms a natural trap for all the higher mammalia of this region. When excavations are made near the existing outlets of the springs, we find remains of the large mammals brought into the country by man,— the horse, cow, pig, and sheep.

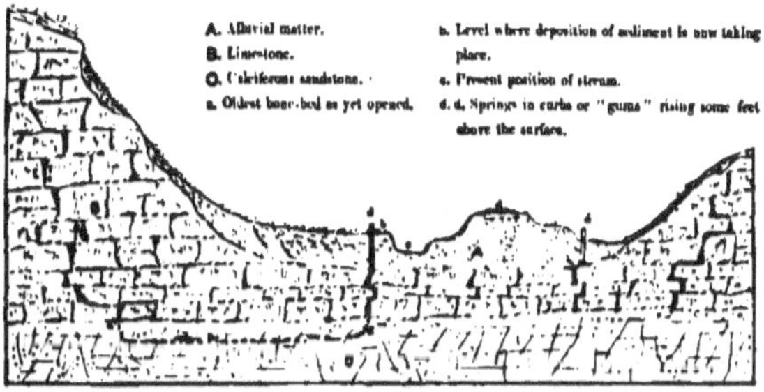

Diagrammatic Section of the beds at Big Bone Lick.

In the frequent change of outlet of these springs, it comes to pass that at many points near the surface of the thirty or forty acres that lie in the little basin where Big Bone Lick is found, there are old spring vents, about which bones are found, that no longer give forth saline waters. It is a fact bearing on the history of the buffalo, that their remains about Big Bone Lick are, when found, always near the present position of the springs and never at any depth beneath the surface. In the recent springs they are very abundant, and not much more ancient in their appearance than the remains of the domesticated animals. The evidence obtained at this point leads to the conclusion that the first appearance of this species in the country was singularly recent, and also shows that their coming was like an irruption in its suddenness. These buffalo bones are wonderfully abundant in some of the shallow swampy places of this neighborhood. I have seen them massed to the depth of two feet or more, as close as the stones of a pavement, and so beaten down by the succeeding herds as to make it difficult to lift them from their bed.

As will be seen from the accompanying diagram, there seems to have been some degradation of the surface of this swamp after the deposition of many of the mastodon remains, and before the coming of the buffalo. This lowering of level was apparently consequent on the erosion of the bed of the small creek that drains the valley. The old elevated beds had probably washed a good deal when the buffalo came, but it was principally by its wallowing and stamping that the bones of the mastodon, elephants, &c., were exposed to the air.* At no point in this old ground did I find a trace of the buffalo, though in some of it the bones identified by Mr. Allen as belonging to *Ovibos* were found. There, too, were found the bones of the moose and caribou. I am inclined to believe from these investigations that the *Bison americanus* did not appear at Big Bone Lick until a very recent time.

All the observations made by the Kentucky Survey in the caverns of the State, and the neighboring district of Tennessee, have led to the discovery of no bison remains in these subterranean receptacles, where the bones of the beaver, deer, wolf, bear, and many other mammals have been discovered. The observation of the officers of the Survey to be published hereafter will show that our caves have been used as the homes of the living and the receptacles of the dead by more than one of the earlier tribes of this region, but they seem never to have brought the bones of this animal to the caves.

Some years ago I ventured to call attention to the general absence of the remains of this animal in all the mounds of the historic or prehistoric races, and to the fact that on their pipes and pottery, though they figure every other indigenous mammal and some of the birds of this region, seeking their models even in the manitee of Florida, I have never been able to find any trace of buffalo bones in any of the mounds which so often contain bones of other animals, nor have I been able to ascertain that they have ever been found in such places. At an ancient camping-ground on the Ohio River, about twelve miles above Cincinnati, where the remains are covered by alluvial soil of apparently some antiquity, and where the pottery (hereafter to be figured in the Memoirs of the Survey) is rather more ancient in character than that made by our modern Indians, I found bones of deer, elk, bear, fox, &c., but none of buffalo. At a number of other old camps on the Ohio River

* For the habits of the buffalo in this regard, see the preceding Memoir of Mr. Allen, p. 64, *et seq.*

there is the same conspicuous absence of the remains of this animal. These evidences, negative and incomplete as they are, make it at least probable that the buffalo was unknown to the people who built the mounds and preceded the tribes which were found here, by the whites, in the seventeenth century. The same arguments warrant us in supposing that the *Bison latifrons*, with its contemporaries, — the musk ox, the elephant, and the mastodon, — had vanished before the advent of this race, or at least before the time of which we have evidence in the fossils already found.

I have long been of the opinion, without claiming originality therein, that the tribes which built the mounds and the shapely measured forts of this region were driven to the southward by an invasion of other tribes coming from the northward and northwestward. In the Memoirs now in preparation, concerning the ancient peoples of this region, it will be claimed, on what seems to Mr. Lucian Carr, ethnologist of the Survey, and to myself, sufficient evidence, that these mound-building peoples were essentially related to the Natchez group of Indians, and were driven southward by the ruder tribes of the somewhat related tribes which occupied the northern parts of the Mississippi Valley, when we first knew it. All this seems to me to have a possible significance in the problem of the coming of the buffalo; when we remember that the Indians north of the Ohio were much in the habit of burning the forests, and so making open plains, or prairies, and that, as Mr. Allen has well pointed out, the buffalo cannot penetrate far into the denser forests, it may be that it was this destruction of forests that laid the way open to their entrance. The so-called Barrens of Kentucky, the southward extension of the Wabash prairies, give us evidence on this point. As soon as the Indians were driven away, these Kentucky prairies sprang up in timber, and are now densely wooded. The same is in part true of the other prairies of the Ohio Valley. I am inclined to think that the forcing back of the timber line from the Mississippi is principally due to the burning of the forests by the aborigines in their eastward working, aided by the continued decrease of the rainfall, which I believe to have been a concomitant of the disappearance of the glacial period.* The question of the origin of the buffalo and its relation to the earliest tribes of people in this district is made still more complicated by the fact that there is no doubt that there was an earlier and closely related species of buffalo in this district, probably coeval with the mammoth and mastodon, and possibly with the caribou and elk,

* Notes on the cause and geological value of variations in rainfall. Vol. XVIII, p. 170, *et seq.* Proceedings of the Boston Society of Natural History.

which had doubtless disappeared before the coming of any race of men that has as yet been identified in this country.

The succession of events in this region, as far as the species of bison are concerned, seems to have been somewhat as follows, viz.:—

1st. The existence of the *Bison latifrons* in company with the mammoth and its contemporaries,—the mastodon, musk ox (*Bootherium cavifrons*), etc. This species, like its contemporaries, by its size gave evidence of the even climate and abundant vegetation of the time just following, and probably in part during the glacial period.

2d. The disappearance of this fauna, followed by the coming of a race (mound-builders) that retained no distinct traditions, and have left no art records of the presence of any of the large animals of the preceding time.

3d. The disappearance of this race from the region north of the Tennessee, probably leaving representatives in the Natchez group of Indians, followed by the occupation of the country by a race that greatly extended the limits of the treeless plains to the eastward, and so permitted the coming of the modern bison into this region.

I have long been disposed to look upon the succeeding glacial periods as the most effective causes of the changes that led to the determination of new specific characters among animals, and I am strongly disposed to think that in the *B. americanus* we have the descendant of the *B. latifrons* modified by existence in the new conditions of soil and climate to which it was driven by the great changes closing the last ice age.

When the exploration of Big Bone Lick is completed, it will doubtless show that there was an interval of some thousands of years between those two species.

INDEX.

MAP.

The portion of the accompanying map south of the forty-ninth parallel is based mainly on the map of this region by Stulpnagel and Berghaus in Stieler's Hand-Atlas; the portion north of the forty-ninth parallel is based on Johnson's map and recent surveys, including Mr. W. H. Dall's map of Alaska and adjoining regions, recently published by the United States Coast Survey.

Owing to the influence the overland emigration and the construction of the different railroads across the Plains have had in restricting the range of the Bison, the course of the overland trail and the Union Pacific and Kansas and Colorado railroads has been laid down on the map. The routes of De Soto and Coronado have been added on account of their historic interest in connection with the former range of this animal, the former being from Schoolcraft's map of De Soto's route (Hist., Cond., and Pros. of Ind. Tribes of U. S., Part III, Pl. xliv), and the latter from Mr. R. H. Kern's map of Coronado's route, published also by Schoolcraft (Hist., Cond., and Pros., etc., Part IV, Pl. iii).

In order to better adapt the map to the illustration of the geographical distribution of animal and vegetable life (the need of such a map being apparent), isothermal lines have been added, based on Mr. C. A. Schott's Temperature Charts of the United States; permission for their use being kindly granted by Professor Joseph Henry, Secretary of the Smithsonian Institution, under whose direction they were prepared. Only the lines of mean annual temperature have been extended across the continent. The isocheimal and isotheral curves, owing to their great complication over the more broken country to the westward of this limit, are carried merely from the Atlantic coast to the eastern base of the Rocky Mountains.

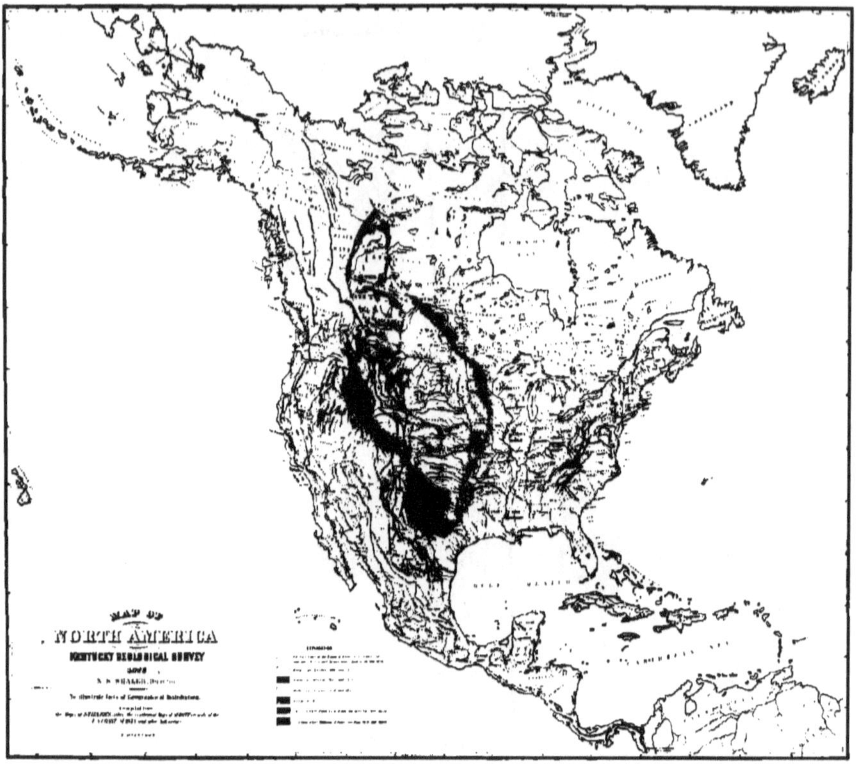
MAP OF
NORTH AMERICA
KENTUCKY GEOLOGICAL SURVEY

PLATE I.

Horn-cores of **Bison latifrons**, from Adams County, Ohio. (From a photograph kindly furnished by Dr. O. D. Norton of Cincinnati. Figures about one fifth natural size.)

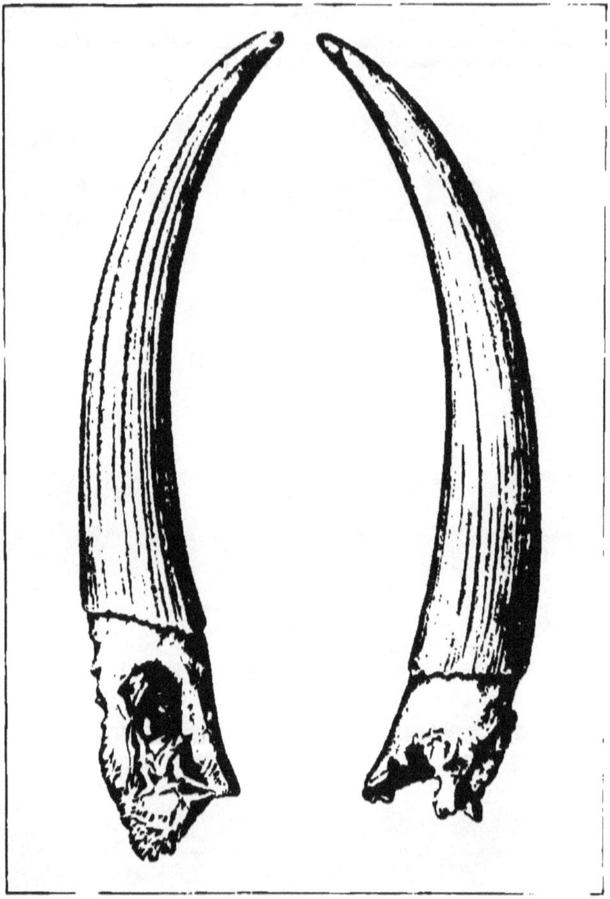

PLATE II.

Atlases of Bisons. (Figures one half natural size.)

Figs. 1 – 4. Atlas of *Bison latifrons?* from Darien, Georgia. (The specimen described by Dr. Leidy.)
Figs. 5 – 8. Atlas of a very large old male *Bison americanus.*

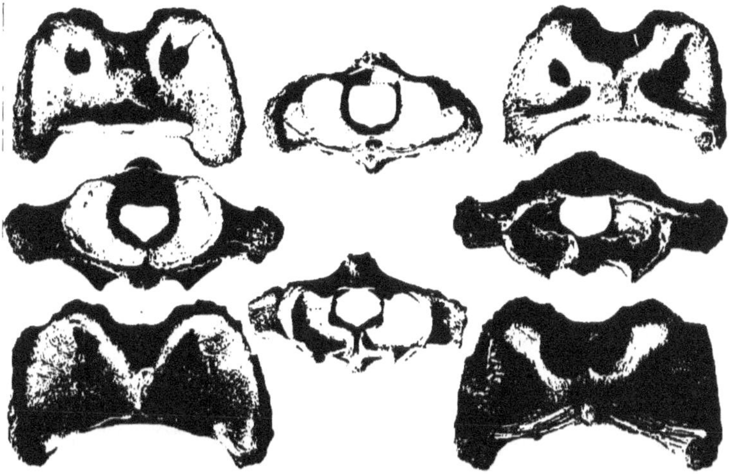

PLATE III.

Rami of Bison antiquus and B. americanus. (All natural size.)

Fig. 1. Fragment of a jaw of *Bison antiquus*, from California. (Specimen received from Professor J. D. Whitney.)

Fig. 2. Corresponding part of the jaw of *Bison americanus*.

Fig. 3. Fragment of a jaw of *Bison antiquus*, from California. (Specimen received from Professor J. D. Whitney.)

Fig. 4. Corresponding part of the jaw of *Bison americanus*.

Fig. 6. Teeth from above of the jaw-fragment of *Bison antiquus*, represented in Fig. 1.

Fig. 7. Corresponding teeth of *Bison americanus*.

Fig. 8. Teeth from above of the jaw-fragment of *Bison antiquus*, represented in Fig. 3.

Fig. 9. Corresponding teeth of *Bison americanus*.

Fig. 10. Section showing the thickness of the jaw-fragment of *Bison antiquus*, represented in Fig. 1.

Fig. 11. Corresponding section from *Bison americanus*.

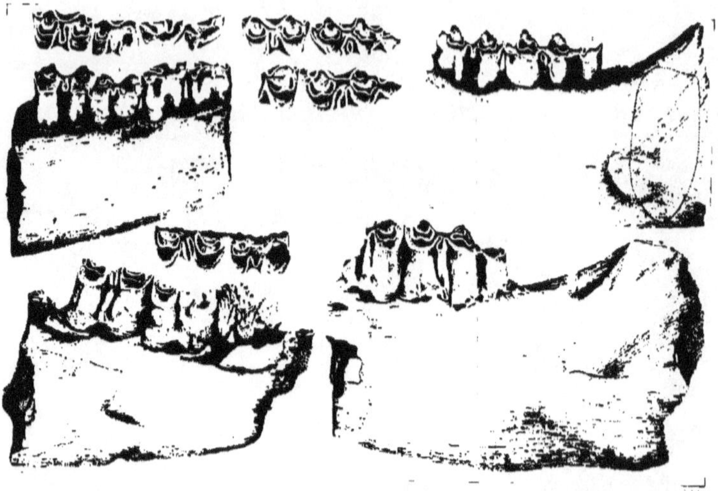

PLATE IV.

Imperfect skull of **Bison antiquus** (probably a female) from St. Michael's, Alaska. (Specimen received from the California Academy of Sciences, through W. G. W. Harford, Esq., Director of the Academy.)

Fig. 1. Occipital view. (One fourth natural size.)

Fig. 2. View from above. (One fourth natural size.)

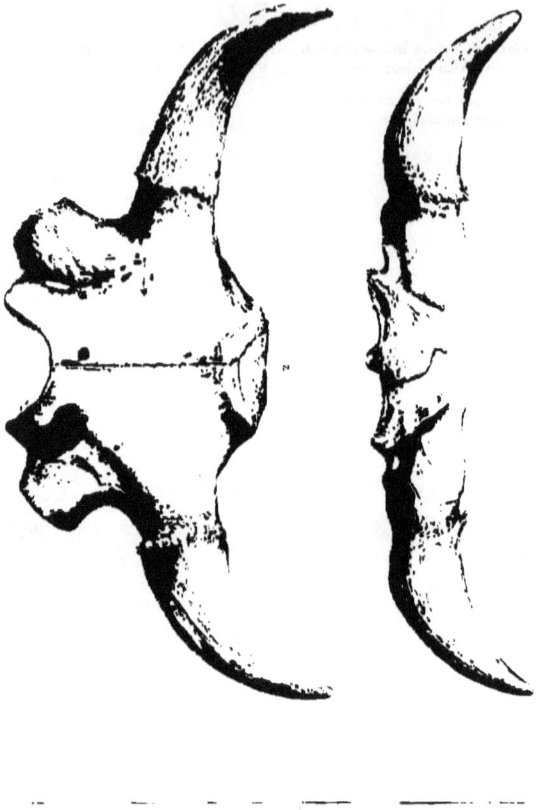

PLATE V.

Skulls of **Bison americanus**, males, showing the great diversity of form that obtains in adult individuals of the same sex. (One fourth natural size.)

Fig. 1. Occipital view of the skull of an old male from the plains of Kansas (specimen No. 1215).

Fig. 2. Occipital view of the skull of a male five or six years old from Kansas (spec. No. 94).

Fig. 3. Occipital view of the skull of an old male from Big-Bone Lick, Kentucky (spec. No. 2047).

Fig. 4. Occipital view of the skull of a middle-aged male from Big-Bone Lick, Kentucky (spec. No. 2050).

Fig. 5. Occipital view of the skull of a male about six years old from Kansas (spec. No. 102).

Fig. 6. Occipital view of the skull of an old male from Kansas (spec. No. 10).

Fig. 7. Occipital view of the skull of a male about six years old from Kansas (spec. No. 11).

Fig. 8. Occipital view of the skull of a male four or five years old from Kansas (spec. No. 100).

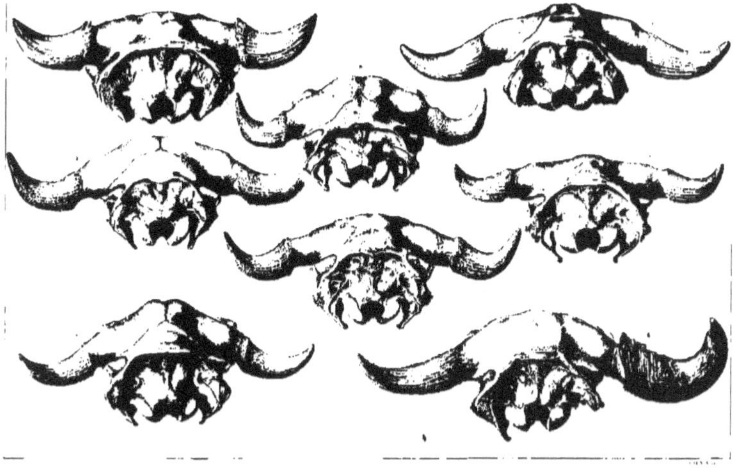

PLATE VI.

Skulls of Bison americanus, males, showing the great diversity of form that obtains in adult individuals of the same sex. (One fourth natural size.)

Fig. 1. View in profile of the skull of an old male from the plains of Kansas (specimen No. 1215).

Fig. 2. View in profile of the skull of a male five or six years old from Kansas (spec. No. 94).

Fig. 3. View in profile of the skull of an old male from Big-Bone Lick, Kentucky (spec. No. 2047).

Fig. 4. View in profile of the skull of a middle-aged male from Big-Bone Lick, Kentucky (spec. No. 2050).

Fig. 5. View in profile of the skull of a male about six years old from Kansas (spec. No. 103).

Fig. 6. View in profile of the skull of an old male from Kansas (spec. No. 10).

Fig. 7. View in profile of the skull of a male about six years old from Kansas (spec. No. 11).

Fig. 8. View in profile of the skull of a male four or five years old from Kansas (spec. No. 100).

Pl. V.

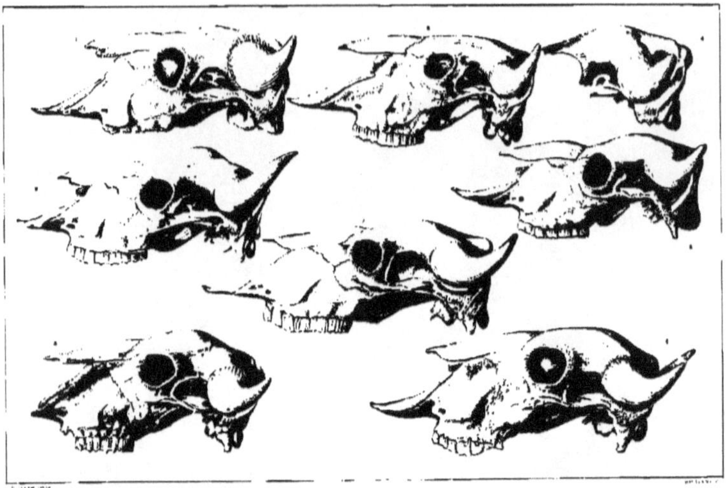

PLATE VII.

Figures of three skulls of **Bison americanus**, females, showing the great diversity of form that obtains in adult specimens of the same sex. Also figures of a skull of **Bison bonasus**, female, and of metatarsal bones of **Bison americanus** and **B. latifrons** ! (Skulls, one fourth natural size; metatarsal bones, one third natural size.)

Fig. 1. Occipital view of a skull of a female *B. americanus*, about six years old, from Kansas (specimen No. 105).

Fig. 2. Occipital view of a skull of a female *B. americanus*, about six years old, from Kansas (spec. No. 12).

Fig. 3. Occipital view of a skull of a female *B. americanus*, about six years old, from Big-Bone Lick, Kentucky (spec. No. 2050).

Fig. 4. View in profile of a skull of *B. americanus*, female, about six years old, from Kansas (spec. No. 105).

Fig. 5. View in profile of a skull of *B. americanus*, female, about six years old, from Kansas (spec. No. 12).

Fig. 6. View in profile of a skull of *B. americanus*, female, about six years old, from Big-Bone Lick, Kentucky (spec. No. 2049).

Fig. 7. Occipital view of a skull of *B. bonasus*, female, about six years old (spec. No. 1790).

Fig. 8. View in profile of the same.

Fig. 9. Metatarsal bone of *B. americanus*, female (spec. No. 12).

Fig. 10. Metatarsal bone of *B. americanus*, male (spec. No. 10).

Fig. 11. Metatarsal bone of *B. latifrons*? from Darien, Ga. (The original specimen described by Dr. Leidy, now in the Museum of the Boston Society of Natural History.)

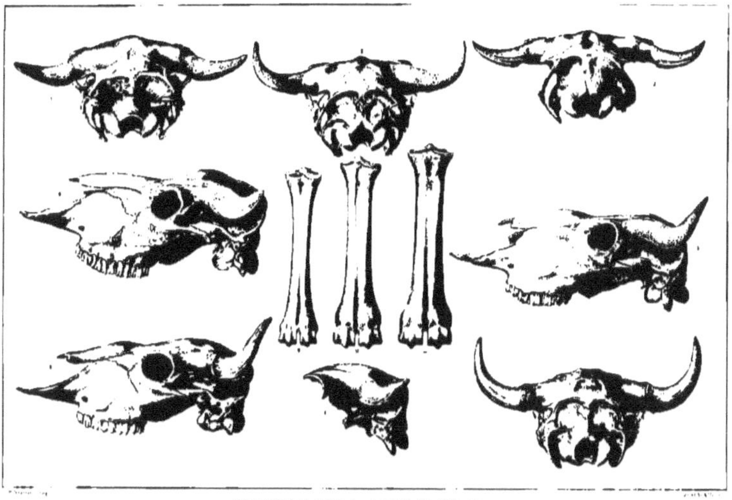

PLATE VIII.

Horns of **Bison americanus** and **B. antiquus**. (One third natural size.)

Figs. 1–5. A series of the horns of the male *Bison americanus*, showing variation in size and form with age. (Fig. 1, from a specimen about six months old; Fig. 2, from a specimen about one year old; Fig. 3, from a specimen about three or four years old; Fig. 4, from a specimen about ten or twelve years old; Fig. 5, from a specimen twenty to twenty-five years old.)

Figs. 6 and 7. Horns of very old males of *B. americanus*, showing diversity in size and form in males of corresponding ages.

Fig. 8. Horn of a six-year-old female of *B. americanus*.

Fig. 9. Horn of a six-year-old female of *B. bonasus*.

Figs. 10 and 11. Horns of old females of *B. americanus*.

Fig. 12. Horn of *B. antiquus* (male !), from St Michaels, Alaska. (Specimen presented by W. G. W. Harford, Esq., Director Cal. Acad. Sciences.)

Pl.VIII.

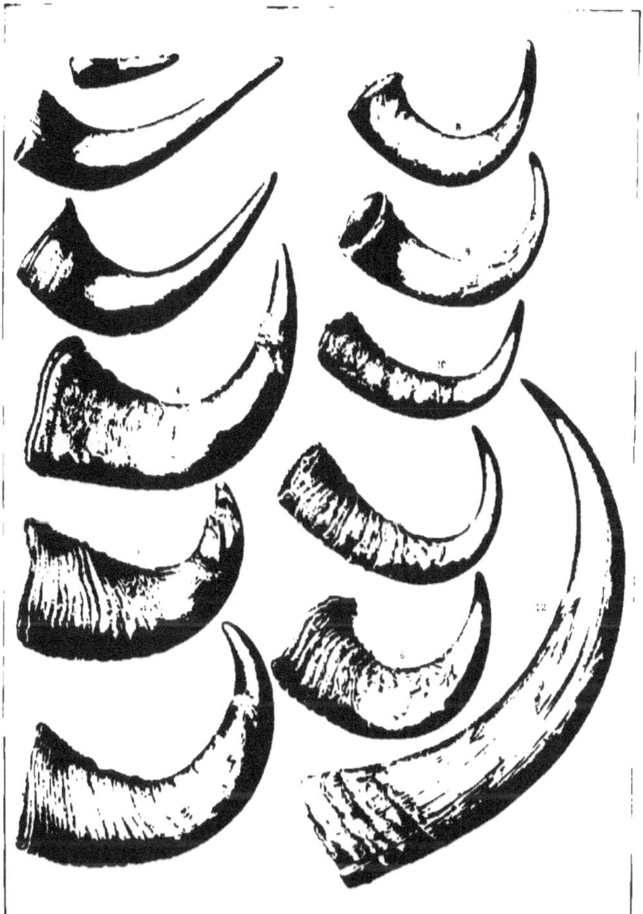

PLATE IX.

Milk Dentition of *Bison americanus*. (All the figures natural size.)

Fig. 1. Right lower pre-molars seen from above, from a very young individual (the first true molar is just in sight). Specimen No. 580.

Fig. 2. The same seen from the outside.

Fig. 3. Right upper pre-molars seen from above, from the same specimen.

Fig. 4. The same seen from the outside.

Fig. 5. Right lower pre-molars, seen from above, from a somewhat older specimen, in which the first true molar is fully in sight. Specimen No. 1153.

Fig. 6. The same, seen from the outside.

Fig. 7. Right upper pre-molars, seen from above, from a specimen of about the same age as No. 1153. Drawn from specimen No. 1155.

Fig. 8. The same, seen from the outside.

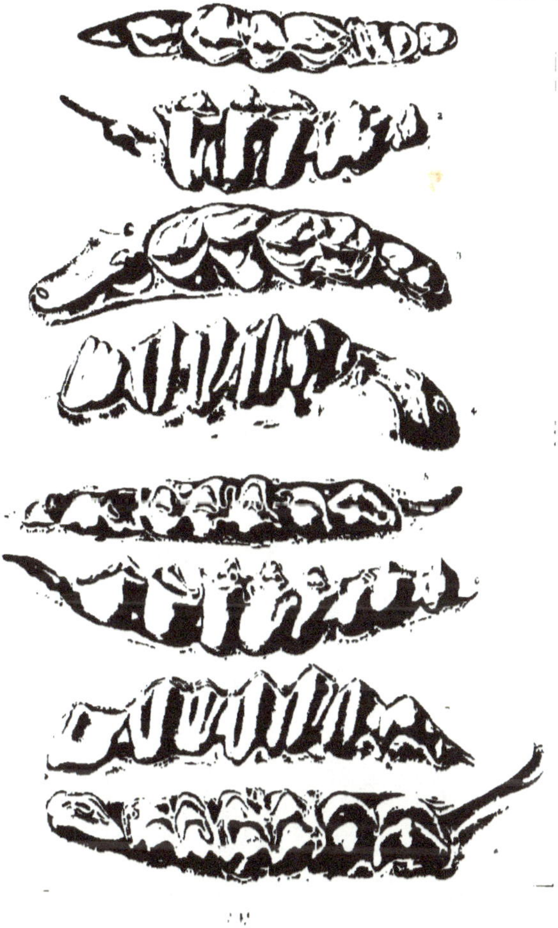

PLATE X.

Teeth of *Bison americanus*, showing different stages of attrition, etc. (All the figures natural size.)

Fig. 1. Left lower molars, seen from above, of a very old specimen from the plains of Kansas (No. 10), showing an extreme stage of attrition.

Fig. 2. The same, seen from the outside.

Fig. 3. Left lower molars, seen from above, of an aged specimen from the plains of Kansas (spec. No. 105), showing a less advanced stage of attrition.

Fig. 4. The same, seen from the outside.

Fig. 5. Right lower molars, seen from above, of a middle-aged specimen from Big-Bone Lick, Kentucky (No. 2046), showing the small amount of attrition.

Fig. 6. The same, from the outside, showing the deeply serrated outlines of the crown surface of the molars.

Fig. 7. Left upper molars, from above, of a middle-aged specimen from Big-Bone Lick, Kentucky (No. 2132), showing the small amount of attrition.

Fig. 8. The same, from the outside, showing the deeply serrated outline of the crown surface of the molars.

Fig. 9. Right lower molars, seen from above, of a rather young or middle-aged specimen from the plains of Kansas (No. 108).

Fig. 10. The same, from the outside, showing the nearly even outlines of the crown surface of the molars.

Fig. 11. Upper molars of the same specimen, seen from above.

Fig. 12. The same, from the outside, showing the nearly even outlines of the crown surface.

N. B. Figs. 11 and 12 are strictly comparable, as respects the age of the specimens, with Figs. 9 and 10. If there is any difference, the specimen illustrated by Figs. 11 and 12 is *younger*, rather than older, than the specimens from which Figs. 9 and 10 were made.

Figs. 9–12 also serve to show the mature dentition of *B. americanus*.

Pl.X

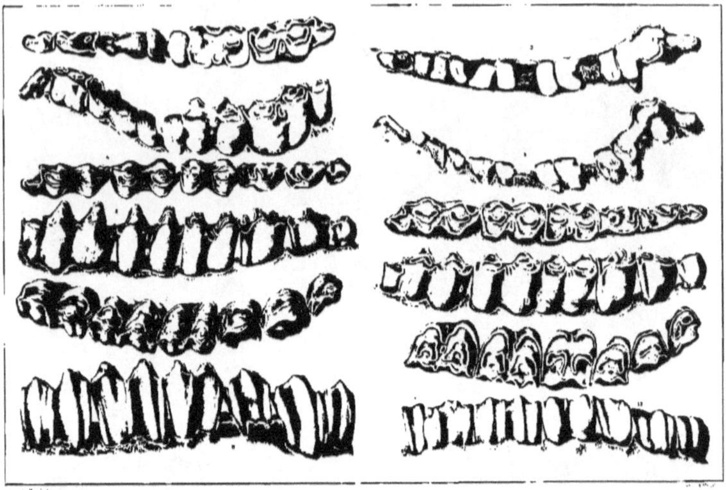

Bison Americanus – Nat. S.

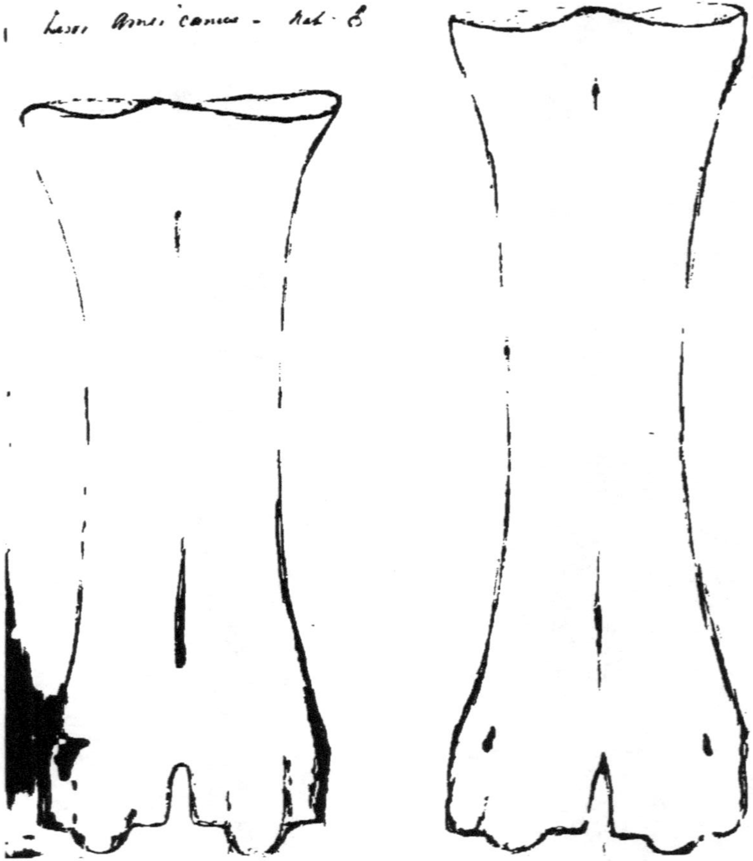

PLATE XI.

Metacarpal bones of **Bison americanus**, showing Individual and Sexual Variation in size and form. The specimens are all from Big-Bone Lick, Kentucky. (All the figures one third the natural size.)

Fig. 1.	Female.	Specimen	No. 2466.
" 2.	"	"	" 2470.
" 3.	"	"	" 2490.
" 4.	"	"	" 2476.
" 5.	"	"	" 2463.
" 6.	Male.	"	" 2483.
" 7.	"	"	" 2467.
" 8.	"	"	" 2489.
" 9.	"	"	" 2488.
" 10.	"	"	" 2486.

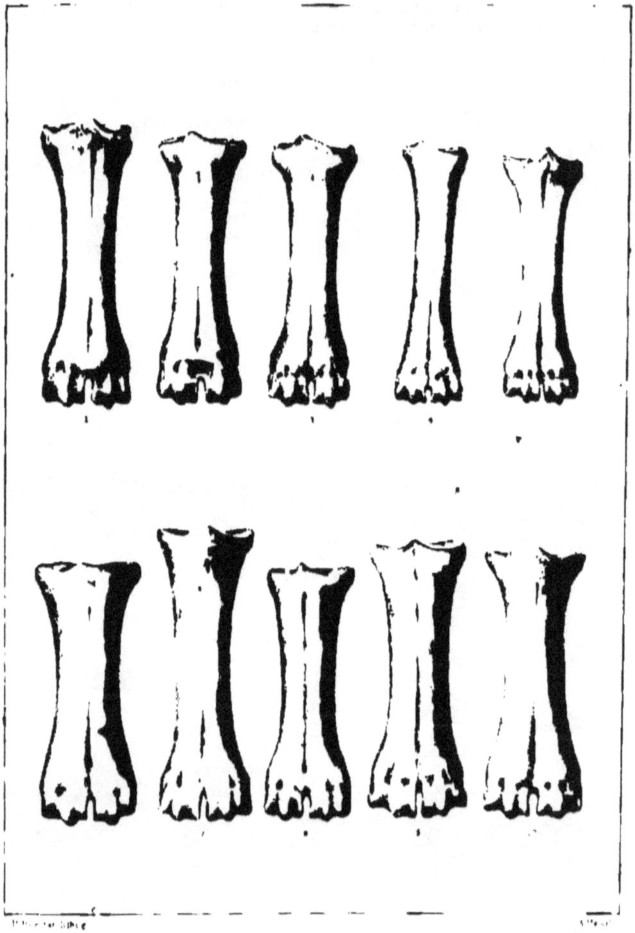

[illegible]ON AMERICANUS

PLATE XII.

Upper molar teeth of **Bison americanus** and **Bos taurus**. (All natural size.)

Fig. 1. Right upper molars, from above, of *B. americanus* (specimen No. 12). In this specimen the last true molar is just through its alveolus, and the last pre-molar of the temporary set is about two thirds grown; the second true molar is still almost unworn.

Fig. 2. Right upper molars, from above, of *B. americanus*, from a specimen (No. 100*) somewhat older than that represented in Fig. 1.

Fig. 3. Right upper molars, from above, of *B. americanus*, from a specimen (No. 94) of the same age as that represented in Fig. 2.

Fig. 4. Right upper molars, from above, of *B. americanus*, from a specimen (No. 11) somewhat older than those represented in Figs. 2 and 3.

Fig. 5. Right upper molars, from above, of *B. americanus*, from a specimen (No. 102), still older than that represented in Fig. 4.

Fig. 6. Right upper molars, from above, of *B. americanus*, from a specimen (No. 3940) still older than that represented in Fig. 5.

Fig. 7. Right upper molars, from above, of *Bos taurus*, from a specimen (No. 4500) corresponding in age with the specimen of *B. americanus* represented in Fig. 1, the last pre-molar of the temporary set being still in place.

Fig. 8. Right upper molars, from above, of *Bos taurus*, from a specimen (No. 4501) corresponding in age with the specimens of *B. americanus* represented in Figs. 2 and 3.

Fig. 9. Right upper molars, from above, of *Bos taurus*, from a specimen (No. 4) corresponding in age with the specimen of *B. americanus* represented in Fig. 4.

Fig. 10. Left upper molars, from above, of *Bos taurus*, from a specimen (No. 5003) a very little older than the specimen represented in Fig. 9.

Fig. 11. Right upper molars, from above, of *Bos taurus*, from a specimen (No. 3) corresponding in age with the specimen of *B. americanus* represented in Fig. 5.

Fig. 12. Right upper molars, from above, of *Bos taurus*, from a specimen (No. 2) corresponding in age with the specimen of *B. americanus* represented in Fig. 6.

Fig. 13. Second right upper molar, from Gardiner, Me., corresponding in age with the specimen represented in Fig. 12. The resemblance of this tooth to the corresponding tooth (second molar) of *Bos taurus*, represented in Fig. 12, with which it is strictly comparable in age, is very close, while it differs quite tangibly from the corresponding tooth of *B. americanus* represented in Fig. 6, with which it is also strictly comparable in respect to age. (This specimen is one of the original lot found at Gardiner, Me., and now belongs to the Boston Society of Natural History. It bears the following label: "Bison

* This specimen is the only one among a large series of skulls of *Bison americanus* in which the crescents of enamel of the first and second true molars have a prominent entering fold on their anterior and posterior borders, not, however, exactly corresponding in this respect with the infolding seen in *Bos taurus*. The specimen, in every other respect, is apparently normal. The specimen represented in *Fig.* 3 exactly corresponds in age with this, and illustrates the usual form of the enamel crescents in *B. americanus* in specimens of this age.

tooth from Gardiner, Me. Presented by Dr. C. T. Jackson." Some of the blue clay of the original matrix still remains between the fangs of the tooth.

Fig. 14. Third right upper molar, from Gardiner, Me., from Dr. Packard's Plate (Mem. Bost. Soc. Nat. Hist., Vol. I, Pl. vii, Fig. 18 a). Strictly comparable with the corresponding tooth in Figs. 12 (*Bos taurus*) and 6 (*B. americanus*). Its much closer resemblance to that of *Bos taurus* than to that of *B. americanus* will be at once noticed.

Fig. 15. First right upper molar, from Gardiner, Me., from Dr. Packard's Plate (Mem. Bost. Soc. Nat. Hist., Vol. I, Pl. vii, Fig. 18). Strictly comparable with the corresponding tooth in Figs. 12 and 6. The infolding of the enamel at the inner posterior corner of the hinder crescent marks it distinctly as a tooth of *Bos taurus*, and as not at least a normal tooth of *B. americanus*.

NOTE. — In the text of this work (pages 90, 91, put in type over four months ago) I left the question of the identity of the teeth from Gardiner, Me., a somewhat open question, though stating it to be my conviction that they were those of *Bos taurus*. A re-examination of the subject, in the light of a larger series of specimens of the latter, fully confirms this conviction. Of such identity I now believe there is not a reasonable doubt.

To complete the history of the subject I have copied Dr. Packard's figures of the two molar teeth of which I am unable to give original figures.

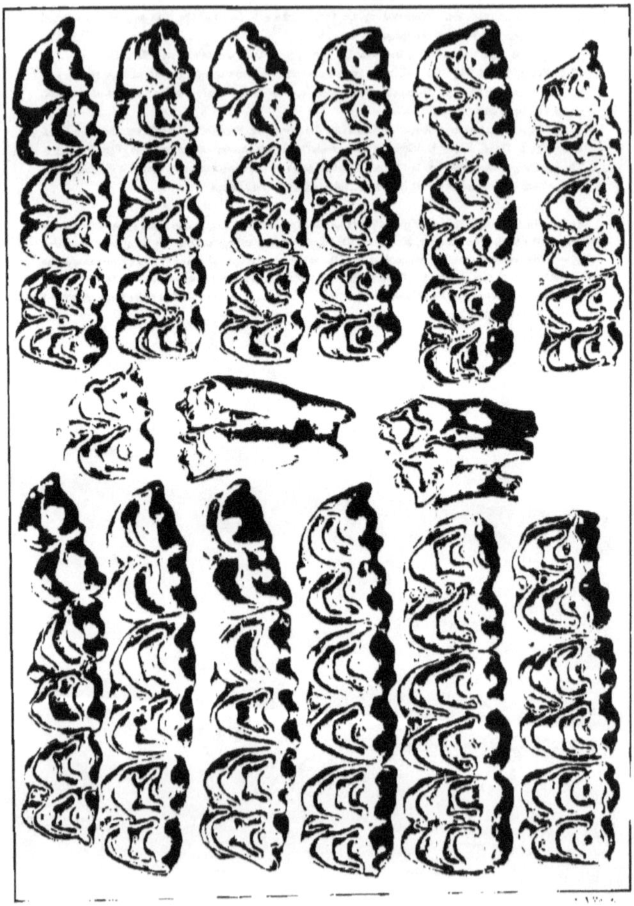

www.ingramcontent.com/pod-product-compliance
Lightning Source LLC
Chambersburg PA
CBHW031902220426
43663CB00006B/735
* 9 7 8 3 3 3 7 7 1 6 7 9 0 *